Jan 1999

Happy Birthday Clarence —
Hope you enjoy this Book on
your favorite Sport

Charlee

100 YEARS OF HOOPS

100 Years of Hoops

Years of

Hoops

By Alexander Wolff

100 YEARS OF HOOPS

by Alexander Wolff

CRESCENT BOOKS

New York • Avenel

Copyright © 1991
Time Inc.

SPORTS ILLUSTRATED is a
registered treademark of Time Inc.

100 Years of Hoops
Project Director: MORIN BISHOP
Copyreader: LESLIE BORNSTEIN
Reporter: KELLI ANDERSON
Photography Editors: BRADLEY M. SMITH
JEFFREY WEIG
Production Manager: ANDREW HUGHES
Designers: STEVEN HOFFMAN
BARBARA CHILENSKAS

100 YEARS OF HOOPS was prepared by Bishop Books, Inc.
611 Broadway, New York, New York 10012

Cover photograph (Michael Jordon, Charles Barkley, 1993): John W. McDonough

This 1995 edition published by Crescent Books,
distributed by Random House Value Publishing, Inc.
40 Engelhard Avenue, Avenel, New Jersey 07001

Random House
New York • Toronto • London • Sydney • Auckland

Library of Congress Cataloging–in–Publication Data

Wolff, Alexander, 1957–
Sports illustrated 100 years of hoops : a fond look back at the sport of basketball / by Alexander Wolff.
p. cm.
Originally published: Menlo Park, Calif. : Oxmoor House, 1991. With new pref.
Includes index.
ISBN 0–517–14690–8
1. Basketball—History. 2. Basketball—United States—History.
I. Sports illustrated (Time, Inc.) II. Title.
GV883.W65 1995
796.323'09—dc20   95–33205
CIP

Printed and bound in the United States of America

10 9 8 7 6 5 4 3 2

contents

Original Thirteen Rules of "Basket Ball"

The game began with this somewhat awkward, sometimes ungrammatical set of sentences, typed and then posted by Dr. James Naismith on December 21, 1891 in the gymnasium of the International YMCA Training School in Springfield, Mass.:

1. *The ball may be thrown in any direction with one or both hands.*

2. *The ball may be batted in any direction with one or both hands (never with the fist).*

3. *A player cannot run with the ball, the player must throw it from the spot on which he catches it, allowance to be made for a man who catches the ball when running at good speed.*

4. *The ball must be held in or between the hands, the arms or body must not be used for holding it.*

5. *No shouldering, holding, pushing, tripping or striking in any way the person of an opponent shall be allowed. The first infringement of this rule by any person shall count as a foul, the second shall disqualify him until the next goal is made, or if there was evident intent to injure the person, for the whole of the game, no substitute allowed.*

6. *A foul is striking the ball with the fist, violation of rules 3 and 4, and such as described in rule 5.*

7. *If either side makes three consecutive fouls it shall count a goal for the opponents (consecutive means without the opponents in the meantime making a foul).*

8. *A goal shall be made when the ball is thrown or batted from the grounds into the basket and stays there, providing those defending the goal do not touch or disturb the goal. If the ball rests on the edge and the opponent moves the basket it shall count as a goal.*

9. *When the ball goes out of bounds it shall be thrown into the field, and played by the person first touching it. In case of a dispute the umpire shall throw it straight into the field. The thrower in is allowed five seconds, if he holds it longer it shall go to the opponent. If any side persists in delaying the game, the umpire shall call a foul on them.*

10. *The umpire shall be the judge of the men, and shall note the fouls, and notify the referee when three consecutive fouls have been made. He shall have power to disqualify men according to rule 5.*

11. *The referee shall be the judge of the ball and shall decide when the ball is in play, in bounds, and to which side it belongs, and shall keep the time. He shall decide when a goal has been made, and keep account of the goals with any other duties that are ususaly performed by a referee.*

12. *The time shall be two fifteen minute halves, with five minutes rest between.*

13. *The side making the most goals in that time shall be declared the winner. In case of a draw the game may, by agreement of the captains, be continued until another goal is made.*

The Roots of the Game

The place: Springfield. The man: Naismith. Together they brought forth the sport with which they would forever be associated

Picture a game invented by a future Presbyterian minister of Scottish descent and Canadian upbringing. Imagine that this game was conceived at a school for missionaries, to tide a class of 18, mostly white men, through the ennui of a New England winter and help them fulfill a moral duty to exercise. Imagine, too, that the very first practitioners of this game were studying to be ... secretaries.

Now think of your garden-variety high-flyin' death-defyin' 360-degree slam dunk.

Good gawd. However did we get here from there?

It took only 100 years for basketball to go from those uptight Apollonian beginnings to today's loose and Dionysian result. En route, all sorts of thrilling things happened, and all manner of folk joined in. Women. People in wheelchairs. Folks from virtually every nation on earth. Muggsy and Bevo and Dancin' Harry. Danny the bowling alley proprietor and Dick Vitale. The Seattle Browns, Sweet Charlie and Downtown Freddie. And the St. Joseph's Hawk, basketball's best mascot.

James Naismith: the inventor of basketball.

A few shots can still be heard 'round the world: Plump's last as a high schooler; Luisetti's first in the Garden; West's from beyond half court; Belov's from under the basket; Erving's from some distant galaxy beyond the baseline. Black Americans, still barred from some hoops precincts as recently as the 1970s, nonetheless made a mark so indelible that basketball would be completely transfigured in style, argot and the very plane on which it was practiced. And the game supplied a brace of towering figures, known by nouns with definite articles attached, titles that together defined a century. The Original Celtics and the Wonder Five. The Bear and the Baron. The Cooz and the Pearl. And a couple of Promethean physicians, the Doctor (James Naismith, the original preacher man) and the Doc-tah (Julius Erving).

When the big guys came along—from Kurland and Mikan, through Wilt and Russ, to Kareem and Hakeem (or Lewis and Akeem, as we first came to know them)—the game conferred upon them majesty and dignity where there might otherwise have been mere ungainliness. To document his season of covering the NBA in 1988–89, a mischievous San Francisco sportswriter named George Shirk asked sundry Golden State Warriors to pose in front of his Polaroid camera while wearing a funny-nose-and-glasses getup. Coach Don Nelson agreed. So did forward Chris Mullin. Not so Manute Bol, the Dinka tribesman who stands 7' 7" and wisely avoids sidewalk grates.

Bol took the glasses from Shirk. He studied them. And he thought for a moment.

"No, man," he said finally, shaking his head. "It make me look funny."

As basketball blows out the candles on its cake—devil's food with vanilla frosting, angel food with chocolate, either will suit this multicolored game just fine—more than 250 million people worldwide play some organized and sanctioned version. Many millions more play whenever, however, wherever. "The ground," Naismith wrote shortly after inventing basketball, "may be the gymnasium floor cleared of apparatus...though it could be played in the open air at a picnic, etc." At a picnic, et cetera, indeed. *Yo! I got winners. Pass the mustard.*

Such pastoral pursuits were hardly uppermost in Naismith's mind in December 1891, when he took over the Phys-Ed Class from Hell at the International YMCA Training School in Springfield, Mass. Two other men had tried and failed to bring some order to this incorrigible group of 18 future YMCA executive secretaries. Most of the class consisted of rugby and football players out of season, and they chafed under the regimen of leapfrog, Indian clubs and tumbling that passed for indoor sport during the winter months. They were unmanageable in December, and Naismith, then 30, could only imagine what hellions they would be as cabin fever set in a few months deeper into the New England winter.

"Those boys," Naismith would remark later, "simply would not play drop the handkerchief!" But what *would* they play? Dr. Luther Gulick, head of the physical education department, gave Naismith 14 days to come up with something to tame the savage secretaries.

Naismith was a curious hybrid of a man. Raised by relatives following his parents's death from typhoid, he spent a frontier childhood among lumberjacks and farmers in rural Ontario. Yet he devoted his late adolescence and young adulthood to the study of theology, philosophy and ancient languages and resolved to enter the ministry. A chance to teach at the YMCA Training School seemed perfectly suited to the dual parts of this man's nature, his robust and athletic instincts on the one hand and his Christian piety on the other.

Bill Bradley: from college standout to the U.S. Senate.

He was also a modest man, untroubled by working for Gulick, who was younger than he. Indeed, Naismith took to heart something his superior had told him. "Dr. Gulick had reminded me on one occasion that there is nothing new under the sun," Naismith noted. "What appears new is just a combination of older things."

Gulick, we now know, was correct. Elements of what Naismith would invent can be found in cultures as far back as 1200 B.C., when the Olmec Indians, the "rubber people" of Mexico (so-called not because they were good rebounders, but because they manufactured objects out of rubber plants), played a ball-and-hoop game and attached religious significance to it. Variations persisted on the Yucatán peninsula, through the heydays of the Mayans and the Aztecs and up until the Spanish conquest in 1521. More recently the Argentines played a game similar to basketball, called *pato,* on horseback; in parts of Indonesia, *'sepachraca* is played by placing a basket in the middle of a village and tossing a "ball" resembling a badminton shuttlecock at it.

Naismith disavowed knowing any of these historical details as he sat in his office sketching out some of the conditions a new game would ideally meet. It would have to have standards of vigor, so the wintering ruggers and footballers wouldn't be made to feel like pantywaists. It had to be simple in outline, so anyone could grasp and play it, but it had to possess a degree of difficulty, too, to attract players of a scientific bent and of course to keep a challenge alive through the long winter. And it had to be safe enough to be played properly within a cramped gymnasium measuring 50' by 30'.

Like any good inventor, Naismith was a problem solver. As he fashioned basketball out of fragments of other games, he sought to ameliorate the flaws he saw in the popular sports of the day. The scourge of rugby and football was the roughness, which stemmed largely from tackling. Who got tackled? Runners. So Naismith decided that, in his game, the ball could be passed in any direction, but not carried.

Yet if passing were permitted willy-nilly, the game might degenerate into little more than keepaway. Thus, this new game needed an objective, a literal "goal"—but not a goal on which violent rushes would be mounted, as in football, rugby or lacrosse. This after all would be an indoor game, and violent collisions would be too dangerous.

Here Naismith reached back to a pastime of his childhood in the hamlet of Bennies Corners, Ont. He

John Wooden: truly a coach for the ages.

and his friends had played a game called duck on a rock. It involved trying to knock a good-sized rock off the top of a boulder by pelting it from a distance with other, smaller rocks. Duck-on-a-rock players, Naismith remembered, soon learned that accuracy was more important than force and that there was an optimal arc to a toss. Station the goal aloft, he thought, out of reach, and the game would encourage such scientific analysis. But what kind of goal? Here Naismith thought back again, this time to his days as a philosophy student at McGill University in Montreal, where rugby players stayed loose in the winter by tossing a ball into a box in the gym. And here, more or less,

Naismith had his game—none too soon, for Gulick's deadline of 14 days was fast approaching.

It took about an hour for Naismith to draft his original 13 rules, most of which can still be found in some form in the game today. Shortly before the class was to meet, the Doctor posted two type-written pages enumerating them.

"Hmmmph!" said one student when he showed up on Dec. 21 for phys ed. "A new game."

But the new game would bring the class to heel. Naismith divided his students into two teams of nine each, and the first scrimmage ended with a YMCA executive-secretary-to-be named William Chase having scored basketball's first—and the first game's only—basket, a toss from about 25 feet away.

Christmas vacation followed shortly, and a number of the players in the first game took "basket ball" back to their hometown YMCAs. The game grew astonishingly quickly thereafter, thanks largely to the far-flung travels of Training School graduates and Naismith's genial willingness to share his rules with anyone showing interest. In addition, despite all Naismith's precautions, many Y's considered the sport to be too rough, and incipient teams banned from Y's found new homes in Masonic temples, dance halls and gymnasiums bounded by chicken wire that came to be known as cages. This introduced the game to even more people. Most fundamentally, however, basketball grew because there was a need for a simple, indoor, wintertime game.

Think for a moment how radically different the contours of today's game might be if the lower rail of the balcony in the YMCA Training School

9

gymnasium hadn't been precisely 10 feet high. If building superintendent James (Pop) Stebbins had been able to find in the storeroom the boxes that Naismith requested and hadn't produced a couple of peach baskets instead. And if the Doctor had permitted his invention to be known, as a student had suggested, as Naismithball.

Today Naismith's game is represented by 176 national basketball federations, including ones in Djibouti, Romania and San Marino. Women play on CBS and for the Harlem Globetrotters and have begun to take their rightful place, belatedly, in the Hall of Fame. A 5' 7" guy has been crowned NBA Slam-Dunk king, and a 53-year-old one has made more consecutive free throws than anyone, ever. Thus has the game claimed its place next to the American bosom, right there with sleepy baseball and overwrought football. Or maybe a little closer than those two, if you examine the evidence. According to a 1987 survey by the National Sporting Goods Association, more boys and girls in the United States aged 7 to 17 play basketball than any other sport. In 1990 a cross section of Americans were asked which single sporting event they would most like to attend. Twenty-one percent named the Final Four—the same percentage that named the World Series and only 2% fewer than named the Super Bowl. That same year a marketing firm released its "Q" ratings, which gauge how popular certain professional athletes are with the public. Basketball players took six of the top 10 spots, with a guy named Jordan outstripping them all.

It is said that basketball is a black game. Yet until the middle of the century, people considered it a Jewish game. This only goes to show that what it is, really, is an urban game, one that flourishes in constricted spaces and among those who might not be able to afford more than a pair of gym shoes, a borrowed ball and a taxpayer's share in a public park. And when, newly prosperous, some of these people flee to the suburbs, they may start playing golf—but they don't entirely "trade up" to another sport. They bring their Cons with them, and teach the game to their children.

But basketball always existed in its own way, on its own terms, in small-town America, too. Its essence, once you lace 'em up, may indeed be deception, as sportswriter Leonard Koppett once said—a con man's series of feints and setups all aimed at swindling the defense out of a couple of points. (A most citified ethos, that.) But there is nothing deceitful in what's communicated by hundreds of thousands of hoops, some jerry-built in alleyways, others mounted like altars over garage doors. These goals are reassuring. They bespeak stouthearted values. They conjure up images of a solitary boy working on "my game" (baseball and football players do not speak of "my game"), or the rituals of a Friday night in February in some fevered high school gym, or the crazy lotto of an office pool in March. Basketball signifies and sanctifies community. And that ideal of five working as one to win a championship defies the disorder that seems so intrinsic to the game. What is the essence of that team ideal? We don't know exactly. But businessmen take graduate seminars trying to attain it; preachers devote a month of Sundays trying to

Julius Erving: perhaps the game's most beloved star.

instill it; jazz aficionados spend smoky evenings trying to describe it. Basketball champions, to coin a phrase, just do it.

"Twelve men are constantly in movement (counting two referees), the rebounds of the ball are unpredictable, the occasions for passing or dribbling or shooting must be decided instantaneously," social commentator Michael Novak wrote in his book *The Joy of Sports*. "Basketball players . . . have a score, a melody; each team has its own appropriate tempo, a style of game best suited to its talents; but within and around that general score, each individual is free to elaborate as the spirit moves him. Basketball is jazz: improvisatory, free, individualistic, corporate, sweaty, fast, exulting, screeching, torrid, explosive, exquisitely designed for letting first the trumpet, then the sax, then the drummer . . . soar away in virtuoso excellence."

And Dr. Naismith thought he was writing a hymn. In fact, Springfield,

Lynette Woodard: the first woman Globetrotter.

an industrial city in western Massachusetts, was as likely a place as any for basketball to get invented. Winters were sufficiently intimidating to drive Naismith's students indoors and keep them there, but not so severe as to suggest ice hockey, already 35 years old, as a worthwhile alternative. And the faculty at the Training School was just prudish enough to be aghast at the violence prevailing in sports like rugby and football during the Gilded Age. Thus Naismith, who remained on the game's rules committee for years, made certain that basketball retained disincentives to contact—provisions that allowed the game to evolve into the aerial ballet that we marvel at today.

At 100, basketball enjoys a more exalted status elsewhere in America than in the city of its birth. Some of its manifestations in the heartland have become archetypes, permanently woven into the national fabric: the Indiana high school gym that brims with more people on one night than will inhabit the town itself the next morning; the community in Utah where the carpeted common room adjoining the temple is given over to "ward ball," a sort of Latter-Day Saints CYO league; the hardscrabble slab outside a towering housing project in Chicago where, for young black males born into a cycle of poverty, basketball can be one of two things—either salutary, an area from which a young man can extract a sense of self-worth and a chance for a free college education; or cruelly deleterious, a seductive dream of an NBA career he might chase unavailingly into young adulthood.

Yet even if today's Springfield loved hoops as conspicuously as it is loved by Hoosiers or Mormons or kids in the Rust Belt ghettos, you sense that Yankee reserve would temper that passion somehow. The whole point of Springfield College, which is what that International YMCA Training School would come to be called, is to go forth and share, not take the credit. And if those young missionaries were going off to every corner of the earth anyway, they might as well take a basketball along.

The Springfield seal features a triangle to indicate the school's mission to develop mind, body and spirit. Basketball, too, often distills to tidy trinities. There's the defensive mantra of ball, you, man. The offensive player's "triple-threat" position, from which he can pass, dribble, shoot. The so-called "three-man game," engaging guard, forward and center, which is as much a staple of three-on-three in the corner schoolyard as of the half-court offense in an NBA game when the shot clock ticks down.

In November 1983, as basketball came up on its 92nd birthday, I decided to plumb Springfield myself, to determine if the heart of the game still beat in the natal city. There was certainly superficial evidence that it did. There was the Hall of Fame, still on campus at the time of my visit, a monument to the man who invented it there. Indeed, it was known officially, then as now, as the *Naismith Memorial* Basketball Hall of Fame. A nondescript brick building, derided by some as Naismith Tool & Die, the old Hall nonetheless had an integrity to it, something redolent of the same Scottish Calvinist who thought up the game. A new shrine, still a couple of years from opening, had become a sort of political basketball, spawning arguments over everything from who would pick up the $11 million tab to what the building would look like. (Why not a basketball? wondered Leigh Montville in *The Boston Globe*. You could turn the air valve into the entrance, and require visitors to wet themselves down to gain entry....) In addition, Springfield featured the Tip-Off Classic, a nonconference, intersectional college game that benefited the Hall and provided the pretext for my visit. A sort of basketball bowl game, the Tip-Off is the culmination of the weeklong Peach Basket Festival, which features ballroom dancing, a parade

Earl (Goat) Manigault: A legend from the playground.

through downtown and a batallion of panjandrums in peach blazers.

Yet in neither of these institutions, not in the musty Hall nor at the Tip-Off Classic, did I get a sense of basketball *discovery*—the feeling that Naismith must have had when he hit upon the notion of a ball and a basket. There was just no eureka factor. Until I stumbled upon Dunbar.

You only stumble into the Winchester Square section of town, because an out-of-towner wouldn't head intentionally into so blighted a neighborhood. The facades of buildings here have an abused and hollow look. The desolate lots every few blocks can't really be described as vacant, because altogether too much broken glass shimmers in them under the midday sun. There's no way of telling which of these sorry patches is the site of the gym where they played the first game, although one of them putatively is. But if you find your way to the Dunbar Community Center, at the corner of Oak and Union, go on in. You have found sanctuary.

Dunbar was once a church. It is no blasphemy, however, that the nave has been cleared out and a floor—parquet, no less—laid down where the pews once were. Instead of stained glass, bright murals depicting African themes and outtakes from Paul Laurence Dunbar's poetry grace the window wells. The supervisor, a man of stout reserve named Bob Jennings, greeted me warmly. He told me how, a number of years earlier, a young work-study student from the University of Massachusetts in nearby Amherst did a tour of duty at Dunbar. The young man's name was Julius Erving.

Every afternoon at three o'clock the gym filled up, and the young legs ran. "They'll say, 'Run with us, Mister J,' " Jennings, then nearly 60, told me. "And I do. I'll wake up the next morning a little stiffer. But I won't play half court. You stand around too much."

A church. Mister J. *Doctor* J. All just steps from where Dr. James midwifed the game. Writers are rightly accused of sometimes reading too much into what they observe, but in this instance I was ready to risk being so charged. To this day, every time I hear someone speak in lofty tones about "basketball's shrine in Springfield, Massachusetts," I can't help but think of Dunbar.

I checked in with Dunbar eight years after that visit, to find out whether Mr. J still ran with the kids. I reached his longtime aide-de-camp, George (Big Will) Williams, who filled me in. Bob Jennings had hung it up, retiring four years before to take a part-time job with Head Start. As his successor, Big Will knows well what he has been entrusted with. "The corner of Sherman and State, that's where the game was invented," he said. "It's only four blocks away. This is the holiest gym in the nation."

Big Will was also feeling chesty about Travis Best, a 5'10" youngster from Springfield's Central High School. Best is the city's birthday gift to the game. He won his first trophy at Dunbar as a 10-year-old. "You'd better become an All-America," his mother had told him as he dribbled heedlessly through the house, whacking his basketball off any which thing. "Because if you're not, I don't want to put up with all this."

A superstar for the next generation?

He did become an All-America, scoring 81 points in one game, and leading Central through an unbeaten season to the state title as a senior. At Georgia Tech, where he would be enrolling in the fall, he may well wind up winning an award named after Naismith's daughter-in-law, Frances Pomeroy Naismith, which is given annually to the best college senior under 6'. Funny: The winner of that prestigious award in 1991 was a kid from East Tennessee State named Jennings, whom everyone calls Mister.

Basketball has taught many lessons over its 10 decades—about courage in the face of long odds, about how individuals can find a place for themselves in a community, about the good and sometimes great things people of all stripes can achieve when they work together. It's pointless to peg the game as black or Jewish or small-town or inner-city or American or Yugoslav or Dinka. The urge to put a ball through a hoop is primevally human, visible in cultures the world over.

Professor Hermann Niebuhr, a former president of the West German Basketball Federation, has studied the works of Omar Khayyam, the 12th-century Persian thinker. Given Niebuhr's love for the game of basketball, it would be best to regard the following with some skepticism. Nevertheless, he has translated one passage of Khayyam's more or less like this: "You are a ball being played by destiny. God plays too, and for a thousand years he keeps shooting from beside the rim."

Bob Jennings isn't Omar Khayyam, but I always try to follow a piece of his advice. Don't play half court. You stand around too much.

The Elements

A simple game in many ways, basketball is nonetheless composed of many parts, each of them indispensible to its structure. Here is a look at the critical elements—shot, pass, dunk and more—and how they evolved along with the sport they would come to define

The
Shot

The Shot

1936 Hank Luisetti of Stanford brings the one-hander to Madison Square Garden and forever alters the course of the game. "It seemed that Luisetti could do nothing wrong," writes *The New York Times.* "Some of his shots would have been deemed foolhardy if attempted by any other player, but with Luisetti doing the heaving, these were accepted by the crowd as a matter of course."

1940 Kenny Sailors of Wyoming is credited with being the first player to use the jump shot in college competition. Sailors will be tournament MVP as the Cowboys win the 1943 NCAA title.

1944 With three seconds to play in overtime of the NCAA championship game against Dartmouth, Utah guard Herb Wilkinson

There are only two great plays—South Pacific, and put the ball in the basket.
—former NBA coach and referee Charley Eckman

Set, jump, hook. Scoop, tap, layup. Runner, bank, follow. Distill basketball to its elements, and the shot sits at the top of the game's periodic table. No sport has at its core a simpler and more ubiquitous act. Hitting a baseball is vexatiously problematic; stickhandling a puck and throwing a tight spiral are only slightly less so. Ah, but to a basketball player, shooting a shot—shooting *your* shot—is that most life-affirming of skills, most fundamental of fundamentals, as quotidian a task as sleeping, eating or breathing.

Perhaps the shot transcends so because it may be honed alone, with the practitioner's thoughts his own. Or perhaps it's because, when a shot is squeezed off in competition, the shooter has rendered the abilities of the other nine players on the floor—for the life of the ball's flight, anyway—irrelevant. If you sink your shots, get on a roll, start cooking, *feel it,* your private little game detaches itself from the larger one, and the larger one becomes momentarily moot.

The shot can be reduced to mathematical formula, but before it can properly take flight it must be given voice in the exhortations of thousands of coaches, whose mantras—elbow in, follow through, eye on that spot just over the front of the rim—apply whether the hand (nay, the *fingertips!*) from which a shot is launched belongs to the most wizened professional or the most callow biddy tyro. To all this, one must add the proper attitude. "My own philosophy is to keep missing shots until I score one," said Jeff Fryer, the superb jump shooter on Loyola Marymount's teams of the late '80s, "and then keep making shots until I miss one."

In its evolution the shot has climbed up the human body, like a frisky dog. It began as a two-hander, released underhand from between the legs. Since then the shot has come to be sighted from points progressively higher—from the waist, then the chest, then the eyes or the shoulder, and ultimately from above or behind the head. Stanford's Hank Luisetti introduced the one-hander (a.k.a. "the stab"), and Wyoming's Kenny Sailors is widely credited with birthing the jumper (later to be called the J). But former Murray State and Philadelphia Warriors star Joe Fulks was their equal as a pioneer, the first player to bring the ball behind his head to good effect. With uncommon strength in his upper body, he would leap and hang until a defender could stay up no longer. Another Philadelphian, Paul Arizin, would take Fulks's antigravitational principles and apply them to the one-hander. By 1958 players were releasing their jumpers from points so high that Bill Roeder of *The New York World-Telegram* wrote, "Today's two-handed shooter looks like a subject being frisked. He lifts both hands over his head, lets the guard go through his pockets and casually flips a soft line drive toward the basket.

"It's our prediction," Roeder added, "that if basketball lasts another 25 years, the boys will be shooting with no hands."

Thirty-three years later, it only sometimes seems that way, what with all the idiosyncratic shooting styles the game has spawned. Jerry West and Geoff Petrie were masters of that last hard dribble, the better to propel the ball up into the sling of their hands for release. Cult shooters like Joe Hassett and Rick Mount made jumpers the sine qua non of their games. Ron King, Jamaal Wilkes and Jerry Lucas let fly an amazing array of misbegotten-looking shots that, nonetheless, found the mark with confounding frequency.

With the ascent of the jumper and one-hander came the decline of the hook. Once even forwards, men like Ed Macauley, Tom Heinsohn and Cliff Hagan, knew the utility of this shot that, in its grace and rarity, remains the spiritual polar opposite of the slam dunk. But as the game quickened, more and more shot opportunities came in the open floor and on the move. In this new order, the hook became as antiquated as the set—except, of course, in the environs of the Forum in L.A., where Kareem Abdul-Jabbar let fly his majestic skyhooks.

Bob Houbregs, who spent his college career at Washington launching graceful parabolas from deep in the corners, mastered the hook because a childhood case of rickets stripped him of his jumping ability. Necessity mothered the invention of Sailors's seminal jumper in the backyard of his childhood home in Hillsdale, Wyo.; older brother Bud stood eight inches taller, and Kenny had no choice but to jump before shooting. And in the college towns of the Midwest during the '50s it was said that, from watching where Indiana's Jimmy Rayl launched his curious-looking shots, and from the trajectory each one traced, you could recreate the architecture of the barn in which he learned the game.

To each his own shot; behind every shot a story.

West's quick release made him one of the league's most dangerous jump shooters, particularly in the clutch.

launches a shot from just beyond the top of the key. It hangs on the rim for what seems an eternity, then drops through, giving the Utes a 42-40 victory.

1947 Howie Dallmar of the Philadelphia Warriors goes 0 for 15 in a game against the New York Knicks.

1948 Howie Dallmar goes 0 for 15 again, this time against the Washington Capitols.

1956 In a youth league game in Cornwall Heights, Pa., nine-year-old Lew Alcindor gathers in a rebound and, largely out of reflex and disorientation at finding himself with the ball, throws up his first hook shot. His future coach with the Lakers, Pat Riley, will describe the Jabbar skyhook as perhaps "the most awesome weapon in the history of any sport."

1957 Pittsburgh sports publicist Beano Cook tries to persuade polio vaccine pioneer Jonas Salk, a member of the Pitt Medical School faculty, to pose with Pitt All-America candidate Don Hennon for a photo to be billed "The World's Two Greatest Shotmakers." Salk refuses.

1970 Los Angeles guard Jerry West throws in a 65-foot shot to force overtime in Game 3 of the NBA Finals between the Knicks and Lakers. The Knicks, however, go on to win the game and the series.

1973 UCLA's Bill Walton makes 21 of 22 shots against Memphis State in the NCAA championship game. No individual has ever shot so well in so important a game.

New York's Bernard King (left) tossed in this one-hander against Detroit in 1984; Ralph Sampson's love of the J, an asset in college, hurt him in the pros.

1985 Bruce Morris of Marshall, after picking up a loose ball just before the end of the first half of a game against Appalachian State, hurls a line drive shot that covers 89' 10" before going through the hoop. Morris, who is credited with the longest measured field goal ever, says, "I probably couldn't hit the backboard from there in a million tries."

1987 Indiana's Keith Smart throws in a 16-foot jump shot from the left baseline with time ticking down to give the Hoosiers the NCAA title over Syracuse 74-73.

1992 After taking a three-quarter court pass from teammate Grant Hill, Duke's Christian Laettner sinks a turnaround jumper as time expires to give the Blue Devils a 104-103 overtime victory over Kentucky in the NCAA East Regional final. Duke will go on to win its second straight national title.

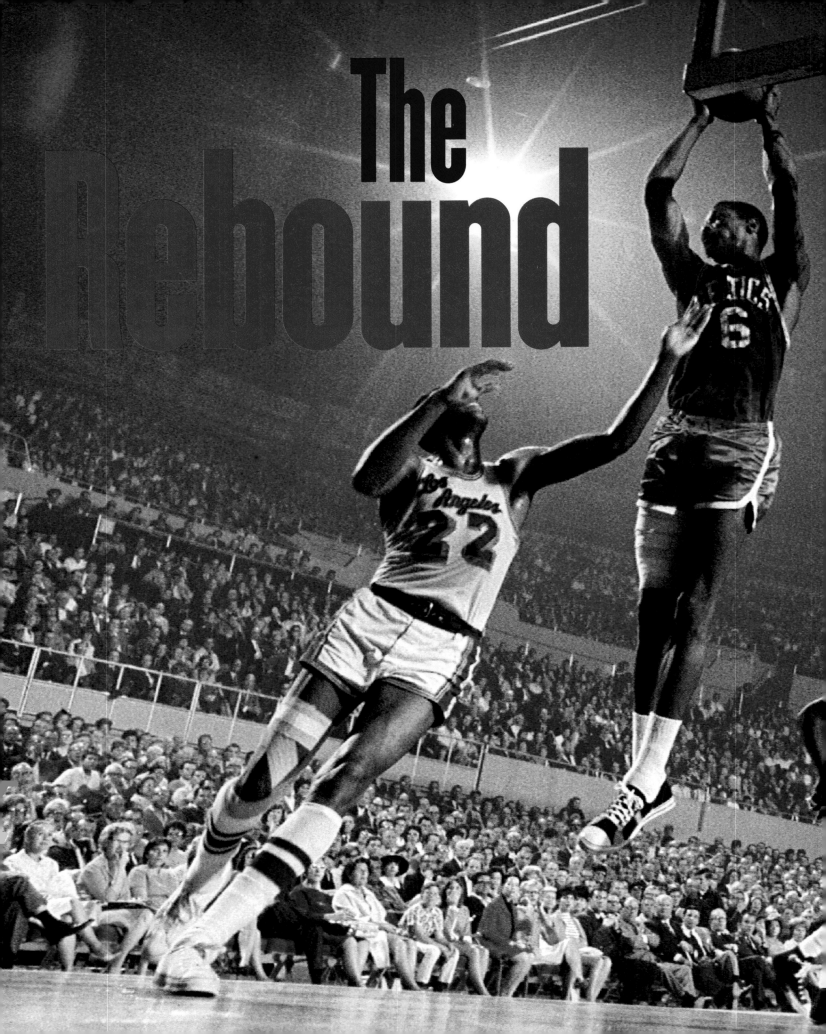

The Rebound

The Rebound

1896 To keep spectators sitting behind the basket from reaching out from the stands and interfering with a shot as it approaches the goal, a rule is passed requiring that the basket be attached to "a flat perpendicular screen or other rigid surface measuring at least 6' by 4'." This is the first official backboard, to which generations of rebounders will go.

1938 The baseline is extended to four feet beyond the bottom of the backboard, relieving congestion under the basket and increasing the variety of angles off which a missed shot might come. As a result, rebounding becomes a more athletic exercise.

1953 William and Mary's Bill Chambers, in a game against Virginia, gathers in 51 rebounds, an NCAA record likely never to be broken.

Leaning, hooking, grabbing, the bodies array themselves like a Roman frieze beneath the basket every time a shot goes up—more than a hundred times a game, untold thousands of times a season. If the ball should find its mark, the tension releases and the scrum disbands for a few moments until it is time to form again. But as often as not, the shot is off the mark. The ball caroms away, eligible to be claimed by any one of these burly homesteaders, or perhaps by a smaller, quicker interloper with a running start and stout heart.

Over the years, a few eminences have risen with particular frequency and style above that primordial cluster of sweat and sinew beneath the rim: Bill Russell, spreading his legs emphatically after grabbing a rebound, then pivoting in search of a teammate upcourt. Paul Silas, gathering in his rebounds where coaches say 90% of them are found—below the rim. Bob Pettit, always, somehow, finding optimal position to retrieve the ball. And the preposterous Charles Barkley, not even 6' 5", clearing space with the convex line of his body while leaping and snaring, then signaling his success by slapping the ball with his free hand.

Rebounding is a skill of subtle satisfactions, perhaps none so acute as that nirvana experienced when defensive players have blocked out their respective opponents so perfectly that they construct a hermetic box into which a missed shot falls to the floor, untouched. At the same time, no element of the game has distanced itself so much in actual practice from the staid contours of basketball primers. The old instructional materials counsel, more or less, the establishment of position, the exposure of one's armpits and, well, the "getting" of rebounds. This is how you *really* execute a "pull," as the modern rebound is known: Find a corridor of air space. Sky. Herald your claim, Barkley-like, with a percussive report. Then come down and pivot, elbows out. (Menacing glare and flaring nostrils are optional.) Indeed, what is arguably the game's most riveting play, the tap dunk, is in fact a rebound *garni*.

Listen to them talk, and rebounders sound like old bluesmen. They speak of blue-collar pride. They point to welts, scars and bruises on their person. The best have been largely taciturn men, unassuming in temperament and workaday in style—more like NFL linemen than the dunkers and leapers who find their way onto the 11 o'clock highlights package every night. Listen to Moses Malone: "Basically, I just goes to the rack." Wes Unseld: "That's my job—rebounding." Buck Williams: "My rebounding motto is, 'The ball belongs to me.' "

There is no more regular challenge in basketball than the one these men take up. A player is asked to stop his man on defense only on every other possession and to sink a shot even less often. A rebound, on the other hand, may conceivably be yours every time a shot goes up, whether you're on offense or defense. Late in one game when Unseld was at Louisville, his coach, John Dromo, gave him word that he was closing in on the school's single-game scoring record. Unseld specifically asked that his teammates not feed him the ball. "Just let 'em shoot, and I'll get it off the board," he said.

UCLA coach John Wooden conditioned his players to assume every shot would be missed and to bring their hands automatically to their shoulders when one went up. (Even Bruins on the bench, it was said, would sometimes react accordingly.) Jack Ramsay, as coach of the 76ers, devised a system of fines that docked a player $15 if his man grabbed an offensive rebound and $25 if the shooter did so.

Defensive rebounders are counseled to box an opponent first with body contact and only then go to the glass. Offensive rebounders, on the other hand, must rely more on tenacity and concentration. They're usually opportunistic forwards, lithe bolts able to insinuate themselves into the cracks between the space-eaters who have dutifully seized position. Yet, beginning in the late '70s, the game's greatest force on the offensive glass turned out to be Malone, a relatively slow 6' 10" center from the bullrushes of tidewater Virginia. He was so dominant at Petersburg High that his teammates refused to feed him the ball inside. Thus he *had* to go to the rack. (Once, he picked off 45 rebounds there.) By 1977, when he had reached the undermanned Houston Rockets, a good third of their offense consisted of Moses getting second and third shots in the paint.

Malone's prodigious boardwork stood out all the more because it came at a time when rebounds were becoming more and more scarce. In the NBA, soaring shooting percentages were to blame. Where the Celtics of 1960 averaged more than 70 rebounds a game, a typical pro team 30 years later would be pleased to pull down 50.

But that only serves to make the skill that much dearer. Rebounding seems woefully short on glamour until you consider this: In a clean game, one devoid of steals and turnovers, there are only two ways to gain possession. One is the cheap way, when the ball turns over to you after an opponent's score. The other way is every bit as substantive as the first one is hollow.

This shot of Robertson rebounding against Kansas State left Olajuwon in awe.

1956 Bill Russell grabs an NCAA-tournament record 27 rebounds as San Francisco defeats Iowa 83-71 for its second consecutive NCAA championship.

1957 Apparently unaffected by the keener competition, Russell, now an NBA rookie, pulls down 32 rebounds in Boston's 125-123, double-overtime defeat of St. Louis for the NBA title.

1959 Oscar Robertson is photographed gathering in a rebound in the lane against Kansas State with his legs in a full split. Years later, upon touring the Naismith Memorial Basketball Hall of Fame, Hakeem Olajuwon will see this famous photograph and remark, "Serious rebound."

25

1959 In the final minute of the NCAA championship game, California's Darrall Imhoff tips in his own missed shot to give the Golden Bears a 71–70 victory over West Virginia.

1960 Wilt Chamberlain pulls down an NBA-record 55 rebounds in a game against Bill Russell and the Boston Celtics.

1961 Chamberlain grabs an average of 27.2 rebounds per game, the NBA single-season record and a mark that will probably stand forever. By the time he retires 12 years later, he will have four of the five most prolific rebounding seasons in NBA history.

1963 Vic Rouse rebounds Les Hunter's missed jump shot with four seconds to play in overtime, then scores to give Loyola of Chicago a 60–58 victory over heavily favored Cincinnati in the NCAA championship game. "I felt suspended in air—you could almost say it was an out-of-body experience—and totally focused," says Rouse, who like Hunter attended all-black Pearl High in Nashville. "It was like a blessing."

Chamberlain (left), the game's greatest rebounder, skied against Boston in '67; Patrick Ewing was a fearsome presence on the boards for Georgetown in '84.

1970 Smaller UCLA wins the NCAA title by outrebounding Jacksonville 50 to 38, even though the Dolphins' start two seven-footers across their front line.

1973 Offensive rebounds are recorded by the NBA as an official statistic for the first time. Moses Malone will go on to dominate the category, pulling down an NBA single-game record of 21 against Seattle in '82 and setting the regular-season mark of 587 in 1978-79.

1979 Malone grabs 38% of the Houston Rockets' boards, a figure believed to be the largest percentage of a team's rebounds ever claimed by a single player. Malone averages 17.7 rebounds a game over the 1978-79 season—a third more than runners-up Rich Kelley and Kareem Abdul-Jabbar.

1982 Washington State coach George Raveling writes *War on the Boards,* a textbook devoted to the importance and technique of rebounding.

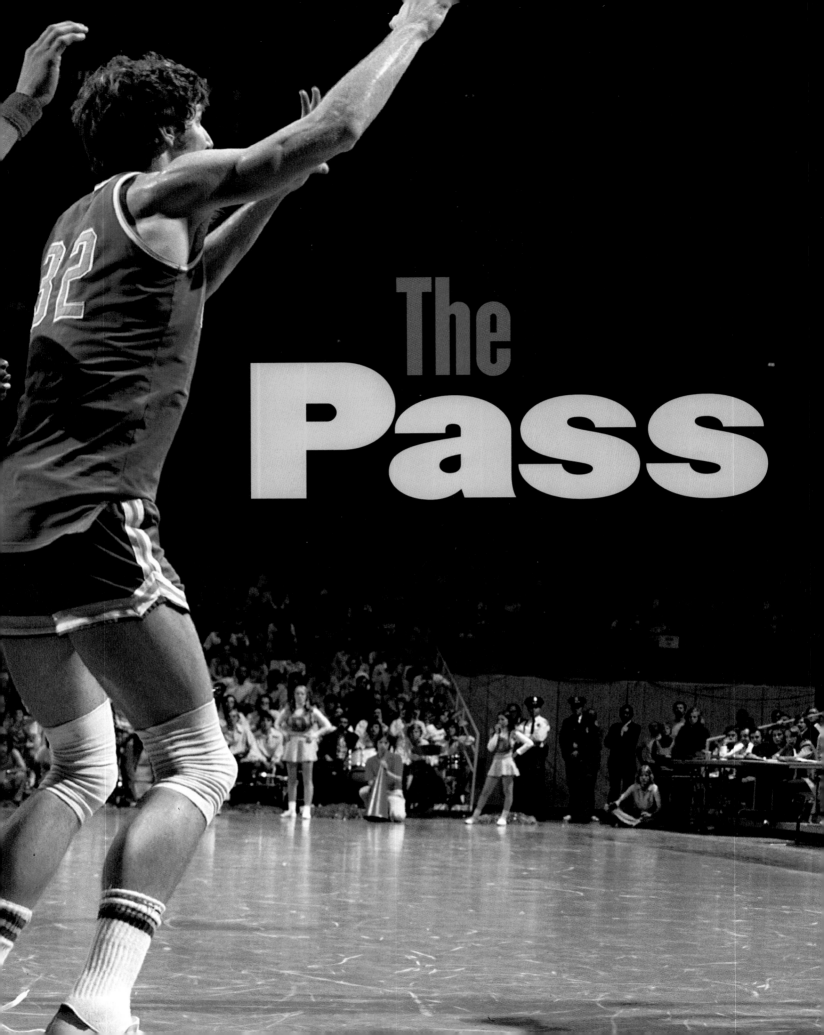

The
Pass

The Pass

1891 In the first basketball game ever, played in the gym at the YMCA Training School in Springfield, passing is the only sanctioned means of advancing the ball. The first of James Naismith's original thirteen rules reads, "The ball may be thrown in any direction with one or both hands."

1921 Manager Jim Furey signs Nat Holman, and the Original Celtics go on to become the dominant pro team of the '20s. Relying on a methodical motion offense, the precursor of today's passing game, the Celtics are also credited with perfecting the give-and-go.

1946 Bob Cousy, the New York-raised son of French immigrant parents, enrolls at Holy Cross. During his four seasons with the Crusaders, and later with the Boston Celtics, Cousy will popularize such passes as the behind-the-back and the no-look.

Faster than the dribble, rarer than the swish, so much subtler than the dunk—that's the good pass. While great shooters are made with long hours of lonely practice, the skilled passer owes his gift to things given by God, not acquired by man: peripheral vision, ambidexterity, uncommon hands, intuition.

If you doubt that the superb passer is the most esteemed player on the floor, just drop in on basketball's speakeasies, the schoolyards or steamy rec center gyms where the game is at its most unalloyed. Few plays executed here will touch off more spirited dealing of digits—on the part of both teams—than a shoveled no-look that finds its mark in full stride. The most coveted compliment on the playground isn't "nice slam" or "great shot." It's "nice look" or "good find."

There are passes, and then there's the right pass. To a driving cutter, it's the bounce pass; to an open shooter, the chest pass; to a man standing alone on the far side of the zone, the lobbed "skip" pass. Bob Cousy, Hot Rod Hundley and Pete Maravich went behind their backs. Larry Bird, Bill Bradley, Magic Johnson and Tom Gola looked away. Bill Walton, Willis Reed and Wes Unseld lit the fuses of their teams' fast breaks, turning the outlet pass into a prologue to the dunk and proving that the pass is a skill no player on the floor can afford to ignore.

The pass is what finally ran Kansas's Wilt Chamberlain from the college ranks. He was so frustrated by having to play twice a season against Henry Iba's glacially slow Oklahoma A&M offense—the Cowboys once threw 160 passes on a single possession before taking a shot—that he fled the Big Eight for good and took up with the Harlem Globetrotters, where every pass promised to be an adventure. Yet before his epic career was through, Chamberlain would discover the glories of the pass and find somewhere within him the ability to throw it to good effect. In 1968 he led the NBA in assists, the only time a center had done so. "It's like helping an old lady across the street," he once said of the pass. " 'Here, ma'am, here's my arm.' "

Those who have the gift assume a special station and are worshipped accordingly. When UNLV coach Jerry Tarkanian spoke of the doomed Lloyd Daniels, the crack-addicted playground star whose talents Tarkanian tried in vain to bring to big-time college basketball, the skill he raved most about was Daniels's ability to pass. Or, more precisely, the blessing it was to receive a pass from him. "So *soft,*" Tarkanian said of Daniels's passes, notwithstanding the hard world from which Daniels came.

Not necessarily the greatest pro teams, but the ones that captured the nation's imagination, did so with their passing: the Original Celtics; the Boston Celtics of the early '60s and early '80s; the Knicks of 1970; the Trail Blazers of '77. The '83 76ers and '89 Pistons worked every bit as hard in their post-and-pound systems as did the aforementioned in their pass-and-move schemes. But without the pass, they didn't have the same élan that the others did. And they aren't remembered nearly so vividly.

Cousy's Holy Cross teams of the late '40s were so enamored of the pass, it was said, they sometimes forgot to shoot. The Knicks' Dick McGuire, it was also said, was so smooth and so untouchable that he could play in a tuxedo. UCLA's Greg Lee lofted passes to teammate Walton for alley-oops so often that the two friends might have been Siamese twins joined at the eye.

If coaches can't actually throw passes, they surely think them. Those who cogitate most over this stark skill are the linguists of clipboardom—men who see in each movement of the ball, from one player to another, the game's smallest units of meaning, the very morphemes of hoop. At Boston College, Stanford and Iowa, Tom Davis insisted on bounce passes around the periphery of a zone, the better to stretch the defense at its edges, whereupon an entry pass could be whipped into that defense's softened midsection. When Princeton coach Pete Carril learned of a prospect, the first thing he wanted to know was, "Can he see?" He meant, "Can he pass?" The 1988 Soviet Olympic team of Alexander Gomelsky, with its knack for spreading the floor and moving the ball around the forecourt to any one of three ingeniously spaced three-point shooters, proved that the old hockey adage—no one's faster than the puck—is relevant to basketball. (The Russian word for pass, by the way, is *pass*.)

Coaches have never given up on the notion that the pass can be taught. But in the hurly-burly of a game, with "passing lanes" constantly narrowing, openings always evanescing and the exigencies of decision-making forever forcing his hand, a player has little time for thought. The pass may be practiced, preached and parsed, but, ultimately, it can only be thrown. In this way, the pass unfetters a player from a coach.

"If I can get the ball to a man with a pass behind my back as well as I can with a regular chest pass," Maravich said, "what's the difference?"

What's the difference, indeed. In high school Maravich had five coaches in five years. But in its 100 years, basketball has had only one Pistol Pete.

Cousy, the master of the no-look pass, dished this one off against the Lakers in the 1962 NBA Finals.

What's more, he will often throw them at the most tense moments of a game.

1966 As a 10th-grader at Daniels High in Clemson, S.C., Pete Maravich throws a behind-the-back bounce pass through an opponent's legs to a teammate for a layup. "I think, right then, showtime was born in me," he would say.

1972 The U.S.S.R.'s Ivan Edeshko throws a full-court pass to Aleksandr Belov for a last-second layup to defeat the United States 51-50. It's the first time the Americans fail to win the gold medal in Olympic basketball competition.

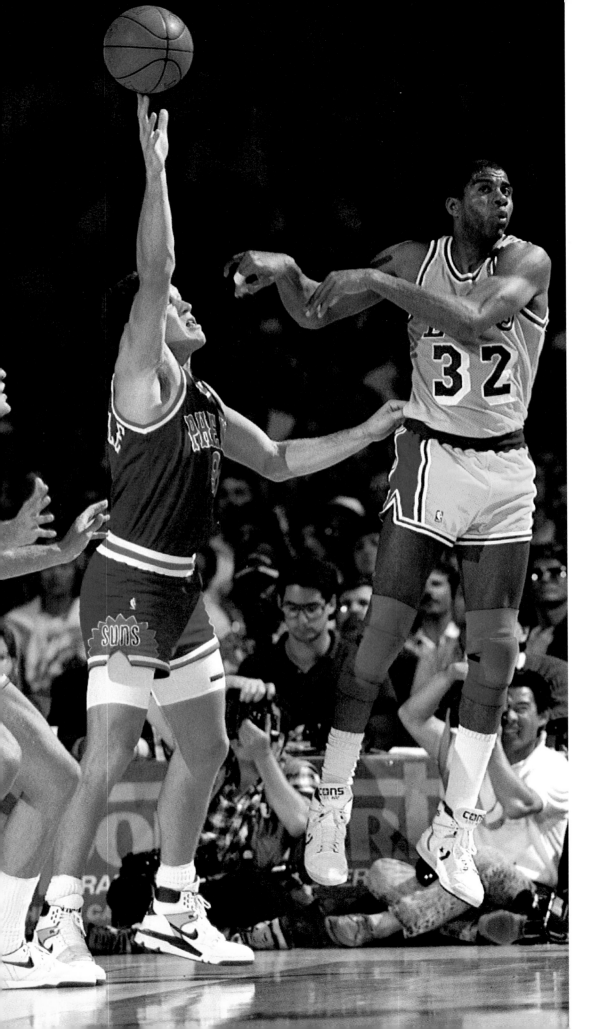

1973 Providence's Ernie DiGregorio whips a no-look, half-court, behind-the-back, through-a-crowd pass under pressure to teammate Marvin Barnes for a layup in the first half of the NCAA semifinals against Memphis State. Barnes goes down with a knee injury, however, and misses the second half, in which the Friars go on to lose.

1973 In the NCAA championship game, UCLA guard Greg Lee has 14 assists, most on lob passes over the Memphis State defense to Bruins center Bill Walton. "Our eyes meet, and I wail it up there," says Lee after the Bruins' easy 87-66 win.

1988 Utah's John Stockton dishes off 24 assists in a Western Conference semifinal game against the Lakers to tie Magic Johnson's single-game playoff mark.

1990 New York City high-schooler Adrian Autry, a swingman bound for Syracuse, introduces a new fast-break pass—a sort of on-the-move football hike to a trailing teammate—while playing for St. Nicholas of Tolentine High.

Magic (left) took the no-look one step further: He actually looked away; the Sixers' Andrew Toney went behind the back—not his own, an opponent's.

1990 Scott Skiles, a guard for the Orlando Magic, passes off for an NBA-record 30 assists in a game against the Denver Nuggets. His total surpasses the previous mark of 29 set by New Jersey's Kevin Porter in 1978. Skiles also scores 22 points in the 155–116 win.

1991 In a season in which he has already surpassed Oscar Robertson as the NBA's alltime assist leader, Magic Johnson makes yet another creative pass, to clinch the Lakers' 91–90 Game 6 semifinal playoff win over the Portland Trail Blazers and propel L.A. to its ninth appearance in the NBA Finals in 12 years. With five seconds remaining and the Lakers ahead by one, Johnson rebounds a jump shot by the Blazers' Terry Porter. Not wanting to run the risk of being fouled, he flips a soft, no-look, over-the-head, 10-bounce pass into the empty backcourt. Only .1 of a second remains on the clock when the ball finally bounces out of bounds.

The Dribble

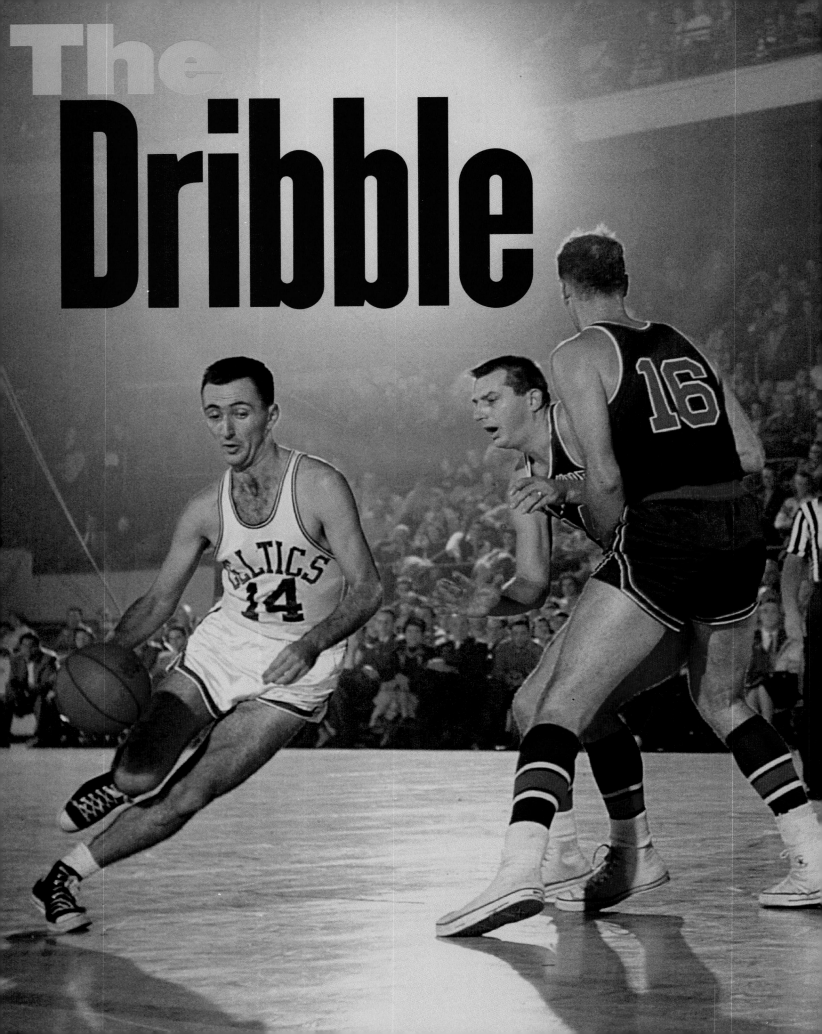

The Dribble

1896 Players on the Yale team first use the dribble in competition. Rules are hastily introduced to restrict the practice.

1896 Dutch Wohlfarth, a member of the Trenton YMCA team that played the first pro game, begins attracting attention for his ability to dribble without looking at the ball. "The Blind Dribbler" is arguably basketball's first gate attraction.

1898 The double dribble is outlawed.

1929 All restrictions on dribbling are eliminated, due largely to the lobbying of Nat Holman, star of the Original Celtics and later the coach of C.C.N.Y. Although the Celtics are noted for their passing, not their dribbling, Holman believes that college players can't be expected to pass as proficiently as the pros do,

James Naismith made no mention of dribbling in his original thirteen rules. He stipulated only that there be no running with the ball and that a player throw a pass from the same spot he received it. Naismith's was a nettlesome oversight. (You can imagine the early practitioners of the game, much like today's Supreme Court justices, chewing over the issue: "Whatever did the Founding Father *intend?*") And thus for most of basketball's first 40 years dribbling existed as a shadowy stepskill, always frowned upon by some reproachful regulation.

Not until 1929 were the shackles on dribbling removed entirely, and when they were, players didn't know quite what to do with it. The dribble had previously been a defensive maneuver, a tactic that allowed a player to stay free from the defense until he became favored with an opportunity to pass. But with the arrival of the great innovator Hank Luisetti, and with the cross-pollination of playing styles brought on by the widespread intersectional play of the '30s, players and coaches began to see its offensive possibilities. The dribble slowly evolved into an element of attack.

It took the 6' 1" Bob Cousy to bring the dribble to its widest audience. Cousy's legerdemain gave new appeal to a game previously best known for thyroidal curiosities like Bob Kurland and George Mikan. Fans accustomed to gawking upward suddenly derived an entirely new kind of wonder from watching a basketball player they could look directly in the eye. In 1949 Cousy, then a junior at Holy Cross, dribbled behind his back for the first time, in the final seconds of a game against Loyola at the Boston Garden. Ramblers guard Gerry Nagel had overplayed Cousy to the star's right, so the Cooz dodged Nagel with a sweep of the ball around his own body, then tossed in a lefthand hook to give the Crusaders the win. "I had him covered, and then he sort of disappeared," Nagel said afterward. "The guy is a magician."

To Cousy, the move wasn't calculated vaudeville but inspired pragmatism. "The fact of the matter is that I had never even thought of such a maneuver until the moment the situation forced me into it," he said. "It was purely and simply one of those cases when necessity is the mother of invention. I was absolutely amazed myself at what I had done. It was only much later that I began to practice it so that I could make it a reliable part of my repertoire."

It took a few years for the generation of kids wowed by Cousy to make their way into basketball. But once they did—once the skill had filtered down to the schoolyard, and eventually percolated back up through the organized game again—the flashy dribble went legit. From Pete Maravich, who grew up sitting in the aisle seat at the movie theater so he could practice dribbling in the dark, it acquired the plumage of style. From Earl Monroe, a dervish so creative that he forced referees essentially to suspend the palming rule, it found a fusion of form and function every bit as coach-friendly as it was crowd-pleasing. From Bob Nickerson of Gallitzin, Pa., who once dribbled four balls at the same time for five minutes, it even got a place in *Guinness*.

As the dunk was to the little guy, the dribble was to his goony counterpart—the Walter Mitty skill he just had to prove he could master. Tennessee coach Ray Mears felt likewise, developing an entire series of exercises integrating reverse dribbles, dribbles upcourt against pressure and dribbles between the legs. The Vols devoted themselves assiduously to this regimen in practice and became so adept at it that Mears put together a lavishly choreographed pregame show, which, during the '60s, riveted those parts of the Southeastern Conference that had always thought of their league as consisting of nothing more than Kentucky and various stooge teams.

If solitary shooters are blessed by that trinity of player, hoop and ball, the dribble reduces to player and ball, no hoop required. Thus some of the game's greatest ball handlers were also among its most notorious loners, whether their solitude was the result of choice or circumstance. Kentucky star Cliff Barker, a member of Adolph Rupp's Fabulous Five of the late '40s, learned to dribble as an Air Force sergeant during a stay in a German P.O.W. camp. Hot Rod Hundley, a star at West Virginia and with the Lakers, developed his handle by playing hooky and going down to the Charleston YMCA. With no one else around, he eventually would become bored shooting and step into an empty handball court. There he would dribble alone, whipping the ball off the four walls, his hands always active.

To the adept dribbler sailing down the floor, the ball is no burden. It becomes instead a sort of antiweight, a hedge against the customary laws of nature. "Everyone on that team could beat me in a sprint," said Ernie DiGregorio, star of the 1973 Providence Friars. "But no one could beat me in a sprint dribbling a basketball."

Even with mediocre teams like the Atlanta Hawks, Maravich's ball handling skills continued to shine.

and thus should have dribbling as a recourse.

1934 A rule change providing for a slightly smaller ball, reduced from 32" in circumference to about 30", makes dribbling easier.

1938 Taking his inspiration from the exploits of Stanford's Hank Luisetti, Bob Davies uses the behind-the-back dribble in a game as a high school senior in Harrisburg, Pa. He will eventually go on to stardom as a slick ball handler for Seton Hall and the NBA's Rochester Royals.

1945 As payback to Southern University, which had shown up another league school earlier that season, Langston University guard Marques Haynes launches into a 2½-minute behind-the-back, through-the legs, sliding-onto-his-side, all-the-while dribbling routine as the clock runs out with Langston leading Southern in the finals of the Southwestern Athletic Conference tournament. Haynes will go on to become known as "the World's Greatest Dribbler" in a career with the Harlem Globetrotters and Harlem Magicians that spans more than 40 years.

1946 Bob Cousy enrolls at Holy Cross, where he will hone his astonishing dribbling repertoire. By the time he retires from the game, after four years at Holy Cross and 14 more in the pros—all but one of them with the Boston Celtics—Cousy will have greatly expanded the universe of ball handling possibility, having perfected the behind-the-back and reverse dribbles, among other creative maneuvers. His legerdemain will help produce one NCAA and six NBA titles.

Frazier's slick skills (left) produced two titles for the Knicks in the '70s; Scottie Pippen helped bring three to Chicago in the '90s. Will there be more?

1972 In a game against Milwaukee, the New York Knicks, led by point guard Walt Frazier, commit just four turnovers, the fewest by any team since the NBA began keeping the statistic in 1970. The mark will go unbeaten until 1991 when Portland commits just three in a game against Phoenix.

1981 Brigham Young's Danny Ainge slalom-dribbles through the Notre Dame defense, then tosses in a layup as the buzzer sounds, to give the Cougars an NCAA East Regional semifinal victory over the Irish. Ainge's feat will become known as "the March through Atlanta."

1987 In an early-round playoff game against Atlanta, Detroit's Isiah Thomas taunts the Hawks' Glenn (Doc) Rivers with his "speed dribble," a rapid, low-to-the-ground ball movement akin to the Ali shuffle. The Pistons go on to defeat Atlanta in five games before losing to Boston in the Eastern Conference finals.

The Dunk

The Dunk

It's as likely to provide a moment of grace (thank you, Julius Erving) as one of destruction (that's you, Darryl Dawkins). High stakes ride on it, for a missed one can sap a team of its momentum as surely as a successful one, brought off with a high degree of difficulty, can springboard a team to unprecedented heights. And it's a star turn, reserved for those elite men—and women, too—who must be credentialed (the Doctors of Dunk; Phi Slama Jama) before their flamboyance is accepted.

Yes, there are those who find the dunk boring in its high percentage and sameness. But even if the actual throwing down of a shot may lack style or excitement, it's the context of a dunk—was it on the break? off the business end of an alley-oop pass? *in traffic?*—that frames and flatters it. Best of all, coaches have nothing to contribute to the pedagogy of the dunk other than their furrowed brows and usual admonitions to their eager charges not to mess it up. If the dunk ever dies, we shall rue the day, but we will have an epitaph ready in the words of Lloyd Hill, the Brooklyn playground regular who figured in Rick Telander's classic *Heaven Is a Playground:* "I think I may put my bed out under the basket, sleep right there, and take a few jams when I get up in the morning."

Within the genus dunk are two species, *punk dunk* and *funk dunk.* With punk dunk, "face" is at stake. Certainly a player wants to score, but the act of punk dunking has as its goal the humiliation of any defender who has impudently imposed himself between the dunker and the basket. Funk dunk, by contrast, has to do with style points. It's gutbucket, improvisational, involving just the dunker and the ball, a solo thrown to the trumpeter by the other guys in the band.

George Gervin's specialty was the *afterthought.* He sailed past the rim, seemingly otherwise occupied, then jackknifed the ball back through the hoop—"Oh, by the way . . .," he seemed to say—before passing out of range. Darrell Griffith had the power and strength to do the *circle,* in which he described a full 360 degrees, floor-to-ceiling, with his shooting hand while levitating toward the hole. New York City playground legend Earl (Goat) Manigault made his rep on the *corkscrew,* turning his body a revolution or two during his ascent. Masters of timing and spring can perform the *tap,* spearing an offensive rebound above the rim and driving it home in one sudden motion. Legions of playground court jesters have messed with the *midwife,* in which the ball is stashed under a loose fitting T-shirt, then "delivered" in midair.

Dawkins carefully cultivated his notoriety as a destroyer of backboards, shattering two during his career. But the father of broken backboards remains Baltimore's Gus Johnson, who destroyed three, including one in 1963 during his rookie season, thereby spawning an addition to the hoops lexicon (to *gusjohnson* (vt): to shatter a backboard by dunking. *I gusjohnson, you gusjohnson, he gusjohnsons*). When Johnson dunked at home, the recorded sound of a gunshot would play over the Bullets' P.A. system. Johnson once recalled what it was like to "pull the trigger" on a dunk: "When I dunked that ball and heard that shot for the first time, I said to myself, 'Uh-oh, Gus. Somebody done gotcha.' But man, that was sweet music. It sure did make me feel good inside."

Like anything once forbidden, the dunk redoubled in allure by withstanding its own Prohibition. For eight seasons, from the late '60s to the mid-'70s, the college game outlawed it. Many people considered the rule the last desperate act of a grounded majority frustrated at watching basketball become an increasingly high-wire, black game. Others saw more than coincidence in the fact that the dunk was proscribed just when 7' 1" Lew Alcindor, then a UCLA sophomore, began to dominate so. The irony of the ban, of course, is that Alcindor only became more dominant because of it, using the slamless interregnum to add an array of short shots to his repertoire, and further hone his skyhook.

"It was hard to live with," said Minnesota's Ray Williams of those lean years. "There were so many times I'd be flying up above the rim, ready to jam, when I'd hear this voice saying, 'No, no, no.'" Sometimes Williams, like others, would ignore the voice and throw it down anyway, incurring a technical foul. No matter: "Those slams always felt better than any technical could ever hurt."

When the rule makers finally came to their senses and the lid came off again, a celebration broke out above the rim. Wiley Peck of Mississippi State dunked so emphatically in one game in 1976 that the ball came through the net and hit him in the face, knocking him cold for two minutes. And Claude (Snowflake) English, an erstwhile high-flyer at little Christian College of the Southwest, opened a gash on his head from hitting it on the rim while dunking.

All things considered, English would say, "it was worth it."

The author of many a monster slam, Dawkins performed this one against L.A. in the 1980 NBA Finals.

the Chicago Stags. A visiting rodeo provides a replacement board and the game goes on.

1963 In perhaps the most storied schoolyard dunk ever, 6' 2" Earl (Goat) Manigault throws one down over two college stars, 6' 5" Vaughn Harper and 6' 9" Val Reed, at a gym on 113th Street in Harlem. Oral historians differ, but the shot is said to have begun at the foul line and included two full corkscrew revolutions in flight. "I have personally never seen its equal," Harlemite Bobby Hunter will say. "And I was in Detroit at the time."

1967 The dunk is banned in college and high school play, ostensibly to curtail injuries and damage to equipment, but probably also to limit the incipient dominance of 7' 1" UCLA center Lew Alcindor.

1976 To the delight of fans and players alike, the dunk is restored to the amateur game.

1979 Philadelphia 76er Darryl Dawkins shatters two backboards in 22 days with slam dunks, thus inspiring the invention of the snap-back collapsible rim. Dawkins christens his first dunk, which brings a hail of glass down on Bill Robinzine of the Kansas City Kings, the "Chocolate-Thunder Flyin', Robinzine-Cryin', Teeth-Shakin', Glass-Breakin', Rump-Roastin', Bun-Toastin', Wham, Bam, Glass-Breaker-I-Am Jam."

1983 In the NCAA semifinal game between Houston and Louisville, the brothers of Phi Slama Jama and the Doctors of Dunk cut each other up in a back-and-forth dunkfest won by the Cougars and highlighted by a full-flight slam by Houston's Clyde Drexler.

A pair of legendary dunks: Sidney Moncrief's two-hander against Texas in '78 (left) and Spud Webb's high-wire act in the NBA Slam-Dunk contest in '86.

1984 In a 110-82 victory over the University of Charleston in Elkins, W.Va., 6' 7" Georgeann Wells of West Virginia becomes the first woman to perform a dunk in competition. "I made two or three dribbles," she would say, "and then I took the glide."

1986 Spud Webb of the Atlanta Hawks, just 5' 7", wins the Slam-Dunk contest at the NBA All-Star Game. Although he is unable to palm a basketball, Webb uses his 42-inch vertical jump—and two brilliant dunks that draw perfect scores of 50 from the judges—to edge out teammate Dominique Wilkins for the title.

1993 Upon the completion of his rookie season with the Orlando Magic, No. 1 draft pick Shaquille O'Neal can claim responsibility, in one NBA season and two at Louisiana State, for three broken rims, two shattered backboards and two torn-down standards.

The Steal

The Steal

The cognoscenti have had an abiding love-hate relationship with the steal. When it works—when a ball handler is fleeced at midcourt, his offensive foray turned instantly into a reversal of fortune—the defense seizes an advantage twice over. Statistically it has scored. Psychologically it has devastated.

Yet basketball purists have come to regard the steal with suspicion. The steal, they believe, runs its own cruel con game on basketball's would-be wiseguys, the lure of its payoff seducing players into wanton gambles that only make the entire team's defense vulnerable. Red Auerbach's attitude toward the steal is typical. As kind as the play has been to his Boston Celtics, delivering them three times—Havlicek stole the ball; then Gerald Henderson; then Larry Bird—from possible or likely playoff losses, Auerbach never much cottoned to it. "Steals give very little indication of a guy's defensive ability," he once said. "After a while a kid starts thinking about steals and doesn't play defense. Nobody keeps a record of how many times they miss a steal and the guy goes by them."

And so the steal has entirely bypassed the primers of the hidebound hoops fundamentalists, taking its place in the game thanks instead to the élan of its most captivating practitioners. Basketball's best thieves tend to be the game's savvier players. They play by the seat of their shorts. They're more likely to be city-bred than country, to play backcourt than fore, and without exception they share a clannish pride in their oft-scorned craft.

It has been this way at least since Walt (Clyde) Frazier turned the steal into a sort of cult ritual as floor leader of the New York Knicks of the late '60s and early '70s. Clyde even dressed like bankrobber Clyde Barrow, with wide lapels and natty fedoras, and squired would-be Bonnies conspicuously through the New York night. Frazier never actually claimed to have stolen hubcaps off a moving car, but he didn't discourage speculation that he could. "Clyde," teammate Willis Reed once said, while the Knicks were waiting for a tardy motorcoach, "go steal us a bus." Eventually NBA teams began positioning their guards far apart from one another to keep the Knicks' backcourt—the similarly predatory Dick Barnett and Mike Riordan were the other guards—from double-teaming the ball. Wags along press row, remembering baseball's Ted Williams, called this maneuver the Frazier Shift.

Speed is no requisite for practicing the art of the steal; witness the lead-footed Dean (the Dream) Meminger. Strong hands are as valuable as quick ones. Long arms—consider Sidney Moncrief—help immensely. Reggie Bird, a hard-nosed white kid from the hardscrabble streets of Boston, didn't even start for Ivy League Princeton, yet wound up being drafted by the pros, solely because of his larcenous heart.

Don Buse was a specialist at picking off a crossover dribble, and Jerry West expert at poaching into the path of a pass. No one could double back and pick off a lazy inbound better than Alvin Robertson. Larry Bird mastered the front-the-post pirouette that can foil the entry passes most offenses rely on in the forecourt. Tyrone (Muggsy) Bogues, said Ernie Nestor, the assistant who recruited him to Wake Forest, "activates the greatest fear a guard has—to be stripped at half court in front of God and the whole world." (If you don't see the 5' 3" Muggsy, the rule of thumb went, he's about to steal the ball.) And no one better learned the skill of "doubling down" on an unsuspecting big man than Maurice Cheeks.

Cheeks has a visage that, even more than Frazier's, begs to be framed by the brim of a hat and the turned-up collar of a trenchcoat. He has stolen the ball more often than any other professional since 1973, when the NBA began keeping track of crime rates. Most of the time, it seems, Cheeks does so by foraging through the low post.

The steal, like every other element of the game, has evolved. As point guards got bigger, it became ever harder to strip a dribbler outright. Thus more and more steals are in fact interceptions, not ball-liftings. They come off traps, tips and roadblocks of the passing lanes. "He knows how to play the passing lanes" was once the most damnable compliment in the basketball lexicon, sort of the "she has a nice personality" of defense. Now, however, that description is no longer reserved for ballplayers who can't move their feet.

Shooters are made by practice, rebounders by will and passers by vision and knack. While the steal draws on many of those attributes, no act in the game follows more directly from study and guile. Seeing tendencies, in an opponent or an offense. Registering how to turn those patterns to your advantage. Disguising this realization until the most opportune time, when that inner voice—anticipation, any thief will say, is at the heart of all this—tells you to go for it.

The old-fogey second-guessers be damned.

After Texas Western's Hill stripped Kentucky's Dampier, the Miners were off and running to their historic win.

the first half of the NCAA championship game, Bobby Joe Hill of Texas Western strips Kentucky guards Tommy Kron and Louie Dampier on two consecutive possessions. Hill's steals, and the layups that follow, set the tone for the all-black Miners' historic victory over the all-white Wildcats.

1969 Trailing the Cincinnati Royals 105–100 with 16 seconds to play, the New York Knicks steal the ball twice in succession and score each time. The Knicks' 106–105 victory is their 18th in a row, then the longest winning streak in NBA history.

After Havlicek stole Greer's pass, the Celtics won the game, Most went ballistic and Boston was one step closer to another banner for the Garden rafters.

1982 James Worthy of North Carolina records an easy but critical steal when Georgetown's Freddie Brown mistakes him for a teammate and passes him the ball with eight seconds left in the NCAA title game. Brown's gaffe allows the Tar Heels to run out the clock and win the game 63-62.

1986 Alvin Robertson of San Antonio makes 301 steals to set an NBA single-season mark.

1987 Larry Bird, in an eerie reprise of Havlicek's steal, steps in front of an Isiah Thomas inbounds pass, then feeds to a cutting Dennis Johnson for the winning basket as Boston defeats Detroit in Game 5 of the Eastern Conference finals. This time, Most is more subdued: "Now there's a steal by Bird ... underneath to DJ ... he scores!"

1990 Nevada-Las Vegas routs Duke 103-73 in the NCAA title game, running off with the victory thanks largely to a tournament-record 16 steals.

The Block

The Block

1891 The second of Naismith's original thirteen rules reads: "The ball may be batted in any direction with one or both hands."

1944 Motivated by the dominance of Oklahoma A&M's Bob Kurland and DePaul's George Mikan, who would position themselves under the basket and swat shots away from the rim with impunity, the college game adopts the goaltending rule, which prohibits a defensive player from touching a shot on its downward flight.

1950 C.C.N.Y.'s Gene Dambrot blocks a final shot by Bradley star Gene Melchiorre to clinch the Beavers' 71-68 victory in the NCAA championship game. Coached by Nat Holman, City College had already won the NIT title and thus became the only team ever to win NCAA and NIT crowns in the same season.

If basketball really is the big man's game it has so long been made out to be; if "the last piece of the puzzle" coveted by so many recruiters and general managers truly is that long cutting from a jigsaw; if the future every coach fondly envisions is in fact one in which the vertical hold has gone haywire—if all this is true, then surely the blocked shot must stand as the reason.

A center will score baskets. He'll grab rebounds. He'll even kick out an outlet pass or two in good time. But if the man in the middle can also block two or three shots a game, alter a few more and begin to mess with the minds of the other team's shooters, he has enhanced his value immensely. Blocking a shot is like planting a tree: You never know how much your effort will yield—what exactly will blossom—until late in a game when you benefit the most.

In the game's peculiar argot, the blocked shot goes by colorful aliases, words that conjure up images of repression and claustrophobia. *Gate. Grill. Check. Snuff. Stuff. Rejection.* It is also, curiously enough, a skill that favors the ingenue. A great shot blocker isn't yet so much a party to basketball's rhythms that he will be deceived by a pump fake, a look-off or any other sort of mambo. Either that, or he has so rigorously disciplined himself that, though aware of those rhythms, he nevertheless moves to his own cadence.

Georgetown brought together two of the college game's greatest shot blockers during the late '80s, one from each of the two species. Alonzo Mourning at 6' 10" had a spare and savvy style of rejection, in which he had learned to leaven his intensity with discipline. Dikembe Mutombo, a tad taller at 7' 2", came to the game late while growing up in Zaire and never picked up any of the bad habits borne of the playground. Thus he would look down almost bemusedly at offensive players as they lurched through their feints, pumps and other futile gestures; when the shooter was finally ready to shoot, Mutombo was ready, too.

If you were to convene the game's great shot blockers, men like Mourning, Bill Walton and Bill Russell, for a clinic, they might walk you through their art. You would find that much of blocking shots involves the mind—exercising judgment, showing discipline, laying down a good psych. First you hang back, to goad an adventuresome shooter into testing the lane. Then you show discretion. You don't want to exhaust yourself by going after every shot, only enough so a notion begins to prey on the shooter's mind that there's a possibility you'll up-

and challenge him. When you do rise to block a shot, you try at all costs to keep the ball inbounds, so possession won't revert automatically to the offense. Finally, it is your job to start the break, and not necessarily be an integral part of it—unless, of course, you have rare speed and a knack for finishing, like David Robinson.

It helps to be lefthanded, like Russell, to "mirror" the right hand, which most shooters use, and not have to reach across your body—but it isn't necessary to possess Russell's array of skills to be effective. Unlike Russell, such centers as Mark Eaton, Manute Bol, Caldwell Jones, Marvin (the Human Eraser) Webster, George Johnson and Wayne (Tree) Rollins—he of the 42-inch sleeve length—did little more than block shots. Nonetheless, during the mid-80s the woebegone Utah Jazz built their offense around Eaton's single skill and were able to change their fortunes. Though they would be routinely outrebounded the Jazz taught their guards to treat an Eaton block as if it were an outlet pass, and scamper off with it.

Tied up in the blocked shot is also a one-upmanship every bit as profound as the in-your-face ethos at play when dunking over someone. Consider the experience of Tom Wilkinson, a guard who played at Penn State during the late '70s. Wilkinson found himself shopping for clothes at a New York City haberdashery one afternoon, a good decade after the end of his relatively undistinguished college career. Across the floor he spotted the distinctive profile of Darrell Griffith, who was killing some time before his Jazz were to meet the Knicks.

Wilkinson went up to Griffith to introduce himself. He reminded Griffith of their brief moment of shared history: Penn State had had the opportunity, back in 1978, to play Griffith and Louisville's Doctors of Dunk in the Seawolf Classic. And though they had been thumped by 31 points, the Nittany Lions, as the moment receded, had come to consider the game to be an honor and a thrill, for Griffith and his teammates had gone on to win the NCAA title at the end of the next season.

Wilkinson said all this. But he made no mention of one other memory from that game, one seared deep into his mind: getting loose on a breakaway, seemingly uncatchable, and sailing up toward the basket . . . only to have Griffith materialize to fix the ball fast against the glass.

He and Griffith exchanged farewells, and repaired to different parts of the store.

Moments later Wilkinson heard a voice behind him. It was Griffith. "Yeah, I remember you," Griffith said. "Didn't I pin your shit?"

Notre Dame's Keith Tower had no chance to get this shot over Mutombo in the 1989 NCAA tournament.

1965 The New York City playground scene, now in its golden age, features such shot-blocking innovators as Jackie Jackson and Connie Hawkins. "[Some] noted leapers were famous for 'pinning'—blocking a layup, then simply holding it momentarily against the backboard in a gesture of triumph," wrote Pete Axthelm in *The City Game*. "Some players seemed to hold it for seconds, suspended in air, multiplying the humiliation of the man who had tried the futile shot. Then they could slam the ball back down at the shooter or, for special emphasis, flip it into the crowd."

1970 Sidney Wicks (6' 8")
blocks a shot by Jacksonville's
Artis Gilmore (7' 2") early in
UCLA's national title match
against the Dolphins. UCLA
coach John Wooden had
moved 6' 9" Steve Patterson,
nominally the Bruins' center, to
forward so Wicks could guard
Gilmore.

1973 The NBA adds blocked
shots as a statistical category,
and L.A.'s Elmore Smith leads
the league in blocks during
the 1973-74 season, with an
average of 4.85 per game.
"You can push and shove
underneath," says Smith. "But
is there any better way to
protect the basket than to
stop the ball before it gets
there?"

1974 In the first minute of
North Carolina State's NCAA
semifinal game with UCLA, the
Wolfpack's David Thompson
blocks a shot by Bill Walton.
N.C. State goes on to defeat
the Bruins, interrupting their
string of seven titles; two
days later Thompson's
teammate, 7' 4" Tom
Burleson, blocks an NCAA-
record seven shots in the
Pack's championship game
defeat of Marquette.

LSU's Shaquille O'Neal left no doubt on his emphatic '91 stuff (left), but in '72 Wilt Chamberlain found Kareem Abdul-Jabbar's skyhook a bit of a reach.

1977 Portland's Bill Walton blocks eight Philadelphia shots in a 109-107 victory that clinches the Trail Blazers's first NBA title. Walton also scores 20 points, grabs 23 rebounds and passes off for seven assists as the Blazers defeat the 76ers in six games.

1985 Utah's Mark Eaton plays in his 94th consecutive game with at least one blocked shot. "Wilt once told me, 'The only way you're going to survive is to think of yourself as the last line of defense,' " Eaton says. "That's how I've approached the game ever since."

1986 Navy's David Robinson blocks 207 shots over the course of the season, more than the total of any Division I team except national champion Louisville.

1988 Alonzo Mourning, a 6' 10" senior at Indian River High in Chesapeake, Va., blocks 29 shots in an AAU tournament game. Mourning goes on to Georgetown, where he leads the nation in blocks as a freshman.

The Free Throw

he

The Free Throw

1894 James Naismith, who is still keeping the game's official rules, adds the free throw: "Whenever a foul had been made, the opposite side shall have a free throw for goal at a distance of twenty feet from the basket and directly before it." Up to that time, the team that had been fouled received a single point automatically. That led to objections that the offended team could score points without really earning them. A year later the shot's distance is shortened to 15 feet, and in **1896** the value of a field goal is doubled to two points, with the free throw remaining at one.

1911 To discourage the proliferating practice of fouling a player just as he is about to shoot, the two-shot foul rule is introduced for fouls committed in the act of shooting.

Basketball's players have usually outstripped its coaches in pushing the game to new heights. Quite rightly, players over the years have ignored the killjoy urgings they've heard from the bench, calls like "Don't dunk!" and "Use the glass!" and "Make the simple pass!" The game is richer because of the incorrigibility of a handful of its visionaries. Yet it is entirely fair that, at the opposite end of the spectrum from the 360 throwdown, there should be the free throw. It is basketball's Norman Rockwell painting, the one skill frozen in time, a redoubt in which all the finicky pedagogues can hole up. It rewards fastidious allegiance to every coaching buzzword—repetition, practice, concentration, practice, discipline, practice, composure, practice, mental toughness and more practice. Coaches tell you that if you don't make your free throws, it's gonna getcha. And you know what? Coaches are right.

As early as 1897, Thomas J. Browne, writing in *Spalding's Official Basket Ball Guide,* spoke truths about shooting free throws that still hold up today. He proposed that the shooter adopt a consistent way of "goal-throwing"—with the lacing pointed in a particular direction, and the seams oriented just so—so he might better become "familiar with any peculiarities in the shape of the ball." In the same article, Browne counseled teams to send their best shooter to the line at every opportunity—a strategy already in wide practice, and one that would remain legal for another quarter century.

Routine would be every bit as essential to the free throw nearly 100 years later. Larry Bird, in a sort of genuflection to the altar of the basket, reached down and touched the bottoms of his sneakers before squeezing his off. Willis Reed took the deepest of breaths to relax his body, breaths that caused the medallion around his neck to quiver slightly as he exhaled. Kyle Macy, who always looked as if he had been plucked straight from the church choir, dried his hands on his socks, kept his feet a perfect shoulder's width apart, took three dribbles and two deep breaths, laid his fingers on the seams just so and launched his foul shot in a single, fluid motion.

Are we laying on the religious imagery a little too thick here? Perhaps. But why then do they call it the charity stripe?

Over the years the free throw has attracted a community of free throw acolytes, men like Bunny Levitt, Ted St. Martin and Ernie Hobbie, who are almost rabbinical in their devotion to the shot's proper practice. (In 1935 Levitt, then a Chicago schoolboy, made 499 straight at a sports carnival, missed one, and made 386 more, all underhand.) They examine such minutiae as depth of knee bends and angles of elbows, but largely they counsel concentration, confidence and practice, practice, practice. "Constant practice," Levitt said, "should make a foul shot a reflex."

If it's not a reflex, of course, you think your way through the shot. And that's where the trouble starts. There has emerged a sort of cult of free throw defense—fans who defend the indefensible shot by somehow getting the shooter to think. They do this by unfurling posters of pinup models, waving arms or audibly counting the number of preparatory dribbles the shooter takes to get loose. (The Duke student section has prided itself on this skill, but over the years opponents have shot at least as well in Cameron Indoor Stadium as they have at home. Total silence, the Dookies may soon discover, is the biggest distraction.)

The free throw's most fascinating legacy over the years may have been its ability to utterly bamboozle so many of the game's greatest athletes. Their failure to sink a simple, wide-open 15-footer at least 70% of the time keeps both sports psychologists and armchair theorists busy. Curiously, even as Rick Barry shot fouls better than anyone else in the game, no one imitated his style, despite its demonstrable advantages. (Two hands offer more control than one; an underhand delivery results in a softer shot, more likely to drop in after hitting the rim; and relatively little stress is placed on the legs and arms, which are likely to be tired at the end of games, when most critical free throws are attempted.) As sports shrink Bruce Ogilvie told *The Wall Street Journal,* ego has a way of impeding. "With athletes, the big things are their masculinity and physical approaches," said Ogilvie. "They don't want to be caught looking clumsy or uncool no matter how much something might help them in the long run. Everyone knows the Barry method will work for anyone who gives it a decent try. The trouble is it looks awkward and even a little feminine."

All things considered, it may depend on how the man toeing the line chooses to look at matters—whether he considers it *free throw* or *foul shot.* Free throws are free, tossed off, blithe and easy. They go without saying, and it's best to think of them that way. Foul shots? They're rancid, *most* foul, and the buckshot from a foul shot can wind up in your foot. "The foul line is the one place on the basketball court where you can choke," Bob Cousy has said. "Everything else is action and reaction. You don't have time to choke."

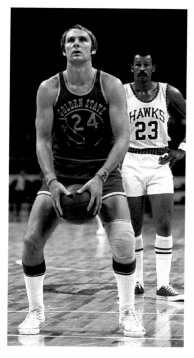

It may not look macho, but Barry's underhanded approach made him the best free throw shooter in NBA history.

1923 A new rule requires that free throws be shot by the player who has been fouled, rather than by the team's most accurate free throw shooter as had previously been the practice.

1953 Playing before a hostile crowd in Kansas City, Indiana's Bob (Slick) Leonard steps to the line with 27 seconds to play in the NCAA title game against Kansas. He misses his first shot but sinks the second, wrapping up the Hurryin' Hoosiers' 69-68 victory.

1968 Wilt Chamberlain, shooting his free throws underhand, connects on just 38% of his attempts in the 1967-68 season.

1969 Against Oregon State, Pete Maravich of Louisiana State sinks 30 of 31 free throws, an NCAA record for most free throws made in a single game.

1971 Boston rookie Garfield Smith pulls off what's known informally around the NBA as the hat trick, missing all of his free throws in a three-to-make-two bonus situation. But Smith does the hat trick one better. Each of his three missed foul shots is an air ball.

1977 Ted St. Martin, 41, makes 2,036 consecutive free throws over three days during an appearance at a shopping mall in Jacksonville. The mark breaks his own record, set two years earlier, of 1,074 straight.

1979 Rick Barry, shooting his free throws in the same way that Chamberlain did, makes 94.7% over the 1978-79 season.

Two sides of a champion: Robinson took aim on the game-winning free throw (left), then celebrated the outcome—an NCAA title for the Wolverines.

1979 Daryl Moreau of de LaSalle High in New Orleans makes 126 straight free throws over two seasons, the longest in-game streak at any level.

1981 Over two months, Houston's Calvin Murphy sinks an NBA-record 78 straight free throws on his way to the league's single-season free throw percentage record of .958. In 1993, Michael Williams of Minnesota will eclipse Murphy's mark by knocking down 84 straight—a streak that would still be alive as the 1993-94 season began.

1989 Michigan guard Rumeal Robinson sinks two free throws with three seconds to play in overtime to defeat Seton Hall, 80-79, and win the NCAA title.

1989 Cleveland's Chris Dudley, on one trip to the free throw line, misses five straight free throws—both ends of a two-shot foul and three more shots on three consecutive Washington lane violations.

Speed

Speed

1893 After two years of existence as a game made up of 15-minute halves, basketball is altered such that a game consists of "two halves of twenty minutes each or such time as the captains may mutually agree upon"—a length that has remained the amateur standard ever since.

1897 Another rule change reduces the number of players on a team from nine to five. This unclogs the court and encourages movement.

1915 The Troy (N.Y.) Trojans, known as Wachter's Wonders after star (and coach) Ed Wachter, go 29-0 on a 39-day tour of the Midwest. Their offensive tactics aren't particularly organized, nor do they have a name. But the Trojans are considered the first fast-breaking team.

James Naismith fed rabbit to his track athletes the day before big meets because he believed it would make them run faster. No hoops coach is known to have done that, not even on the eve of a game with the Hurryin' Hoosiers, the Runnin' Rebels or any of the many other track clubs that have formed over basketball's first century. But if what philosophers tell us is true—that our world distills to the two fundamentals of time and space—then coaches have little choice. Basketball's space is unalterable: 94 feet here, 10 feet there, the ball 30" in circumference. Time, on the other hand, can be played with.

Is it mere coincidence that so many of the coaches who have tinkered with time were academics or teachers of one sort or another? Rhode Island's Frank Keaney, the first real fast-break coach, was a chemistry teacher who actually invented the light blue dye that is still the Rams' official color. College and pro coach Paul Westhead, the Chuck Yeager of offense, was a Shakespearean scholar who liked to quote Macbeth mulling over the murder of Duncan to illuminate his theory of basketball: "If it were done when 'tis done, then 'twere well it were done quickly." Princeton's Pete Carril, the supreme advocate of a prudence borne of antispeed, had a master's in education, while Iowa's Tom Davis, a pioneer in the relationship between pressure defense and speed, had a doctorate in history.

The eggheads can only theorize, of course. It takes talented truants like Pete Maravich to make those theories real, to see the wondrous possibilities in a developing fast break. "That's what I really love," Maravich said. "Blasting down the middle on a three-on-one or three-on-two. Sometimes when we start out and I see the play developing, I just want to shout out, 'Here we go! Hey everybody, watch this!' "

But basketball fast doesn't necessarily mean endline-to-endline fast. It may mean spot-to-spot quickness: I'm here when you're still there; I'm up when you're still down. And while most associate speed with offense, speed can insinuate itself into the game in unexpected ways. It may come from defense, like John Wooden's UCLA 2-2-1 zone pressure and Dean Smith's North Carolina "run-and-jump" scramble, both of which could send gas to a game's engine every bit as quickly as could a crisp outlet pass and fill-the-lanes choreography. Or speed may defer to its evil twin, tempo. If you're curious about the effectiveness of tempo, ask any of the players who tried to run against Carril's Tigers or Henry Iba's Oklahoma A&M Aggies.

When Keaney took over at Rhode Island State College, basketball was a Clydesdale's game, with scores rarely pushing beyond the 40s. In 1937–38, the first season after the elimination of the center jump, the Rams were suddenly unfettered, averaging 67.3 points a game as Keaney's players pressed man-to-man, coast-to-coast, tap-to-horn. Not surprisingly, their coach was an impatient man. He never called timeout, and when an opponent did, Keaney wouldn't permit his players to sit down. When another team stalled, he once ran into the stands to lead the students in the school song. "If we shoot more," he reasoned, "we'll make more." He loved the full-court pass and despised the dribble. "What are you trying to do?" he would ask self-indulgent dribblers. "Prove there's air in the ball?"

The conservatives in the East objected at first to Keaney's chaotic ideas, but the break caught on in precincts out west—with Ed Diddle at Western Kentucky, where the Hilltoppers used their entire bench; with Purdue's Ward (Piggy) Lambert, who coached a guard named John Wooden and taught "racehorse basketball"; and with Indiana's Branch McCracken and his Hurryin' Hoosiers. All discovered that, when practiced by athletes with agility as well as size, the break was an irresistible way to get advantageous offensive position without going through the tedium of running a half-court set. The fans never doubted its appeal, but the legitimacy of the fast break wasn't assured until the early '60s, when both the Boston Celtics and the UCLA Bruins won the first crowns of their respective dynasties, and in each case stormed the palace runnin'.

A quarter-century later, Westhead vowed to "flirt with speeds no one else has reached." First at Loyola Marymount, then in Denver with the NBA's Nuggets, he laid down for his players the simplest parameters: Shoot within seven seconds of gaining possession; grab at least 20 offensive rebounds a game; force no fewer than 25 turnovers; and take at least 100 shots. "Speed isn't essential," he explained. "What is, is the willingness to use *all* your speed *all* the time."

Westhead would have liked the spirit of his forebear and fellow pusher of the game's envelope. When someone pointed out to Keaney that the shooter's staple, the two-handed set, couldn't be used in the Rams' system, the chemistry prof was unmoved. "Hey," Keaney said, "if the music plays faster, you dance faster."

Men like Keaney and Westhead weren't so much Nutty Professors as visionary maestros under whose batons the game found its ability to reach and captivate audiences.

Westhead, one of the game's most avid speed demons, brought his running offense to both the college and pro ranks.

1929 The point-a-minute barrier is broken when coach Frank Keaney's Rhode Island State team finishes the season averaging 41 points a game. Two years later the Rams will accomplish the feat again.

1932 In an effort to discourage stalling tactics, a rule is adopted requiring an offensive team to advance the basketball into the forecourt within 10 seconds after gaining possession.

1937 The center jump after each basket is eliminated.

1950 The Fort Wayne Pistons, trying to end the defending NBA champion Minneapolis Lakers' 29-game winning streak over two seasons, hold the ball for long stretches of a 19-18 victory. To forestall a recurrence of the Fort Wayne freeze, the NBA will adopt the 24-second clock four years later.

1956 The college game eliminates the shooting of so-called "common," or one-shot, fouls when a team isn't yet in the bonus or penalty situation.

1957 An assistant coach at the Air Force Academy, which has strict height restrictions for cadets, devises a spread offense "delay game" to neutralize the height advantage enjoyed by the Falcons' opponents. The coach, Dean Smith, calls the set the Four Corners. Years later there will be a restaurant in Chapel Hill, N.C., with that name.

1964 UCLA, using a 2-2-1 zone press and a lineup with no starter taller than 6' 5", wins

Johnson's uncanny outlet passes (left) ignited the Lakers' devastating fast break; Johnny Dawkins tried to play the same role for Philadelphia.

the NCAA title. The Bruins will win nine of the next 11 national championships.

1979 Magic Johnson joins the Lakers, and L.A.'s signature fast break is born. Predicated more on crisp passing than raw speed, it will propel the Lakers to five NBA titles in the '80s.

1985 Taking its cue from pro and international basketball, which have 24- and 30-second clocks, respectively, the college game adopts a shot clock of 45 seconds.

1988 Loyola Marymount, led by stars Bo Kimble and Hank Gathers, scores 164 points in a win over Azusa Pacific. "Like an amusement park," says Gathers of coach Paul Westhead's offense. "So many rides!"

1990 Westhead installs his fast-break offense with the NBA's Denver Nuggets, who average a league-leading 119.9 points per game but finish the season a disappointing 20–62.

Flight

Flight

1891 After each basket scored in the original game in Springfield, the ball must be taken out of the peach basket, whose bottom is still intact. School custodian Pop Stebbins has the chance to become the game's first high flyer, but chooses to do the honors while standing on a ladder.

1933 Kenny Sailors, growing up in Hillsdale, Wyo., discovers that he can successfully shoot over his taller, older brother by jumping before letting fly.

1949 Using a jumper that was commonly referred to as an "ear shot," "Jumpin'" Joe Fulks of the Philadelphia Warriors scores 63 points against the Indianapolis Jets.

1957 Seattle's Elgin Baylor blocks a layup attempt by Temple's Guy Rodgers in such a way that the ball caroms to teammate "Sweet" Charlie Brown for a layup. "Elgin," said

It doesn't happen. Can't be done. *Basketball players don't fly.* O.K.? *There's no such thing as "hang time."* It's an illusion. With regard to all that soaring and swooping we see, or think we see, listen up:

A basketball player's center of gravity follows the path of a parabola determined by the amount of vertical thrust he generates at the moment of takeoff. It helps to have high muscle mass and low body fat, but the only thing that determines how long a human being will stay in the air is how efficiently he converts horizontal momentum into vertical force. The majestic spreading of arms and raising of knees make it *seem* that a player is flying. But the only way to actually stay in the air longer is by jumping farther and jumping higher.

The preceding dissertation notwithstanding, who can deny that a select few basketball players *can* rise, levitate, hang, hover and otherwise cut Isaac Newton up?

As does so much else in basketball, flight traces its origins to Hank Luisetti. Out at Stanford, basketball's Kitty Hawk, he became the first college player to leave his feet and only then decide whether to pass or shoot. A few years later Wyoming's Kenny Sailors would leave his feet specifically to shoot. Then, in the NBA, Joe Fulks and Paul Arizin began showcasing the art of going up for shots—and staying there. "I never really thought about my 'hang time' because I didn't know what it was and nobody wrote about it," Arizin has said. "All I know is other players used to say to me, 'How do you stay up there so long?'"

The original levitator, Elgin Baylor, fielded that question disdainfully, always dismissing the notion that he hung in the air. He simply shot on the way down, he said, thereby seeming to hang. More recent practitioners have their own explanations. "Sometimes on a straight rise," Julius Erving once said, "you sort of put your air brake on and wait for the defense to go down." Michael Jordan added this: "I spread my legs pretty wide in the air. Maybe they're just like wings, and they hold me up there a little bit." Maybe. And maybe not. Such scientific musings aside, what is *not* in doubt is how dominant the black player has been in this category; generations who have witnessed the likes of Gus Johnson, "Pogo" Joe Caldwell, Darnell Hillman, "Jumpin'" Johnny Green, Billy (the Kangaroo Kid) Cunningham and Joey Johnson know why basketball people of all colors speak unself-consciously about "white man's disease." As Baylor has noted, "All of us are black except Cunningham, and maybe you'd better check on him."

Tales of flight are muddied somewhat by the apocrypha of urban storytellers. In New York they tell of Herman (the Helicopter) Knowings, who, it was said, was once pump-faked into the air in the lane during a summer-league game only to have the ref whistle the man with the ball for three-seconds before Helicopter came down. Earl (Goat) Manigault, only 6' 2", could dunk the ball once, then again, all before alighting. "Sidecar" Jackie Jackson was so called because he elevated high enough to dunk from his hip. That story about being able to pick a quarter off the top of the backboard and leave 15 cents change—they told it first about Jackson. (Reality check: The top of the backboard is some 13 feet off the ground.)

Some leapers weren't particularly great hangers: Green, Spud Webb, Bobby Jones, Stevie Thompson. Some hangers, on the other hand, weren't great leapers: Tiny Archibald, Earl Monroe, Connie Hawkins, Baylor. And remember: There are no height restrictions in the frequent-flyer club. The behemoth Wilt Chamberlain could get up, even if he didn't do so very often; at Kansas he would dunk at coach Phog Allen's experimental 12-foot basket and briefly toyed with the notion of dunking his free throws. (He believed the rules would permit it, provided he took off from somewhere within the key behind the foul line. The rule makers rejected the idea.) When Dominique Wilkins was at Georgia, a 5' 9" laundryman named Leroy Nowells would walk into the gym and match him jam for jam. "The Human Highlight Film," wrote sportswriter Scott Ostler, "versus a Selected Short."

Problematic circumstances have at times produced creative airborne solutions. David Thompson played college ball when the dunk was outlawed, so he would finish off alley-oop passes by soaring, snaring, savoring the moment and gently depositing the payload. Darrell Griffith dazzled with his hanging jump shots, bamboozling one opponent, Iowa's Bob Hansen, such that Hansen said, "I've guarded guys who could leap high before. But all of them came down."

If hoops flight is primarily a black thing, don't attribute that fact to any of the spurious physiological reasons often advanced. Better to chalk it up to an imperative of the spirit. Listen to African-American novelist John Edgar Wideman, an erstwhile all-Ivy ballplayer at Penn: "When it's played the way it's spozed to be played, basketball happens in the air, the pure air; flying, floating, elevated above the floor, levitating the way oppressed peoples of this earth imagine themselves in their dreams, as I do in my lifelong fantasies of escape and power, finally, at last, once and for all, free."

One of the game's original Wright Brothers, Baylor developed his airborne repertoire at Seattle University.

Julius Erving, "was always occupying several planes of space en route to the basket."

1970 A Georgian named Herb White, a.k.a. the Elevator from Decatur, spends a season with Atlanta and becomes famed for his pregame dunks. Only 6' 2", White is widely recognized as the greatest white leaper ever. "He never got off the bench," said Wilt Chamberlain, "but in warmups he could dunk better than anyone I've ever seen."

1974 Ten minutes into the NCAA East Regional final against Pittsburgh, David Thompson drives the lane, goes up and flips over the shoulders of teammate Phil Spence. Upon falling, he suffers a gash in his head that will require 15 stitches to close but won't prevent him from leading the Wolfpack to the NCAA title.

1977 Louisville's Darrell Griffith, in Sofia, Bulgaria, for the World University Games, causes a sensation among members of the East bloc press with one ferocious slam dunk, on which he soars over a Belgian player to jam home a teammate's missed shot. "I told them it was a God-given talent," Griffith said later. "That confused them because I don't think they believe in God."

1980 In Game 4 of the NBA Finals, the 76ers' Julius Erving navigates the right baseline, picking up his dribble outside the lane, a good 12 feet from the basket. Forced by the Lakers' Mark Landsberger and Kareem Abdul-Jabbar to drift beyond the backboard and over the baseline, he

A pair of peerless pilots: Erving (left) made a midflight adjustment against L.A. in '82; Jordan was clearly looking hoopward against Portland in '90.

then reappears on the far side of the basket. Extending his arm as if hydraulically, he flips a reverse layup off the board and in. Erving's move will inspire saxophonist Grover Washington Jr. to write and record *Let It Flow (for Dr. J)*.

1985 In a gym in Mesa, Ariz., Joey Johnson, the younger brother of NBA star Dennis Johnson, turns the baseball cap on his head sideways. Then, in street clothes and without a running start, he leaps straight up, tosses his head to the side, and "dunks" his cap.

1989 In a first-round playoff game against Cleveland, Chicago's Michael Jordan goes up for a last-second jumper with the Bulls trailing 100-99. Upon leaving his feet, Jordan realizes the man guarding him, the Cavaliers' Craig Ehlo, is sailing in from the side to block his shot. Jordan waits until Ehlo has flown past, then lets fly. The ball swishes through as the buzzer sounds.

the Culture

The Culture

In Cheech and Chong's "Basketball Jones," protagonist Tyrone Shoelaces drew his skewed world view from the game of basketball.

1938 Former Stanford All-America Hank Luisetti stars with Betty Grable in *Campus Confessions,* a basketball movie in which he performs the behind-the-back dribble in slow motion.

1948 Long Island University coach Clair Bee, who will eventually be inducted into the Hall of Fame with college basketball's alltime best winning percentage (.827), publishes *Championship Ball,* the second of his Chip Hilton

Anyone in search of the essence of the 10-foot culture could do worse than slip on a pair of Converse Chuck Taylor All-Stars. Chucks do more to capture basketball's peculiar dualism than anything else. That peerless cultural arbiter, New York City's *Village Voice,* once described the game's quintessential footwear as being "as familiar and ordinary as the shape of a small-town bungalow, the white ladder of its laces as All-American and old-fashioned as a white picket fence." But Cons are also manufactured in Lumberton, N.C.—the same town in which David Lynch filmed *Blue Velvet,* his film full of ghoulish secrets lurking behind wholesome facades.

Need we say more? Basketball, and the civilization that has sprouted up around it over the past 100 years, exalts in equal measure the neat and the untidy. It puts them in the same place, side-by-side, teammates. The pure jump shooter and the rebounding fool. The dandified, control freak coach and the prodigious dervish of a ball handler. The son of a banker and the son of the ne'er-do-well who skipped town long ago.

Like boxing, basketball encourages braggadocio. (In 1983, when Moses Malone incanted "Fo, fo, fo" in predicting his 76ers' prospects in the playoffs, he sounded like the old prefight Ali.) And it has spawned a Runyonesque periphery, full of characters and their con games, much as the sweet science has. Yet its rules legislate against contact. Indeed, basketball's beauty follows from its very proscription of brutality.

Minimize collision and you maximize movement. Is basketball most like dance? One might watch a game, says social theorist Michael Novak, as one beholds a dance troupe, "occasionally half-closing the eye to blur out the detail and to fasten upon the essential abstract pattern of the movement, to catch its inner ecstasy." Or is a basketball game really more akin to literary art, an unfolding tale with myriad twists of plot? Novak again: "Like the stories and legends of black literature, the [basketball] hero does not let his antagonist guess his intentions; he strings him along; he keeps his inner life to himself until the decisive moment. The other must commit himself first; only then dare the hero strike."

The art form most often invoked for purposes of comparison is neither of these, but jazz, which may be the only facet of American life other than basketball that has proved more able to bridge America's most problematic chasm, the gulf of racial difference. Indeed, that may be the identifying mark of basketball culture—its racial ecumenism. Much of basketball's argot, words with etymologies often traceable to the street, passes on eventually into colloquial use. No pretext other than a basketball game more regularly brings black and white together, indoors, conspicuously affirming the nonracial tribal affiliation represented by the hometown team. And while few white men, given a chance, would really trade places with a black man, how many whites *don't* entertain the delicious prospect of what it would be like to be Magic or Michael or Julius?

If we were to build a museum of basketball culture, we would house in it:

Basketball synonyms, like Hoops. Hoop. The cage game. Ball. Baskets.

Basketball handles, like Jerry (Hound) Baskerville. Hercle (Poison) Ivy. Walter (the Truth) Berry. Jeff (Monkey Jesus) Shepard.

Basketball lit, like *The Basketball Diaries. Heaven Is a Playground. Rabbit, Run. A Sense of Where You Are.*

Basketball celebs, like Jon Voight. Dustin Hoffman. Elliott Gould. Bruce Hornsby. Martina Navratilova. Jack Nicholson.

Basketball pols, like Paul Sarbanes. Mo Udall. Byron (Whizzer) White. Bill Bradley. Tom McMillen. Ray Flynn. (They tend to be Democrats.)

Basketball ads, like Jump higher, run faster. Limousines for the feet. Do you know, do you know, do you know? Bo knows. Lonnnnnng distance. Bill Denby. Rainin' down jumpers like there's no tomorrow.

Basketball clowns, like Abe Lemons. Goose Tatum. Meadowlark Lemon. Jim Valvano. George Schauer.

Basketball music, like Grover Washington Jr. Cheech and Chong. Kurtis Blow. Sweet Georgia Brown.

Basketball argot, like In your face. Basketball jones. Drain the trey. Fall back, baby. Give it up. In the paint. If you don't play ball, you can't hang out (also known as Meminger's Law).

Basketball video, like *Drive, He Said. The Fish That Saved Pittsburgh. One-on-One. The White Shadow. Fast Break. The Harlem Globetrotters on Gilligan's Island.* (Seriously.)

Basketball accessories, like Luther (Ticky) Burden's tassels. Derrick Chievous's Band-Aids. Pistol Pete Maravich's floppy socks. Bill Walton's headbands. Kareem Abdul-Jabbar's goggles. Patrick Ewing's T-shirts.

Basketball voices, like "A ring-tailed howitzer tickles the twine." "Good, like Nedick's." "A PTPer, baby!" "They got to go to the aircraft carrier." "Havlicek stole the ball!" "Yessss!"

And basketball shrines, like Fonde Recreation Center in Houston. The Palestra. Boston Garden. Mackerville U.S.A. Holcombe Rucker Memorial Playground. And Springfield, Mass.

The Nerf ball and hoop made basketball a household game as well as a source of fun for college bands across the land.

sports novels and the first to deal with the game of basketball. He will write 23 books in all, eight of them about hoops.

1958 In his third pro season, Cincinnati's Maurice Stokes is paralyzed after suffering a fall and contracting encephalitis. Teammate Jack Twyman becomes Stokes's legal guardian and rallies the basketball community to support an annual benefit game in New York's Catskill Mountains. Though confined to a wheelchair until his death in 1970, Stokes eventually learns to speak again, thanks in large measure to Twyman's abiding friendship and support.

1970 Parker Brothers toy manufacturers introduces the foam Nerf ball. The Nerf hoop will follow two years later, as basketball becomes an engaging, pacifying diversion for millions in dormitories, family rooms and executive suites.

1973 Novelty musicians Cheech and Chong record *Basketball Jones,* in which Tyrone Shoelaces, the song's protagonist, implores someone to "set a pick for me at the free throw line of life."

1973 As the mercurial James (Fly) Williams leads Austin Peay State University into the NCAA tournament, fans of the school in Clarksville, Tenn., adopt the cheer, "The Fly is open! Let's go Peay!"

1978 Humorist Roy Blount Jr. suggests that basketball box scores include a notation of significant "face jobs" pulled off during the course of the game. Just as a hit batsman is indicated in a baseball box score, e.g., HBP—Guidry (Evans), so too could the perpetrator and victim of a "facial" be accounted for: IYF— Free (Twardzik).

Nicholson and Magic Johnson (left) rode to superstar status in tandem during the '80s; Tatum was the Globetrotters' clown prince in the '50s.

1979 Hirohide Ogawa, a former candidate for the Japanese national team who had quit to devote his energies to "private basketball," publishes *Enlightenment Through the Art of Basketball,* a series of Socratic exchanges with one of his pupils. "If one is anxious before scoring, there is no value in scoring," Ogawa writes. "If one is disappointed after failing to score, there is no value in not scoring. The steady hand, the steady heart, the steady head. . . ."

1986-87 During a ten-month period, *A Season on the Brink,* a book about Indiana coach Bob Knight, reaches No. 1 on the bestseller list, Knight's Hoosiers win the national title and a movie is released called *Hoosiers,* based loosely on Milan High's 1954 state title. "Run the picket fence," Dennis Hopper's Shooter tells the Hickory High varsity in one memorable scene. "But don't get caught watchin' the paint dry!"

The Pantheon

Their talents were varied—from the fearsome presence of Chamberlain (right) to the subtle artistry of Cousy—but together they defined the contours of the game they loved. Here are the most influential figures from basketball's first century.

Phog Allen

If Dr. James Naismith invented the game of basketball, Dr. Forrest C. (Phog) Allen invented the spectacle of it, literally taking the sport from the cramped gymnasiums of its birth to the far corners of the world. An innovator and propagandist as much as an X's and O's man, Allen first played for Naismith at Kansas and then coached there for 39 years. Through the '20s, as the aging Dr. James taught fencing and wrestling in another corner of Old Robinson Gym, he watched the vision and energy that Dr. Phog brought to the job of teaching hoops. "From the father of basketball," read the inscription on a photograph of Naismith that Allen kept with pride, "to the father of basketball coaching."

Before Allen became college basketball's first great coach, he was a pretty fair high school player in Independence, Mo. At Kansas he scored 26 points in a game in 1906, a school record that stood for seven years. After graduation he left basketball for medical school, spending four years studying osteopathy before taking the head coaching job at Warrensburg Normal College (now Central Missouri State) in 1912. After seven successful seasons there, he returned to Kansas and settled in for what would be a historic run.

Allen never let anyone forget that he was unusually schooled for his job. He spoke of the shooter's proper "pronation" and "supination" of the hands and wrists, and he broke down the movements of the game to their elements. "The knees are the only springs in the body," he liked to say. "Bend them!" He was so frightened of the deleterious effect cold feet could have on human performance that he had his players congregate barefoot in front of a fire before games. "I never saw a man with cold feet who wasn't nervous or jumpy," he said. "Keep the feet warm and you keep the nerves of the players calm."

Allen was always espousing some pet cause and taking on sportswriters, particularly those from the East Coast. But many of his projects—they included an NCAA tournament, a national coaches' association (originally formed to lobby against the elimination of the dribble) and the inclusion of basketball on the Olympic program—came to glorious fruition, with the latter, perhaps Allen's proudest achievement, occurring at the 1936 Games. He was less successful in his proselytizing for the 12-foot basket, a proposal he first embraced in the early '30s, but advocated less stridently toward the end of his career, particularly after the Jayhawks lured to Lawrence 6' 9" Clyde Lovellette and 7' 1" Wilt Chamberlain (*pictured at right with Allen*).

Cranky and tendentious, Allen riffled freely through the Zeitgeist in search of touchstones to use in his frequent commentaries. He was superstitious, too, but in a convoluted sort of way; he actually sought out ladders to walk under and considered 13 his lucky number. On the bench Allen drank enormous amounts of water. Four quarts, it was said, signified a routine game; eight, a doozy. A favorite teaching tool was the movie *Killing the Killer,* in which a mongoose subdues a cobra. The film, screened at the first practice of every season, allegedly inspired the pressing defense for which Allen's teams were noted.

Critics had fun with his nickname, a bastardized truncation of Foghorn, which he had earned for his sonorous bellowings as a baseball umpire in his youth. A foghorn, *New York Post* columnist Milton Gross noted wryly, is "an instrument which operates on hot air and indicates the one blowing the whistle has more or less lost his way."

Yet Allen was the first to warn of a possible point-shaving scandal, sounding off as early as 1944 about the growing influence of gamblers. Most of his peers chided him for being alarmist, but within a few years he was proved tragically correct. In 1952, shortly after the full extent of the collegiate scandals had come to light, Allen enjoyed his greatest moment as a coach. The Jayhawks, led by Lovellette, whupped St. John's by 17 points for the NCAA title, in front of all those New York City sportswriters no less, the ones who had called him "the corn-country pop-off."

"Of course I used everything we had to get him," Allen said a few years later, after Kansas raised eyebrows by signing Chamberlain. "What do you think I am, a Sunday school teacher?" (He was, in fact, a Sunday school teacher—there was always an element of gamesmanship to Allen's bluster.) He hoped to be made an exception to the state's mandatory retirement age of 70, so he could actually coach Chamberlain. But he was forced to step down in 1956, a victim of what he liked to call "statutory senility." He had won 771 games overall and brought 24 conference titles to Lawrence. He was still alive in 1968 when one of his old players, Adolph Rupp, passed him at the top of the alltime victory list. Allen took this graciously. "Bless his bones," the old osteopath said.

Bill Bradley

A demographer trying to pick out a basketball star would skip right over Bill Bradley. An only child, the son of a bank president, raised in a family that split its time between the sleepy Mississippi River town of Crystal City, Mo., and Palm Beach, Fla., Bradley hardly had the pedigree that makes for greatness. "He has overcome the disadvantage of wealth," wrote *The New Yorker's* John McPhee in his 1965 profile of the Princeton star. Modest means, McPhee explained, impose on a prospective player "the discipline of having nothing else to do." Bradley, by contrast, had so much else to do—everything from scout meetings to Presbyterian services to lessons in golf, swimming, piano, trumpet, French and dancing.

With discipline and rigor, Bradley set out to overcome this handicap. He slipped lead into his sneakers. He wore blinders to improve his dribbling. And he studied others, borrowing freely. His layup he took from Cliff Hagan, his set shot from Ed Macauley, his jumper from Jerry West and Terry Dischinger. His hook was equal parts Bill Russell, Darrall Imhoff and Cotton Nash. His free throw began as a hybrid of Bob Pettit and Bill Sharman, but as he became more comfortable and confident, it metamorphosed into something all his own.

Only an average athlete and an ordinary jumper, Bradley more than compensated. He had been blessed with ambidexterity, uncommon peripheral vision and preternatural powers of concentration, and he brought science so keenly to bear on his sport that he washed his hands before every game to remove any accumulated oils from his skin and thus maximize friction on the ball. "What is 'touch' but concentration?" he said. "A soft touch is no more than practicing the right way. . . . It is really just a matter of coordinating the various movements into one smooth motion involving the eyes, the hands, the legs. With foul shots you are given time to concentrate, to pull all of the elements together." Indeed, the best any pro had ever done in competition was sink 56 in a row. As a college *freshman* Bradley dropped in 57 straight.

Skeptics first questioned Bradley's decision to choose an Ivy League school, then looked upon his achievements at Princeton as spurious. Only after he excelled at the 1964 Olympic trials, making the team as its youngest member and captaining it to the gold medal in Tokyo, did they desist.

Ultimately it would take three games during his senior year, two of them losses, to bring Bradley his full measure of respect. Against No. 1 Michigan and Cazzie Russell, in the semifinals of the Holiday Festival Tournament at Madison Square Garden, he went for 41 points. Princeton was up 12 when Bradley fouled out with 4½ minutes to play, and the Garden crowd gave him a three-minute standing ovation. Then he watched helplessly on the bench, his head shrouded in a towel, as the lead evaporated and Michigan won 80–78.

To reach the Final Four a few months later, Princeton beat Providence, then ranked No. 4, 109–69. Bradley sank 14 of 20 shots and all 13 of his free throws. One sportswriter filled out his all-tournament team ballot as follows: Bradley, Bradley, Bradley, Bradley and Bradley.

Michigan, alas, prevailed again in the national semis, and it was left to Bradley to deliver a valedictory in the consolation game, a 118–82 win over Wichita State. He already had 42 points when his coach, Bill van Breda Kolff, called time with slightly less than five minutes to play. Then a lefthanded hook from the corner went swish. Another sinistral shot, this one over the shoulder, dropped through. A double-clutch jumper from the left side found the mark, too; then a hook from 22 feet, deep in the right corner. In those few minutes he scored 16 unforgettable points without missing once and finished the game with a record 58.

"We didn't produce," Bradley told the students who met the bus back on campus. "I don't know whether to say I'm sorry. . . ."

"Say it 58 times!" someone called out.

He had chosen Princeton because he didn't want to be typed. "I don't want to end up," he said, "as just old Satin Shorts Bradley." Accordingly, he postponed pro basketball, studying at Oxford for two years as a Rhodes scholar. He joined the New York Knicks in 1967 and eventually mastered two things he had never been asked to do much in college: move without the ball and play intense defense. He made a good living for 10 seasons as an NBA cornerman, winning two titles along the way.

"He is a Christian the best way he can be, through the rigors of Calvinism," a college buddy had said of him. "Bill is always going to come back. Do you know just how hard it is to defeat a 16th-century Puritan?"

It must be hard indeed. Bill Bradley (D., N.J.) is serving out his third term in the United States Senate the same way he played the game—succeeding through discipline, study and concentration. No old Satin Shorts he.

Bob Davies

Among basketball pioneers of ordinary dimensions, Bob Davies was a critical transition figure. He was compared to Hank Luisetti, and Bob Cousy would be compared to him. But coach-author Clair Bee minted the most enduring comparison by modeling Chip Hilton, the impossibly talented and virtuous protagonist of his juvenile sports novels, after the "fancy Dan" from Seton Hall.

Curiously, Bee developed his admiration for Davies while his teams were beating Davies'. In 1941 the Hall, with its 43-game winning streak, met Bee's Long Island University Blackbirds in the semifinals of the NIT. Bee ordered his players to double-team the Pirate star and keep a stream of chatter—"Shoot, Bobby! Dribble, Bobby!"—flowing at him throughout the game. The two-pronged strategy seemed to work: Davies scored only four points and fouled out as LIU won easily en route to the NIT title. New York City sportswriters, who had adopted Davies as their own, criticized Bee for his tactics. Yet Davies defended Bee, going so far as to write the coach a letter forswearing any ill feeling. It was Davies' stoicism in the Garden that night, and graciousness thereafter, that inspired Bee to use him as his prototype.

Chip-like, Davies played four sports at John Harris High in Harrisburg, Pa., and was so accomplished a baseball player that the Red Sox signed him to a contract. (He was also, at age 11, Pennsylvania state marbles champ.) Always a little on the small side—only five feet upon entering high school and just 5' 11" when leaving it—Davies came up in modest circumstances. He first toyed with the game by tossing a tennis ball into a paint can in an alleyway. Unable to afford admission to the local high school games, Davies looked on through a crack in the gym door, his field of vision nothing more than the foul lanes and baskets. The slivers of space he saw there so intrigued him that he decided to become a playmaker.

Davies earned a scholarship at Seton Hall only after leading the freshmen to a victory over the varsity. He was perceived as something of a radical at the New Jersey school, to which he brought the footloose and headlong "Western" style of basketball. (Basketball folks in and around New York City considered Pennsylvania the West in those days.) A three-year postcollegiate hitch on a Navy submarine chaser during World War II didn't extinguish his luminous ballhandling and passing skills. Shortly after the war Davies embarked on his decade-long pro career, all of it with the Rochester Royals, first in the National Basketball League, then the Basketball Association of America and finally the NBA. Even as he led Rochester to the NBL title in 1947 and won the league's MVP award, he showed off the selfless style that had so captivated Bee: Between Royals games, by catching overnight trains and lumbering prop planes, he coached his alma mater to a 24–3 record. If Bee had written a role like that for Chip, the critics would have hammered it as being contrived.

The next season Royals owner Les Harrison, not wanting to fret about botched connections and heavy weather, raised the salary of his star so he could forgo college coaching; he also signed one of Davies' erstwhile Pirate players, Bobby Wanzer, as Davies' new partner in the Rochester backcourt. Together they perfected an offensive system that would seem strangely schizoid today, a little like driving a Lamborghini to church: an adroit fast break that culminated, more often than not, in a set shot. In 1951, when the Royals won their only NBA title, Davies wrapped matters up by sinking a couple of free throws in the final minute of Game 7 against the Knicks.

Davies had to set aside his collegiate signature, the behind-the-back dribble, after the war. The pros resented it, believing it showed them up. Yet he practiced other manipulations of the ball—tricks like the change-of-pace dribble—that would make their way into the game, and in nearly all of his 10 seasons he was among the league leaders in assists. "He was probably years ahead of his time," said Red Holzman, a former Royals teammate, upon Davies' death in 1990.

Shortly after his retirement, in 1955, Davies snuck onto the stooge team playing the Harlem Globetrotters in Baltimore's Memorial Stadium. The crowd gasped as the Harrisburg Houdini, in full flight and on the break, leaped into the air. With his right hand he brought the ball around the front of his body before releasing it, behind his back now, to a teammate bolting in from the right side for a layup.

Fourteen years earlier, against Rhode Island in the 1941 NIT at Madison Square Garden, he had also gone behind his back, though in a more orthodox fashion. A priest happened to be winding his watch at that very moment. Upon witnessing the move, the father tossed the timepiece spontaneously up into the air. In retrospect it seems an unusually apt gesture of respect for a forerunner who, in his own way, messed with time.

Patrick Ewing

For four years in the early '80s, Patrick Ewing was the archangel of the Georgetown teams that bedeviled the college game. He had a presence theretofore never seen: an even seven feet of height, 44 inches of sleeve length, eight feet of wingspan and a bounding speed that permitted him to bring these dimensions to bear, in a trice, virtually anywhere on the court. The shots he blocked, three to four every time out, were the only statistical hint of what it was he produced. "I've seen guys drive the lane and start double-clutching and jerking around when Patrick's over sitting on the bench," said Hubie Brown, the man who would coach Ewing during his rookie season with the New York Knicks. "Now that, my friend, is intimidation."

Ewing's intensity owed much, no doubt, to his mother, Dorothy, who, hoping to better provide for her seven children, came to Cambridge, Mass., in 1971, leaving eight-year-old Patrick behind in their native Jamaica. She took a job in the kitchen of Massachusetts General Hospital; her husband, Carl, arrived two years later. When Patrick joined them in 1975, he had some experience as a soccer goalie but had never played basketball. Patrick's graduation from Rindge and Latin School gratified his mother more than any of his basketball achievements, few of which she witnessed. "Work hard and do it right or don't do it at all," said Dorothy, who died in 1983 after, friends say, working herself to death. "Let people say or think what they will."

Her advice was much like that Ewing would hear from John Thompson, the Georgetown coach who first saw Dorothy's son play by accident. He was visiting his old pro coach, Red Auerbach, when the Celtics' boss urged Thompson to check out the state title game that was about to get under way in Boston Garden. Thompson walked in and instantly saw Ewing, then a sophomore, draw a charge and finish off a steal with a dunk. "Get me him," Thompson told Auerbach, "and I'll win the national championship."

The nation followed the ensuing "wooing of Ewing," noting in particular the demands that Patrick's high school coach, Mike Jarvis, laid out for recruiters as they came by. These weren't the usual stick-'em-up demands of recruiting lore; instead Jarvis was looking for ways to help Ewing overcome the barrier between his native Jamaican patois and American English. News of this led fans to chant things like "Ewing can't read!" In response, Ewing closed himself off to the world, and in the vacuum of public information about who he was or what he thought, the worst assumptions took root. Few knew of his love for drawing still lifes and landscapes or had seen his incandescent smile, or knew how determined he was to follow through on a promise to his mother to graduate. Thompson had to get Carl Ewing's signature on the letter of intent, because Dorothy balked. "Mr. Thompson, you sign for land," she said. "You don't sign for people."

Ewing better than anyone carried the standard of the Georgetown program. He embodied every feature the Hoyas prized and flaunted—defense, athleticism, competitiveness, intensity and privacy. He was largely responsible for Georgetown sitting at or near the top of the national rankings in two of the most meaningful statistical categories, field goal percentage defense and rebound margin, for the duration of his college career. Fear, as such, had never been an operative emotion in college basketball before Thompson's Georgetown teams came along, and Ewing struck it.

He never fully unveiled his offensive skills in college, devoting himself instead to following Thompson's tightly controlled patterns. But his ability to score as a pro was never in doubt. He had shot 62% in college, and his strength (240 well distributed pounds) and agility (his feet, size 13½, are surprisingly small for someone his size) further suited him to be a scorer. Yet as he joined the Knicks, the NBA prototype he most suggested was that of the defensive condor, Bill Russell. "They share an amazingly similar level of sensitivity," said Thompson, who played with Russell in Boston for two seasons. "That's the biggest thing, their pride and their will to win. A lot of people have the will to play, but few have the will to win. Patrick didn't think we could look good if we were losing. Neither did Russ."

Ewing shared the '80s with two other superb collegiate big men, Virginia's Ralph Sampson (*pictured with Ewing at right*) and Houston's Akeem Olajuwon, but Ewing's place in the history of the college game is most secure. Sampson's career veered downward after college, and his travails as a professional obscured his prior achievements. By contrast, Olajuwon's spectacular improvement in the NBA outstripped his fine career at Houston. Ewing was the mean of the two, a *mean* mean: intense and steady through four years, the only one of the three to win an NCAA championship.

Henry Iba

Severe and reproachful, with hair parted straight down the middle, Henry Iba was basketball's fundamentalist country preacher. In mien and temperament he faithfully reflected both the prairie outpost of Stillwater, Okla., where he coached Oklahoma A&M (later Oklahoma State) for 36 seasons, and the puritan style of play for which his teams became famous. Disciples of Iba—of *Mr.* Iba—called it ball control; critics preferred "stall ball" or "the deep freeze." Either way, in a popular phrase that all could agree on, playing an Iba team meant "slow death." "I'm not against shooting," he said. "I'm against bad shooting. I want my boys to shoot. I love my boys to shoot. But glory be, make it a good shot—his shot."

Iba first developed his philosophy of the game in his hometown of Easton, Mo. As a player, after suffering a 62–14 loss to a high school rival, young Henry resolved to find a way to play an opponent with superior talent and still win. He coached with distinction through the Depression—at Oklahoma City's Classen High School, Maryville Teachers College (now Northwest Missouri State) and Colorado—before landing, in 1934, at A&M. He stayed until 1970, winning 14 league titles and a total of 767 games, which puts him just behind Adolph Rupp and Phog Allen on the alltime list. He coached A&M to NCAA titles in 1945 and '46, yet he had only one consensus All-America in 36 seasons, the anchor of those championship teams, Bob Kurland.

Even Iba's basketball precepts bore names evocative of the smalltown, turn-of-the-century America in which he seemed permanently rooted. His offense, a rigorous choreography of weaves and cuts, was "the horse and buggy." His defense, the "swinging gate," was a half-court man-to-man that brooked no switching, but encouraged "help." Iba despised extended defenses. He believed that defenders in a press would all foul out within minutes if referees whistled the game correctly. Late in his career, even after UCLA had begun its run of invincibility with a withering 2-2-1 zone press, Iba said flatly, "Defense was never intended to be played all over the court."

Perhaps Iba understood instinctively that full-court pressure put giddyup in a game, necessarily lengthening the reins on which a coach kept his team. Iba, of course, wanted to keep those reins short at all costs. And he disdained the role recruiting now played in the profession. "I used to be able to see a boy in June, ask him to come to OSU, and, by golly, there he'd be come fall," he noted. "Now, after I see a boy, I've got to hound him and flatter him, flatter his parents, flood him with letters." Flattering others wasn't what Mr. Iba had been constituted for. In 1970, at the age of 66, he hung up his whistle.

Iba won only one of his 14 league titles over the final 16 years of his career. That's seen variously as a tribute to his willingness to stand by his principles, and as evidence of his unwillingness to adapt to a changing game. Never was Iba second-guessed more intensely than in 1972, when he took himself out of mothballs to coach the U.S. Olympic team. He used tests of personality and hair length to pick his players, then watched as his squad suffered the first American loss ever in Olympic competition, by one point to the Soviet Union. People seemed all too ready to forget the gold medals he had won in 1964 and '68.

Iba was nonetheless an original thinker, a man whose contributions—the motion offense and the man-to-man with zone principles, to name just two—are still very much in evidence. In fact, his influence is everywhere. The Iba family alone includes six other coaches: younger brothers Earl, Clarence and Howard; son Moe and nephew Gene; and grandson Bret. Figuratively, the clan is even more far-reaching. If you study the "bloodlines" of college coaches since the '20s, and trace them back to men who either coached or played for the Iron Duke, five generations of Iba disciples have carried clipboards in the collegiate ranks.

A coach with no direct lineage to Iba, but who counts himself a follower just the same, is Indiana's Bob Knight. Knight made Iba an adviser to his 1984 Olympic team. In a scene that must have taken some of the sting out of the debacle at Munich a dozen years earlier, the Americans carried both Knight and Iba off the floor after winning the gold in Los Angeles.

Even in retirement, until the fall of 1992 when old age began to take its toll, Iba faithfully looked in on the game he loved every afternoon, never missing an Aggie practice. Upon his death scores of coaches turned out for the funeral, sharing tales of the man they all knew as "Mister"—tales like the one about the time Iba's Maryville squad was returning in the team bus after getting beat, and the driver indicated they were low on gas.

"You're the driver, period," Mr. Iba said. "I'll tell you when we need gas."

Five minutes later the motor quit.

"O.K., kid," he said. "Now I'm the driver. All of you, out. And push."

Bob Knight

Somehow Bob Knight imparted discipline to legions of Indiana basketball players even as he demonstrated little of it himself. Perhaps his lapses were calculated; maybe he hoped to make himself so frightening that, out of fear of being met with some projectile or profanity, no player would dare stray, no booster would dare cheat and no ref would dare err. Whatever, the list of Knight's indiscretions—assaulting a Puerto Rican policeman, hurling a chair across the court, taking a team off the floor because he was displeased with the officiating, and so on—is so long that the wire services ran a boilerplate "Chronology of Knight Incidents" after each new one occurred. That list, alas, will always cast a shadow over another list that's just as peerless, the one that details his accomplishments over 28 seasons as a college head coach: three NCAA titles, 11 Big Ten championships and more victories sooner in his career than virtually anyone else in the profession.

While growing up in Orrville, Ohio, during the '50s, Bobby learned discipline from his father, Pat, a railroad worker who took out a 20-year mortgage on the family home and paid it off within 4½ years. Today Knight's working definition of discipline is "doing what you have to do, and doing it as well as you possibly can, and doing it that way all the time." But if Bobby learned this lesson as a youth, he didn't practice it. He was kicked off his high school team for refusing a new coach's order to come out of a game. And when he arrived at Ohio State, the Buckeyes' courtly head coach, Fred Taylor, quickly dubbed him "the Brat from Orrville."

Knight nevertheless contributed to the John Havlicek and Jerry Lucas–led teams that reached the NCAA championship game in 1961 and '62. With his low-slung outside shot he could break up a zone, the defense he would, years later, almost never permit his own teams to play. Still, he didn't see much action; one sportswriter would note that "Knight began on the bench, and is still on the bench. His space in the Hall of Fame has been fashioned out of pine."

Never as good a player as he wanted to be, Knight's coaching ambitions sprang from that sense of failure. In 1962, in his first game as coach of the jayvee team at Cuyahoga Falls (Ohio) High, he broke a clipboard. He enlisted in the Army in '63 and was assigned to West Point as Tates Locke's assistant. When Locke left two seasons later and Knight was named head coach, he was 24, the youngest man ever to lead a major college program. The Cadets played in four NIT tournaments during Knight's six seasons, and in 1971 he left for Bloomington.

The Big Ten he came to was an up-tempo league. Iowa had won the conference championship two seasons before by averaging more than 100 points a game, and Indiana in particular had a crowd-pleasing reputation as "the Hurryin' Hoosiers." Yet the man-to-man defense Knight instituted was so successful that the Hoosier faithful were won over instantly, and a decade later Big Ten scores had plunged by more than five points a game. His NCAA championships, in 1976, '81 and '87, are spread out so evenly that they can't be attributed to either a run of luck, or a single great class or great player. By the '90s, the IU advertising slogan was succinct: Play four years under Knight and you can expect at least one Big Ten title, and reasonably hope for the whole shebang.

In practice and elsewhere behind closed doors, Knight used methods so dehumanizing that the Bloomington faculty passed a resolution aimed at curbing his excesses. "You know, there were times when, if I had a gun, I think I would have shot him," said Isiah Thomas, the guard who led his 1981 champions. "And there were other times when I wanted to put my arms around him, hug him and tell him that I loved him." The administration tolerated Knight's misbehavior because he made up for it in so many ways: with his graduation rate, his record of compliance with NCAA rules, even his policy of signing over the money from his shoe endorsement deal—"pimp money," he called it—to the school's general fund. Knight suffered under the ambivalence so often expressed by those who appraised him. "It kills me," he said. "I get castigated just for screaming at some official. And the other coach? Oh, he's perfect, he's being deified, and I know he's one of the worst cheaters in the country. It's like I tell my players: Your biggest opponent isn't the other guy. It's human nature."

This, like most of Knight's theories of the game, was derived from others—older and wiser men like Clair Bee, Hank Iba and Pete Newell. He admitted this freely and proudly. And though 15 of his former assistants became college head coaches, Knight more often focused on his debt to the past than on his legacy to the future. So long as the Bees and Ibas and Newells were there for him, and until the last one was gone, he would always go to them contritely, on bended knee. He could still be, would still be, the Brat from Orrville.

Bob Kurland

It was inevitable that Bob Kurland would be called many things, for no one had seen anyone quite like him before. He seemed to beg for all manner of modifiers, metaphors and descriptive phrases, few of them flattering. "A glandular, mezzanine-peeping goon," said Phog Allen, coach at Kansas, a rival of Kurland's Oklahoma A&M Aggies. "A freight elevator," said another coach in the conference, Oklahoma's Bruce Drake. Looking back, the most graceful of Kurland's appellations—"Foothills"—proved to be the most apt. If you think of basketball history as navigable terrain, Foothills was indeed undulating up-country, a precursor of the seven-foot peaks to come.

The secret can now be told: Kurland wasn't really a seven-footer. He was in fact 6' 10¼"; an A&M publicist, believing that public curiosity would redouble over someone purporting to be so tall, embellished the figures on his roster. Kurland was, however, as he himself once said, "as close to seven feet as 98 cents is to a dollar." Which was close enough.

Kurland grew up in St. Louis, the son of protective parents who restricted his participation in sports before he entered high school. The Kurlands feared their boy's size and ungainliness—he stood 6' 6" at age 13—posed a threat to other children his age. As a result, young Bob grew up as something of a contemplative child, contenting himself with less rigorous pursuits, like fishing in the Mississippi River. At Jennings High School, in addition to playing basketball, he won the state high jump championship. Like most young male St. Louisans of that time, he wanted to serve in World War II and play for the University of Missouri. But he was too tall for combat duty, and Mizzou wasn't interested in giving him an athletic scholarship. His high school coach succeeded in jawboning the Aggies' Henry Iba into taking him on.

When Kurland showed up in Stillwater in 1942, he could touch a spot 9' 4" off the floor while standing on his tiptoes. But he couldn't reach much else. During fall practice of his freshman year, the story goes, the first 200 hook shots Kurland tossed up were air balls. By his sophomore season, however, Kurland had figured out the psychological value of knocking a few shots off the rim early in a game. After a 59–40 loss to A&M in 1943, in which Kurland had batted away more than 20 Sooner shots, Oklahoma's Drake persuaded the collegiate rules committee to investigate. The following year a committee representative studied Kurland's tactic from a special observation tower, and by 1945 the goaltending rule would be adopted.

Eventually college basketball would feature such titanic matchups as Spivey-Lovellette, Alcindor-Hayes and Sampson-Ewing. But the first such titanic clash occurred in 1945, when the NCAA champion Aggies and Kurland, now a junior, met NIT titlist DePaul and George Mikan. The game, played in Madison Square Garden to benefit the Red Cross, generated "a helluva lot of hullaballoo," Kurland remembers. He used a scoop shot in the low post—as low a low post as any giant ever played, given how narrow the lane was in those days—to goad Mikan into fouling out within 14 minutes. By game's end three other Blue Demon starters had met the same fate, and the Aggies were victorious, 52–44.

The following season A&M became the first school ever to win two straight NCAA titles as Kurland led the nation in scoring and, in his final regular-season game, burned St. Louis University and "Easy" Ed Macauley for 58 points. Kurland's name had shown up on a few All-America teams after his sophomore season. But now, for the second straight year, he was a consensus pick and NCAA tournament MVP.

It had been hard for Kurland to get his due. The relative height advantage he enjoyed was much like that an eight-footer would have if playing today. Never as deft an offensive player as Mikan, he learned to shoot with both hands and was always the better defender. The slurs of Allen and others had motivated him, and he was an emphatic presence now, not merely a curiosity. "If you take pride in anything, it's not the mechanics of learning how to play," he would say. "It's in having the guts to stay in there and prove you can play when Phog Allen called you a 'glandular goon.'"

Kurland never played pro ball, despite offers of up to $15,000 from teams in the NBL. But after college he nonetheless had a prominent and prosperous basketball career with the Phillips 66 Oilers, an AAU team sponsored by the petroleum company. Three times the Oilers won national titles, and twice, in 1948 and '52, Kurland won Olympic gold medals. An honors student in college, he eventually became a Phillips marketing executive, with vivid memories and no regrets. "People ask me if I wish I had been born 20 years later for the money the pros offer," Kurland says. "I just say I'm glad I wasn't born 20 years earlier."

Hank Luisetti

Coming out onto the floor that night in late December 1936, Hank Luisetti and his Stanford teammates thought they could see fireflies in the far reaches of Madison Square Garden—points of light dancing and flickering. They were in fact the tips of thousands of cigarettes, and they extended up three decks, into the fastness of the old arena. It was a spectacle they had never seen before. Yet by evening's end the Indians, unfazed, had returned the favor, treating more than 17,000 spectators to something they had never seen before and wouldn't soon forget. As Stanford ended Long Island University's 43-game winning streak, Luisetti showcased the art and effectiveness of the one-handed shot. Basketball was changed forever—literally, single-handedly and overnight.

Luisetti, a 6' 3" junior, scored only 15 points, sinking just five field goals. But those were prodigious totals for the era. Filing out after Stanford's 45–31 victory, the spectators could still visualize each of them. The first came near the foul line, after a fake and a pivot, over LIU's 6' 8" Art Hillhouse.

"You lucky so-and-so," Hillhouse muttered to Luisetti, as they repaired to midcourt for the center jump.

Hillhouse didn't say anything when Luisetti's next one-hander dropped through. And by halftime, with Stanford controlling the game and holding a 22–14 lead, the Garden crowd had swung its support from the locals to the interlopers. Luisetti controlled the ball for much of the second half, shooting rarely. *New York Times* columnist Arthur Daley described the ballplayer who today would be one of thousands, but in the '30s stood alone: "What the cold figures do not reveal is his blinding speed, his uncanny ability to control the ball on a dribble, his twisting shot making that sends the sphere whipping through the nets and his beautiful 'feeding' that sets up the plays for his mates." Thirty years later Daley reflected on the meaning of that game and concluded that Luisetti "drove the Original Celtics into the dusty archives and made the Boston Celtics possible."

Indeed, Luisetti was the doorman for a floodgate. Heretofore all basketball innovation had flowed east to west—from places like Springfield, Buffalo, Troy and New York City to points in the Midwest and beyond. Here now was the backwash of Naismith's game, returning to the population centers of the Eastern Seaboard with innovative flotsam. Soon all sorts of developments—the behind-the-back dribble, a single and multitalented star playing any and all positions, even the elimination of the center jump after every basket—would filter through the game, and each owed something to Luisetti's unfettering one-hander. "It would be unfair to compare anyone who played then with the modern players," said Howie Dallmar, who played at Stanford after Luisetti. "But no one now—I mean no one—is as far ahead of his contemporaries as Hank was of his."

The New Yorkers so bedazzled by Luisetti that night already knew San Francisco's northeast corner as a mother lode of sporting legends like Crosetti, Lazzeri and DiMaggio. A few blocks from the Luisettis' home was an asphalt slab too small for baseball, and their only son, after shedding painful braces designed to correct his bowed legs, shot baskets there as a grammar schooler. The high school kids were taller, so he stepped back some and began pushing the ball one-handed to reach the goal. At Galileo High he wasn't a scorer, but a playmaker and a defender in an era when scores were commonly in the teens. But in his freshman season at Stanford he averaged 20 points a game.

By the end of his senior season Luisetti had scored 50 points in a single game and 1,596 for his career. Both totals represented firsts for a collegian. "It isn't showmanship as many suspect," he said of the one-hander. "It's merely a matter of efficiency. I don't have to take time to get set when I shoot one-handed. That saves a half second. I can shoot while in motion, and what probably is most important of all, I can shoot with accuracy."

Paramount paid Luisetti $10,000 to appear with Betty Grable in *Campus Confessions,* a forgettable 1938 film that was created to cash in on his celebrity. All it did, alas, was lead the Amateur Athletic Union to suspend him for a year for performing his sport for profit. He soon resumed his AAU career and, after World War II started, excelled in service ball. But before he could be sent into combat he contracted spinal meningitis, spending four months in the hospital and losing 40 pounds. Doctors told him he couldn't play the game anymore. He was all of 28.

Luisetti never played in the NCAA tournament or the pro ranks, yet his role as a pioneer is unchallenged. He did coach a team representing San Francisco–based Stewart Chevrolet, for whom he sold cars after the war, to the 1951 AAU title. But he soon stepped down and left the game for good, content with having started a revolution and letting others see it through.

Pete
Maravich

Pistol Pete Maravich played with an abandon possible only if your dad is the coach. With his floppy socks, shaggy locks and sense of showmanship, he liberated the first three letters from the word fundamentals. He was an oxymoron many times over: an apostate purist, a Dixie hoophead, the closest thing possible to a white Globetrotter. "An American phenomenon," NBA teammate Rich Kelley would call him. "A stepchild of the human imagination."

Maravich's childhood was a cross between that of a gym rat and an Army brat. His father, Press, moved from one college coaching posting to another, from Clemson to Raleigh to Baton Rouge. Press dictated to Pete both his nickname (after little Pete's from-the-hip push shots) and choice of college (LSU, where Press took over in 1966). And he furthered his son's legend not merely by letting him run free, absolved of the usual constraints of conscience, for three varsity seasons, but by confessing to anyone who would listen that he shared the public's awe. "I get to the point where I don't coach him," Press said. "I just watch."

Press, the story goes, was shooting hoops in the Maravich backyard one day when Pete, all of seven, happened by. Press let him try one. Pete missed, but Press realized he had him hooked. Four to five hours a day Pete would play, shooting, working on all manner of ballhandling prestidigitation, hustling bets from other kids that he could keep a basketball spinning on his index finger forever. Once he spun a ball for 50 minutes, until the finger, its nail worn to a nub, was a bloody mess. Father and son collaborated on a movie, *Homework Basketball,* which showcased the results of Pete's études. "My god," exclaimed the coach of an all-black high school in Baton Rouge after seeing a screening. "He's one of us!"

Colonel Parker, the man who said he could make a million bucks if he could find a white boy who could sing like a black one, eventually found Elvis. In the late '60s, the Southeast found Pistol Pete. The body, described by one sportswriter as "a cross between a clarinet and a filter king," seemed ill suited to any athletic endeavor, yet it successfully probed every defense, the hair faking one way while the Pistol went the other. The signature socks,

lovingly washed and dried in Maravich's dorm room after each use, signified that the show wasn't prepackaged or antiseptic, but had grown organically from a little boy's longstanding and loving relationship with a basketball.

The passes rarely failed to please. The shots, on the other hand, came a little too often for some conservative tastes. He shot 50 times and scored 48 points in his first varsity game. He scored 47 one night with a 104° temperature. On another occasion he scored 42 despite a gash over his eye that required nine stitches to close. After going for 41 in the second half against St. John's, Pete was mobbed by the mostly black Redmen.

It mattered little that his team didn't always win; in the basketball void that was LSU, where the Bayou Bengals had experienced only one winning season since the days of Bob Pettit in the '50s and games were still played in a barn belonging to the School of Agriculture, folks turned out to see something even rarer than victories. Maravich played along: "If I have a choice whether to do the show or throw the straight pass, and we're going to get the basket either way, I'm going to do the show."

In each of his three collegiate seasons he led the nation in scoring, averaging 43.8, 44.2 and 44.5 points per game. "My average has gone up every year since I was in high school," he noted, correctly enough. When he was done, Maravich wasn't merely the college game's alltime leading career scorer; he had scored more in three varsity seasons than anyone had scored in four, before or since.

He won a scoring title in the NBA and made the All-Star team four times in a 10-year career. But he never came close to a championship. And so Maravich began facing questions, never posed to crowd-pleasers in other sports, like Ernie Banks or O.J. Simpson, about his desire to win. He reacted to the inquiries, and debilitating knee problems, by becoming a paranoid loner.

By definition, a showman must go on the road. "I much prefer playing away than at home," Pete had said in college. "At home the same people are watching you who have seen it all before. On the road you have new places, and you're playing to people who don't know about the show. I can do things that they haven't seen before."

Yet Maravich was happiest after leaving the game that had consumed him. The irony was this: At the end of his life, before his heart quit on him at age 40 during a pickup game in a church gym, he had unpacked his bags and settled down. He had set aside his considerable pride and chosen family life, rural living and an austere Christianity. He had chosen home, at long last, over away.

Pete Newell

He spent only 13 seasons on the bench, from 1947 through '60. But by the end of Pete Newell's brief transit of the college game, he had become the first coach ever to win amateur basketball's three jewels—the NIT, NCAA and Olympic championships. And long before UCLA's John Wooden (winless in his final eight games against Newell) began dominating West Coast basketball, the California coach was perfecting his simple strategy of counter-punching. Roust an opponent out of what he most wants to do, Newell believed, and victory will be yours. It was a principle so simple and captivating that, three decades after his retirement from Berkeley, he was still acclaimed overseas as the finest of American coaches.

Raised in Los Angeles, the youngest of eight children, Pete was only 13 when his father died. Earlier, his mother had pushed him into acting, and family legend holds that he nearly beat out Jackie Coogan for the starring role in Charlie Chaplin's *The Kid*. He also displayed precocious management skills, getting himself a paper route and quickly subcontracting the folding and delivering duties to friends.

At Loyola of Los Angeles, now Loyola Marymount, he played for coach James Needles, who was so impressed with Newell's leadership ability and attention to detail that he switched him from forward to guard. In 1947, Needles, now working in the athletic department at the University of San Francisco, gave Newell his first college coaching job.

His mentor may have been the only person not astonished when Newell guided the Dons to the NIT championship in 1949. *(Newell is pictured at right celebrating with his team after an upset of Utah en route to the title.)* At Michigan State, where he took over in 1950, Newell presided over another unlikely renaissance, bringing back a program that had gone 4–18 the previous season. In 1954, with his family homesick for the West Coast, he moved to Berkeley. The Golden Bears won the 1959 NCAA title without a single high school all-state selection, and only one player, captain Al Buch, who would receive any collegiate honors of note. As Cal beat Cincinnati and West Virginia, the man of the moment was Darrall Imhoff, the 6' 10" center, who blocked two late shots by Oscar Robertson to secure Cal's semifinal victory, then rebounded his own miss and scored to defeat the

The Bears reached the NCAA championship game the following season, too, losing to an Ohio State team led by John Havlicek and Jerry Lucas. Again, their success followed from Newell's belief that basketball success could be distilled to minimizing mistakes. He had calculated that a turnover was worth roughly 1.5 points; California's two great teams typically lost the ball six times for every 15 times their opponents did and thus could expect a 14-point advantage whenever they stepped on the floor.

Newell had also learned the importance of controlling tempo. Usually that meant bringing a fast-breaking opponent to heel by pressuring a defensive rebounder and choking off outlet passes. But it often entailed goading a deliberate team into pushing the ball upcourt and then defeating it with a prudent running game. "They become like a guy who takes a certain amount of time each day to shave a certain way," Newell said. "One day he's five minutes late, so he has to hurry and he cuts himself."

Another obsession of Newell's was conditioning. His players could often be seen scaling the hills overlooking the Berkeley campus, sweating themselves into shape. Like a basketball Balanchine, he spent hours breaking down the footwork of every common move in the game. He believed everyone has a dominant foot, as everyone has a dominant hand, and he worked assiduously to develop among his players agility in both feet. Also, he reasoned, everyone bends his knees before moving. So why wait to get into a crouch? Thus, for 20 minutes at every Berkeley practice, players would shuffle, knees bent, one hand up to obscure a shot, the other down to deflect a pass, until the pose became second nature.

Newell fussed over details so much that it was no surprise when he chose to forgo the daily grind and leave the bench at the age of 45. But he did so only after winning, with the help of Robertson, Lucas and Jerry West, the gold medal at the 1960 Olympics. He went on to spend the next 30 years variously as athletic director at Cal, and as a general manager and scout for several NBA teams. But he missed the basketball classroom, and soon enough a brace of NBA players, from Kermit Washington to Kenny Carr to Kiki Vandeweghe, came to study at his knee, at a tutorial he held each summer back on the Loyola Marymount campus, where he had learned the game himself. For his time, Newell asked nothing; for his wisdom, these young millionaires didn't pay a dime. "We'd run drill after drill," Washington recalled, in as high a compliment as a coach can receive. "People would leave the court, throw up and come back for more. Pete was there out of the goodness of his heart, so you weren't going to tell him you were tired. Instead, you'd just go home and die."

Adolph Rupp

The mien fit the man perfectly: Brown suits for games, starched khakis for practices. Jowls you'd summon a bellhop for. An unwavering aversion to joviality. Adolph Rupp was emphatically not a picnic in the park. Yet he didn't merely concede his curmudgeonliness; he cultivated it, nurtured it, and made it work for him. "One of those eastern writers is trying to get people to believe the only reason I win is because I'm an s.o.b.," he once said. "But I know a lot of losers who are s.o.b.'s, so that's not the answer."

A Kansan by birth and breeding, Rupp played for Phog Allen in Lawrence. When he arrived at Kentucky in 1930, the Wildcats had muddled through some 15 coaches over the previous 26 seasons and desperately needed the stability Rupp would bring to the program. Rupp used 10 set plays for the bulk of his career, and upward of 80% of his players came from the Bluegrass State. (He was fond of quoting Scripture: "I will lift up mine eyes unto the hills, whence cometh my help.") Only after World War II did the Wildcats really begin to assert their dominance; they won the 1946 NIT thanks to a star named Jack Parkinson; two years later the Cats had gotten so good that Parkinson, now a senior, no longer started. Kentucky raced through the back half of the '40s, winning 155 of 170 games and NCAA titles in 1948 and '49. "No joking, no laughing, no whistling, no singing, no nothing," said Alex Groza, a member of those "Fabulous Five" championship teams, of life under Adolph. "Just basketball."

The Wildcats' winning percentage against the point spread, however, was suspiciously lower over this stretch, and authorities later learned that Groza and teammates Ralph Beard and Dale Barnstable, in a 1949 NIT first-round loss to Loyola of Chicago, had taken money from mobsters—this after Rupp had boasted that gamblers couldn't touch his team "with a 10-foot pole." Authorities of all stripes swooped in to give Kentucky a hidestrapping for these and other indiscretions, and the school canceled its 1952–53 schedule. The forced hiatus embittered Rupp, who vowed not to retire until he had won another NCAA championship.

With three players ineligible to enter the tournament in 1953–54, the Cats, stir-crazy, nonetheless went 25–0 in the regular season. And in 1958 the Fiddlin' Five—so-called because Rupp believed he had nothing but "barnyard fiddlers" when the schedule called for violinists worthy of Carnegie Hall—did indeed win the title he had promised. In the championship game, Kentucky continually fed the ball to whomever Seattle star Elgin Baylor happened to be guarding, thereby forcing him to defend a one-on-one move. With Baylor neutralized by fouls, Seattle was subdued, and Rupp had his fourth and final NCAA crown.

Yet he wasn't about to resign. Instead, like the bourbon whiskey of which he was fond, he began to mellow. "I'm not out to conquer the world anymore," he said by way of explanation. "Just win all the games my team plays." He gradually became more congenial with his players and more permissive in his approach to the game. A hidebound adherent to the man-to-man, Rupp added a combination defense, insisting that it wasn't a zone but "a transitional shifting man-to-man with a hyperbolic paraboloid." But he never did accommodate himself to that canard about how it didn't matter whether you won or lost, it was how you played the game. Said Rupp: "How would you like your surgeon to tell you, It doesn't matter whether you live or die, it's how I make the cut?"

Despite the 41 seasons (42 counting that year of penance), and notwithstanding the 879 victories, the many skeptics of Rupp's achievements—people who were sometimes hard to separate from those who simply didn't like him—questioned the quality of competition in the Southeast. What Rupp did, said Notre Dame coach Johnny Dee, was "like taking five Canadians and starting a hockey league in Texas." And, of course, there was Rupp's failure to recognize in any substantive way the black athlete, until 1966, when Texas Western defeated "Rupp's Runts" for the national championship.

It was a measure of Rupp's aura of invincibility that the social significance of that game—of college basketball's most ardent segregationist being beaten by a team that started five blacks—was left to another generation of historians to consider. At the time, college basketball noted simply that mighty Kentucky had been beaten. "It was a thrill playing against Mr. Rupp, let alone beating him," said the Miners' victorious coach, Don Haskins.

Late in his life, before leaving the bench in 1972, Rupp returned more and more to a favorite pastime, fox hunting. "It's the best sport for a man my age," he said. "You turn the dogs loose and sit down and listen to them with some sandwiches and a fifth of bourbon. The fox holes up and doesn't get caught. The dogs have a happy time running about. Nobody wins and nobody loses. And the alumni don't write letters."

Dean Smith

Well before the end of basketball's first century, there emerged a particular species of college team called "the program." Part corporation and part clan, pledged to lofty standards of success, most of the elite programs were built by, and in the image of, a single man. Knight's Hoosiers, Thompson's Hoyas, Crum's Cardinals—all could count on the fealty of a nearby constituency and a steady flow of top high school talent. But the apotheosis of the modern college basketball program, the game's IBM, could be found at North Carolina, in the Tar Heels of Dean Smith.

Smith seemed at first blush an unlikely CEO. The son of strict Baptist schoolteachers, he was a twice-married, chain-smoking, Scotch-quaffing liberal Democrat who attended Kansas on an academic scholarship. While majoring in math, he was nevertheless an athlete, a reserve on the Jayhawks' 1952 NCAA champions, who always seemed to hold down the coachly positions—catcher, quarterback, point guard. In 1958, after five years in the Air Force, he joined Frank McGuire's staff at North Carolina and, three years later, at age 30, was named head coach.

The circumstances of his hiring hardly foreshadowed the successes to come. The Tar Heels had just served a probation for recruiting violations. The school's chancellor, the story goes, chose Smith because he believed the new coach would flounder around, and a sport sorely in need of de-emphasis could thus be scaled down. "Whoever heard of anybody named Dean?" wondered McGuire, a New Yorker, when he first met Smith. "Where I come from you become a dean. You're not named Dean."

If the name signified a sort of premature maturity, Smith had to draw on all of that precociousness as he struggled through his first few seasons. Returning home after a loss at Wake Forest in 1964, the team bus pulled up in front of the gym to find the coach hung in effigy. Later that year, however, Smith lured Larry Miller, a Pennsylvania high schooler with a national profile, to Chapel Hill. An active integrationist, Smith also signed one of the Atlantic Coast Conference's first black stars, Charlie Scott. And as the state began producing promising players of its own, Smith prevailed on many of them to stay home. In 1967 UNC won its first ACC tournament title and from that year on never failed to earn a postseason bid.

The list of Smith's accomplishments bespeaks an almost numbing, inexorable excellence. North Carolina won at least 20 games for an NCAA-record 23 straight seasons. Smith hadn't even turned 60 when, in 1991, he won his 700th game—the youngest coach to reach that milestone. Over one astonishing period of 29 straight years, the Heels never finished lower than third in the ACC's regular-season standings; every other league team except for newcomer Florida State had finished last at least once in the previous 17 years alone. In 1981–82, just as whispers about his never having won a national title approached critical mass, Smith won an NCAA crown in the most difficult manner possible: by nursing a preseason No. 1 ranking through the entire schedule. His second title, in 1993, was an emphatic riposte to the whispers that had begun anew—that Smith had lost his edge, and that his powder-blue program was being eclipsed by the darker shade eight miles up the road, of Duke and its young coach, Mike Krzyzewski.

The two things about which Smith is most compulsive, privacy and detail, were cornerstones of the Carolina program. A strict pecking order put seniors on the cover of the media guide, regardless of how little they contributed to the box scores, while freshmen, irrespective of portfolio, were conscripted into performing such chores as lugging equipment on road trips and prohibited from talking to the press until they had played in a game. Smith's Tar Heels performed rituals that, taken together, enhanced both the team's spirit and its chances to win—huddles before free throws, hand signals to the coach to indicate fatigue, even an end-of-the-bench bomb squad called "the Blue Team" that played together for brief stretches and outscored an opponent's first-stringers surprisingly often. At the same time, on matters of NCAA compliance and graduation rates, the two litmus tests of virtue in college athletics, Carolina remained unsullied. "He's a mathematician, and in effect he's written a program for winning basketball games," said former Tar Heel Steve Previs. "Or even better, coach Smith is a Japanese car."

That remark would seem to cast Smith as bloodless. Yet he immersed himself in such hot-button public issues as nuclear politics and civil rights and read everything from Sören Kierkegaard to inspirational tracts. Nearly 100 of his 121 lettermen paid their way back to campus to share in a tribute to him in 1980. "I know nobody on the outside can believe all this stuff is that good," said Billy Cunningham, who played on those early teams when the coach's mortality was very much evident. "But I swear it is. I'd hate Dean Smith too if I were a guy who had to coach against him all the time."

David Thompson

During his three varsity seasons at North Carolina State, David Thompson was many things. He was the David who slew the UCLA Goliath. He was the midpoint between two teammates of curious dimensions, the 5' 6" Monte Towe and the 7' 4" Tom Burleson. And he was the extraordinary player who popularized in basketball circles the term "vertical leap." Indeed, once a game tipped off, the ability to rise 42 inches from a standing start made the 6' 4", 195-pound Thompson more intriguing than Towe and bigger than Burleson.

Thompson, the youngest of 11 children, grew up in poverty in the western half of North Carolina, near the milltown of Shelby. His parents cleaned buildings for a living, and the family shared a house at the end of a dirt lane, with tended flowers and abandoned automobiles out front. By the age of four he had been placed in kindergarten because his siblings were too busy picking cotton to look after him. Thompson was reared to defer to his many elders, and thus he acquired a shyness that would recede only when he roamed the red-clay court out back, playing by the light of the moon and experimenting with the rhythms of the game. Only here, it seemed, could he express himself; the recruiters who soon came by found him so cautious and taciturn that they didn't dare believe their entreaties were getting through to him.

The Wolfpack ultimately signed him but wound up on probation for violations committed during his recruitment. As a result Thompson couldn't play in the NCAA tournament at the end of his sophomore season, 1972–73, during which the Wolfpack went 27–0. The following year, however, N.C. State ended UCLA's seven-year run as national champion in an epic national semifinal, a double-overtime 80–77 defeat of the Bruins. Two of Thompson's teammates had missed shots that could have won the game, first at the end of regulation, then at the end of the first overtime. Thompson wasn't going to let the same thing happen a third time. With slightly more than a minute to play in the second overtime, after the Wolfpack had fought back from a seven-point deficit to within one, Thompson took the ball and the game into his own hands. He leaped, then banked in the jumper—more than any shooter in history,

Thompson *jumped* before squeezing off his jump shots—that gave State a 76–75 lead, all it needed for its eventual 80–75 win. Beating Marquette two days later in the final was an easy anticlimax. Thompson did all this despite suffering a gash on his forehead during the regional, the result of literally tripping over the shoulders of 6' 8" teammate Phil Spence. *(Thompson is pictured at right shooting over North Carolina's Phil Ford.)*

Thompson was now 57–1 as a collegian and National Player of the Year. Yet he passed up million-dollar offers from the still-warring NBA and ABA to return for his senior season, during which he won another Player of the Year award. So high did Thompson leap, as a collegian and as the mainstay of the Denver Nuggets for five professional seasons, that the coming down wasn't always easy. Injuries and drug problems plagued him during his last years in Denver and after a trade in 1982 to the Seattle SuperSonics. He wound up going home to Carolina after his pro career concluded in 1984 and taking a community relations position with the Charlotte Hornets.

It's difficult to appraise Thompson because to do so one must separate his gifts from his achievements, and his principal gift was so impressive that it tended to obscure other parts of the package. Indeed, someone once roped him into trying the triple jump at an N.C. State track meet during the spring of his freshman year. Never before had he tried the event, yet after a couple of practice runs he loped down the runway and hopped, skipped and jumped to a mark of 49' 11", a school record that stood for five years. Somehow he translated this singular talent into an efficient way of playing basketball, and that was an achievement, even if other people—the people who likened him to the queen on a chess board, because he seemed to be able to make any move—couldn't fully appreciate how difficult it was. "Great players can just play their normal games and be very good," Thompson once said. "Those are the ones who have the ability to make basketball an art. It comes naturally for them. But not for me—I have to work at it."

It was hard to get anyone to believe that, because the standard David Thompson highlight clip, the one that will play forever in the Hoops Cineplex, is still distinguished by its effortlessness. The prevailing ban on the dunk only served to dramatize Thompson's levitational abilities and make them seem more graceful: up, up he would go, up some more still, to meet one of the passes Towe had learned to lob just off the rim. Softly his payload would be dropped into the net. Only then, having apparently resolved that, yes, the game merited getting on with, would he return to earth.

Bill Walton

Bill Walton scored, defended and won so prodigiously during his three seasons at UCLA in the early '70s that he left us with scores of different ways to recall his impact on the game. But let us try out this image, for it does justice to both his commitment to team play and his leadership qualities, characteristics that were every bit as memorable as any of his outsized skills. Walton takes a rebound off the defensive glass. Then he turns, sometimes even before alighting, with elbows out, to whip an overhead pass to a teammate upcourt. Moments later he's at half court to check out his handiwork, clapping while some Bruin is flicking in a layup.

Basketball may have been the only place where Walton found a piece of the utopia he always seemed in search of. He grew up in a middle-class Catholic family outside San Diego as one of four children who, thanks to a welfare-worker father and librarian mother, were encouraged to think for themselves. Yet unlike some liberal parents, Ted and Gloria Walton believed in competition, and their children all became athletes. Bill, two brothers and one sister engaged in all sorts of contests among themselves, including one to see who could first touch the ceiling in the family living room.

Bill won that one. Indeed, by his junior year at Helix High School he could touch that ceiling with his elbows. He had sprung up six inches over a single summer, to 6' 7", and by the time he was a senior averaging 29 points and 24 rebounds a game, he stood 6' 11".

"Coach," Denny Crum, then an assistant to UCLA's John Wooden, told his boss, "I've just seen the greatest high school prospect ever."

Wooden reminded Crum about Lew Alcindor, who had been scouted by Crum in New York several years earlier.

"Yeah," Crum said, "but this kid is better."

Wooden prevailed on Walton to choose UCLA, and although the two disagreed on many of the issues of the day, they saw the game the same way. "With Bill in our lineup our strategy is simple," the coach said. "You go to him until the opposing team stops it. Then you go to others. If you don't, it's like using Babe Ruth in your lineup to bunt."

Walton was a sultan of swat, rebound, pass and the simple jump shot. Indeed, nearly two of every three shots he launched during his college career found the mark, the greatest exhibition of his touch coming in the 1973 NCAA championship game, when he sank 21 of 22 field goal attempts as UCLA defeated Memphis State. When the Bruins' 88-game winning streak ended at Notre Dame in 1974, it was the first time in five seasons of amateur play that Walton had tasted defeat. So high were the standards to which he had grown accustomed that he would call the 1973–74 season, in which the Bruins merely made the Final Four, "embarrassing."

"There have been many great players in the game," said Wooden, "but not many great team players. Walton is a very great team player." He talked incessantly on the court, warning teammates of impending screens and open opponents. His knack for keeping his blocked shots in play suggested someone who was conscious of much more than statistics. He took it upon himself to upbraid other Bruins for their failings but often added a phrase of encouragement: "Hey, we love ya!"

Unlike many of the game's greats, Walton's career always had about it an air of mortality. Ill at ease with his celebrity, he showed it by slouching low in chairs and walking in the shadows of buildings on the Westwood campus. And he often broke down physically. Tendinitis in the knees troubled him ever since that growth spurt in high school, and other maladies—a bone spur in an ankle, a dislocated finger, allergies and a bum foot—bothered him throughout his career.

In his search for relief, he became more and more fascinated by the counterculture. To heal, focus or relax, he experimented with acupuncture, Transcendental Meditation, vegetarianism and marijuana. On these and other scores, Walton and his coach clashed. Yet when Wooden stood up to him, offering him a choice between his nonconformism and remaining on the team, Walton always backed down. Wooden knew he would: The team meant too much to him. "I don't have blind reverence for authority," Walton said. "People I respect earn my respect. Coach Wooden has earned it."

Infirmities followed Walton into the pros but didn't entirely waylay him until he had once again demonstrated his winning touch. He was voted the NBA Finals MVP while leading one of pro basketball's most unselfish teams, the 1977 Portland Trail Blazers, to a title. The play-for-pays always were a lark to him. To sum up his own philosophy, Walton liked to quote a line from his favorite rock and roll band, the Grateful Dead: *We used to play for silver, now we play for life.* As he once said, "I'd play every minute I could, even if there was no money at all."

John Wooden

He shunned recruiting. He put relatively little stock in the scouting of opponents. Most stubbornly of all, he refused to equate success with winning. Taken together, these traits would figure to make John Wooden a coaching failure rather than the preeminent winner of all time. But he had chosen to become a coach for the long-term rewards, not the short-term payoffs, and it was through longevity—always studying, always learning, finally prevailing as no coach had before or has since—that he made his indelible mark. UCLA failed to win an NCAA title over Wooden's first 15 seasons, but in the last dozen years of his career the fates rewarded him with 10 championships. "John was a better coach at 55 than he was at 50," said California coach Pete Newell, his rival through the 1950s. "He was a better coach at 60 than at 55. He's a true example of a man who learned from day one to day last."

Born on an Indiana farm with a three-holer outhouse out back, Wooden learned to shoot at an iron goal actually forged by his father. He went on to become a three-time All-America at Purdue, where he earned as much fame for his crew cut as for the grit and abandon with which he played. After service in World War II, Wooden, like any midwestern kid, wanted to coach at a school in the Big Ten. In 1948, unbeknownst to him, a snowstorm had delayed an expected phone call from Minnesota officials with news of a job offer. By the time the Gophers' call came through, asking Wooden to come to Minneapolis, he had already accepted a position at UCLA.

He won his first championship in 1964 with an undersized, full-court pressing team. A year later, when glittery Pauley Pavilion opened on campus, Wooden made sure that the university built him no mere arena, but a classroom, in which the bleachers rolled back and he could replicate the atmosphere of a one-room schoolhouse. His pedagogy owed much to the whole-part method, which breaks the game down to its elements ("just like parsing a sentence," he would say, sounding like the English teacher he had indeed once been). It rested, too, on the notion that basketball is a game of threes: forward, center, guard; shoot, drive, pass; ball, you, man; conditioning, skill, teamwork. (The latter was the trinity preached by Wooden's college coach, Ward (Piggy) Lambert, and comprised the three blocks at the heart of Wooden's homespun Pyramid of Success.) Finally, Wooden applied the four basic laws of learning—explanation, demonstration, correction and repetition.

An article of faith among coaches holds that one must be intolerant of mistakes, but Wooden considered errors to be precious opportunities for learning—preferably in practice, of course. When the games finally came around, they were but exams, through which the teacher could evaluate how much had gotten through. "Wooden is not the game coach everybody thinks he is," said Jack Hirsch, who played on the first title team. "He doesn't have to be. He's so good during the week, he sits back, relaxes and has fun watching the game."

Wooden had a saying for that phenomenon, as he did for most things in life. In this case, the quote was from Cervantes: "The journey's better than the end." Improbably, Wooden's sepia-tinted, Hoosier approach to imparting what he knew—he had a pamphleteer's stash of epigrams and used the oft-reproduced Pyramid to codify his folk wisdom—actually got through to the baby boomers in his charge. "He makes you believe you can do anything," one of them said. "You become surprised when you lose."

Behind his courtly manner and whiskered methods, Wooden retained the spirit that had made him a combative player. His reputation as a relentless jockeyer of officials, and even of opposing players, was well deserved. (His comments were profanity-free, of course; he uttered no oath stronger than "goodness gracious sakes alive!") "He has an antiseptic needle—clean but biting," said Walt Hazzard, the star of Wooden's first championship team and one of many men who tried, in vain, to replicate his success as the Bruins' coach. On other campuses, where the expectations weren't as high, he made possible the cult of the coach that would turn many of the dandified men who worked the sidelines into millionaires. (Wooden, for his part, never made more than $32,500 per year.)

He retired in 1975 after defeating Kentucky for yet another NCAA title. Any reservations about his decision evaporated when an alumnus came up to him after that final game. "Great victory, John," the booster said. "It makes up for your letting us down last year."

Makes up, indeed. No other coach in history had won more than four NCAA championships—and here was the Wizard of Westwood with 10, including seven in a row, and four perfect 30–0 seasons. In 1960 he had been voted into the Hall of Fame as a player. In 1972 he was voted in as a coach, the only person ever to be immortalized twice.

Kareem Abdul-Jabbar

Imagine that Baylor, West and Chamberlain found their way into one person, a colossus who embodied Baylor's speed and grace, West's skill and finesse and Chamberlain's size, if not exactly his strength. Kareem Abdul-Jabbar, born in New York City as Ferdinand Lewis Alcindor Jr., was raised a Catholic and sent to Power Memorial, a Catholic boys school. In the first of many independent decisions, Alcindor decided to enroll at UCLA.

Scrutinized relentlessly even as a 15-year-old, he shrank at first from prying eyes. Indeed, the decision to play for John Wooden—to go to California, with its implied promise of freedom and open spaces—seemed a repudiation of New York's close quarters. Just as Abdul-Jabbar would seem put off by the subtle injustices visited upon him in the hurly-burly of his life on the court, away from it he prized his space and privacy. But as he grew older and staked out exactly who he was—a Moslem and a sort of basketball marathoner, more spiritual athlete than sports mercenary—he let fall away the protective layers. Indeed, before he turned 43 he would write two autobiographies.

That first season in Westwood, freshmen still couldn't play varsity ball; with Alcindor, the UCLA "Brubabes" beat the Bruins' defending champions by 15 points in an exhibition. The next year he would score 61 points in one of his first varsity games, against Washington State, which inexplicably chose to play man-to-man defense. In Alcindor's three varsity seasons UCLA won as many NCAA titles, all of them in lopsided championship games.

In 1971, in just his second season with the NBA's Milwaukee Bucks, the Bucks won a championship and Alcindor, who had confessed his Islamic faith in 1968 when he had joined the black athletes' Olympic boycott, went public with his Moslem name. At about the same time, the Bucks' play-by-play man, Eddie Doucette, started calling Abdul-Jabbar's signature shot "the skyhook." (Appropriately enough, years later, in 1984, it would be a skyhook that pushed Abdul-Jabbar past Chamberlain as the NBA's alltime leading scorer.) Yet the legend, in his middle age, became restive. Unable to swing a deal to send him to his hometown and the New York Knicks, Milwaukee in 1975 traded him to Los Angeles.

"I've always been cautious and secretive, so of course people thought I was strange," he would say. He admitted that his standoffishness was a studied cool, learned from a youth spent prowling New York City jazz clubs. Blamed occasionally for lackadaisical play, expected never to lose, he eventually retreated into a kind of stoicism. "I'm a target," he said. "Always have been. Too big to miss."

It took years for Kareem to find serenity in pro basketball, a world marked by nightly collisions and pokes and elbows, all of them at odds with his own sense of grace. Rather than flinch, Abdul-Jabbar, whose eyeballs had been repeatedly scratched, eventually donned goggles.

Nature had dealt him an advantageous hand, one that made him prominent and wealthy. "I've always considered my height a blessing," he has said. On other counts, however, fate was less than kind. A family of Hanafi Moslems, the orthodox sect to which Abdul-Jabbar belongs, was murdered in 1973 in a Washington, D.C., house that he owned. In 1983 a fire destroyed his eight-room Bel Air home and melted his priceless collection of some 3,000 jazz albums. A misbegotten relationship with an agent led to $9 million in lost investments. Migraine headaches that sometimes left him bedridden addled him during times of stress. For years he gunnysacked his troubles, and twice he snapped, making a fist and lashing out on the court and breaking his hand. Otherwise, remarkably, he suffered no major injuries, a testament to his ability to run the long race.

The Lakers of the '80s, thanks to Magic Johnson and the "Showtime" cast of supporting players, made it easier, of course. But at age 38 Abdul-Jabbar met his last great challenge. It was delivered to him in the 1985 NBA Finals, in the form of a 148–114 Game 1 defeat by the Celtics in Boston Garden. The Captain played miserably, scoring only 12 points and getting beat on defense time and again. With the help of a philippic from his coach, Pat Riley, he rededicated himself. Not in years had the aperture of his focus narrowed so. "We may not win," he told his teammates, "but let's make it worthy of us."

He played exquisitely over the remainder of that series, scoring 18 points in the second half of the Game 6 victory that gave the Lakers the third of their five titles during Kareem's sojourn in L.A.

Fourteen years after he had first been named NBA Finals MVP with the Bucks, he had done it again. Those two trophies—he had never, tellingly enough, won an All-Star Game MVP award—were gilded brackets for a golden professional career. "He defies logic," Riley said in the afterglow of that series. "He's the most unique and durable athlete of our time, the best you'll ever see. You'd better enjoy him while he's here."

Rick
Barry

By always insisting on being first, Rick Barry drove himself to become the player he was. Yet by reason of that compulsion, he became at the same time perhaps the least beloved of the game's greats. His temper led to flareups with opponents, officials, even teammates. His blunt manner, and a congenital critical streak, further alienated the men with whom he played in San Francisco, Oakland, Washington, New York, Golden State and, finally, Houston. "It's difficult for me to do things for fun," he would say. "Even a game like charades . . . a dumb clue drives me crazy." He endeared himself to no one by belonging to five teams over five years under three contracts, and twice holding simultaneous contracts to play with teams in both the NBA and ABA.

"Basketball gypsy" was the spin he put on his incessant peregrinations during the 14 years he was a nonpareil forward. "Mercenary" was the less charitable word others chose.

Thus Barry had one of the most breathtakingly underappreciated all-around games of anyone who played for pay. Until Larry Bird came along with his blind conjurings and subtle hunches, Barry was considered the finest passer ever to play his position. He remains the alltime free throw accuracy leader, with a lifetime percentage of .900, notwithstanding his idiosyncratic, granny-style, underhand technique. His jump shot, only passable when he first arrived in the pros, soon matched his instincts as a scorer, which had always been considerable. "He was Larry Bird," said Al Menendez, the longtime scout for several NBA teams, "before there was a Larry Bird."

At Miami his coach was his future father-in-law, Bruce Hale. (He and Pam Hale, now divorced, have four boys. About his sons Barry has said, "If my kids were horses, they'd be worth a million dollars because of their breeding.") Yet by the time he had enrolled at Miami, Barry's nettlesome manner had already taken deep root. As the Hurricanes ran through a three-man drill that called for them to make 10 layups in a row before being excused to the locker room, the two players teamed with Barry would intentionally flub up when they reached nine—so they would have to do it over, and Barry, who would be furious, couldn't be first in the shower.

His rookie season with the Warriors may have been his happiest, for he understood the NBA's pecking order and had no delusions about, or expectations of, bearing a leader's burden. He managed to smile often enough that year to earn the name "Sunshine" from his teammates. (As a youngster growing up in Roselle Park, N.J., he had always been reluctant to smile because his teeth had come in crooked; a severe and petulant visage would keep him from winning over fans and writers as his pro career progressed.) His talent was never in doubt: In his second season he scored 38 points in the All-Star Game, and he averaged more than 40 a game in the championship series against Philadelphia, a record that still stands.

In 1969 he achieved another first, averaging 34 points per game for the ABA's Oakland Oaks to become the only player ever to have led the NCAA, NBA and ABA in scoring. Then in 1975, as the Warriors won their only NBA title, he averaged more than 30 points a game, placed sixth overall in assists and even led the league in steals, a remarkable feat for a forward. Yet he finished fourth in the MVP balloting, a plebiscite of the players. "A joke," said the Warriors' Clifford Ray, who was as close to Barry as anyone on that championship team. "The man had the greatest season I'd ever seen. That vote was a joke."

As critical as he was of his teammates, a few, like Ray, indulged him because he seemed to meet the even higher standards to which he held himself, and because he would disarm them from time to time with fits of generosity. As for his peers, they might justly have cheered him, for his jumps from league to league helped touch off the premerger salary spiral from which so many players of that era benefited. Instead, said Billy Paultz, another former teammate, "Half the players around the league disliked Rick. The other half hated him."

Coming up, Barry was, quite literally, the crossing guard at school, the altar boy at church, the lead in the Christmas pageant. But he was all those things in a figurative sense, too, as he struggled to live up to his own burdensome expectations.

Before the Warriors saw fit to hoist his jersey into their rafters, he was voted into the Hall of Fame. He celebrated that enshrinement as only the most fastidious perfectionist would: by going to a gym in Springfield, Mass., and sinking 91 straight free throws.

Elgin Baylor

Before Hawkins, Erving or Jordan there was Elgin Baylor, avatar of aviators. Baylor's father, glancing at his watch to mark the moment his son was born, ended up taking the brand name on the watch face as Elgin's first name. Many others would be tempted to check their own watches after beholding John Baylor's boy, who seemed to suspend himself in midair during his creative sallies to the basket.

Baylor was a pioneer of the game's third dimension, that uncharted fastness that makes wannabes of fans everywhere. "Watching Elgin Baylor on a basketball court," wrote Jim Murray, the *Los Angeles Times* columnist to whom that privilege fell for a dozen seasons, "was like watching Gene Kelly in the rain." The Knicks' Richie Guerin seemed to be in much the same metaphorical neighborhood in his own appraisal: "He's either got three hands or two basketballs. It's like guarding a flood."

The water imagery was entirely felicitous. Fluidity isn't what one envisions in men of 6' 5" and 225 pounds, yet that was Baylor's signature, whether scoring or claiming rebounds (he averaged more than 13 a game) or dumping off to teammates when he was accorded the customary attention of two defenders. By 1966 he had already suffered serious injuries to first his left and then his right knee, yet he would still return to the form—rock, jab, step, sky, hang, score—of his salad days. Teammates swore that the famous Baylor head fake, prelude to so many of his moves, would appear just as readily when he was about to play a card in a locker room game of hearts.

Russell was a better rebounder, Pettit a better scorer and Cousy a better passer. But for all three skills in one outsized package, Baylor stood alone. "I say without reservation," said Fred Schaus, his old coach, "that Elgin Baylor is the greatest cornerman ever to play pro basketball."

In an era when the individual conjurer, let alone the black superstar, was still rare, there were really two Baylors. The public one was impeccably turned out, regal in bearing, conscious of who he was and what he stood for. Among his teammates, however, Baylor cut up. "I guess the best way to put it," said Jerry West, "is that Elg is the kind of guy that when he's not around, you know he's not around."

The Minneapolis Lakers didn't have much to lose in 1958 when they signed Baylor to a $20,000 deal, wildly extravagant for the time. They had just gone 19–53, finishing last and averaging 2,000 fans per game. On the same day Lakers owner Bob Short signed Baylor, he turned down an offer to sell the franchise because he couldn't get his asking price of $250,000. The team's fortunes reversed themselves as quickly as Baylor became Rookie of the Year. Attendance doubled. In the two years before the Lakers moved to Los Angeles, Baylor established himself as the franchise's sine qua non. When their star forward had to do Army duty at Fort Sam Houston, the entire team up and went to Texas so they could practice with him. In 1965 Short sold the club for more than $5 million.

In Charleston, W. Va., one night to play the Cincinnati Royals, Baylor encountered a hotel clerk who refused quarters to him and his two black teammates. Baylor hadn't started playing basketball until he was 14 because the city playgrounds in his hometown of Washington, D.C., barred people of color, and he refused to suit up that night. Hot Rod Hundley, a teammate and a Charlestonian, implored him to reconsider. "Rod, I'm a human being," Baylor told him. "I'm not an animal put in a cage and let out for the show." He would perform with dignity or not at all.

The single curse of Baylor's career seemed to have been laid on him in college, when his Seattle University team finished runner-up to Kentucky in the 1958 NCAA finals. Seven times Baylor and the Lakers were frustrated by the NBA's Kentucky equivalents, the Boston Celtics, in a championship series. When the Lakers finally won one, in 1972, he made the rounds of their delirious locker room with what must have been leaden ambivalence, for his knees had quit on him nine games into that season, forcing retirement. West and Wilt Chamberlain, always more celebrated, savored the moment; Baylor could only watch from a spectator's distance.

Curiously for one of the game's Wright brothers, Baylor hated to fly when he first came up. But a few seasons of doing so in arenas around the country must have accustomed him to more mechanical takeoffs and landings. In 1960, when the Lakers' plane lost power in a storm, Baylor stretched out in the narrow aisle of the DC-3, draped a blanket over himself and announced, "If I've got to go, I may as well go comfortably."

When the pilot touched down in an Iowa cornfield, he did so gracefully, as if Elgin had been at the controls.

Larry Bird

His sallow flesh had no muscle tone. Two fingers on his shooting hand were disfigured. He had a throwback of an outside shot, launched off his shoulder, that looked as if it would be easy pickings for pro basketball's springy-legged defensive predators. Yet he's acknowledged to be the greatest forward ever to play the game.

Bob Cousy goes further. "Before, I used to vacillate. The question didn't seem relevant. But Larry Bird came along with all the skills, all the things a basketball player has to do. I think he's the greatest." Add the assessments of Jerry West ("He's as nearly perfect as you can get in every phase") and John Wooden ("I've always considered Oscar Robertson to be the best player in the game, but now I'm not so sure that Bird isn't"), and you have a critical mass of opinion. It's left only to the Celtics' eminence, Red Auerbach, to render his judgment. "If I had to start a team, the one guy in all history I would take would be Larry," says Auerbach, who knows a little about Bill Russell. "He's the greatest to ever play the game."

The poor black youngster from the inner city is supposed to be the one who turns to basketball for succor. Yet basketball served every bit as much a refuge for Bird, who grew up in dire circumstances in small-town Indiana, as it has for countless of his black urban counterparts. His mother, Georgia, worked as a waitress; his father, Joe, a laborer, was an alcoholic, a chronic debtor and ultimately, a suicide when Larry was 18. "Basketball was never recreation for me," he said. "It was something I fell in love with." The game reciprocated with its affection.

As an adolescent, Bird drifted. He was 17 when, in the fall of 1974, he ventured 50 miles north to Indiana University. He didn't last a month. At tiny Northwood Institute, a junior college near his home, he survived only slightly longer, eventually landing back in French Lick and taking a job as a municipal garbage collector.

A year later, older and a little more worldly-wise, the fledgling was ready to spread his wings. He went off to Indiana State in Terre Haute, spending a year to get settled academically before allowing his basketball career to take flight. Yet even after the Sycamores went 25–3 in his first season, as Bird averaged 32.8 points a game, and even after Indiana State reached the NIT quarterfinals in his second

season, the 6' 9" forward remained a cipher to all but college basketball's cognoscenti. Only in his final season did the nation finally take notice as the Sycamores reached No. 1 in the polls and didn't lose until their last game of the season, to Magic Johnson's Michigan State team in the NCAA championship game. Bird, the college player of the year, rebounded, scored and raised an otherwise ragamuffin bunch to a level theretofore unimagined.

If there was any doubt about Bird's salutary effect on the ensemble that makes up a team, he banished it in his first NBA season. Within a year the Boston Celtics, 29–53 without Bird the previous season, had improved to 61–21 and tied the 76ers for the league's best record. A year later the Celtics beat the Houston Rockets for the NBA title, the first of three crowns Bird would win in his first seven pro seasons. There was something perfect about how he ended his career—going scoreless in the U.S. Olympic Dream Team's gold-medal finale in Barcelona, and then allowing that the medal wouldn't mean as much to him because the games hadn't been close.

"This game is all confidence, and you know, sometimes it's scary," he said. "When I'm at my best, I feel like I'm in total control of everything."

And he was. He was capable of squeezing off some of the most delicate shots of his generation, a gift that placed him regularly near the top of the league in free throw and three-point percentages. Yet he always had license to take what for others would be classified as "bad" shots—and some of the most misbegotten of these would go in. His shots would go up with either hand—he eats and writes with his left hand—and he would sometimes call out "Left hand!" to opponents while releasing a sinistral shot, so as to cash in a mental dividend when his wrong-handed efforts found the mark, as they so often did.

He excelled in every other phase of the game, too. He had a knack for throwing what Cousy described as "not the unorthodox pass, but the unexpected pass." While no one bothered to rave about his rebounding skill, he averaged more per game than such heralded chairmen of the boards as Paul Silas and Maurice Lucas. And his desire to put away opponents was unrivaled. "Look in his eyes," said Dominique Wilkins, with whom Bird had a number of epic playoff shoot-outs, "and you see a killer."

Throughout he remained unaffected by public approbation. "The same towns over and over," Bird, the Hoosier philosopher, once said about life on the road. "You know where you're going, but you forget where you're coming from." In between, you cover a lot of territory. The game is acutely aware, and very much in awe, of where Larry Bird has been.

Wilt Chamberlain

Even among the behemoths who play professional basketball, Wilt Chamberlain stood alone as the biggest of the big. An outsized talent in an outsized body, he elicited outsized reactions from opponents, fans, coaches and teammates alike. Asked once to cite the most memorable moment of his own career, Bob Lanier, who is 6' 10" and 270 pounds, spoke not of his own considerable achievements but said it was "when Wilt Chamberlain lifted me up and moved me like a coffee cup so he could get position."

When Wilt left basketball he held or shared 43 NBA records, and although some have fallen, many of his marks—like 100 points in a game, a single-season scoring average of 50.4 per game and a single-season rebound average of 27.2—will likely stand forever. Bill Russell won more, and Russell shows up on more ballots when people convene over cold ones to discuss who they would pick to build a team around. But even today it's Russ who's mistaken on the street for Wilt and not vice versa. "What Wilt was on the outside identified him as a person," says Tom Meschery, the sometime poet who once shared a locker room with Chamberlain. "It's that way with many athletes, but it's all the more so with Wilt because there was more on the outside of him than anybody else."

Indeed, the way Wilt commanded the game during his career became intimately tied up with his persona—with how he adjusted to the role of Goliath. You always got the sense that he could have been a decent foul shooter, instead of the career .511 free throw disaster he was, if only he had resolved to be one; he did make 28 of 32 that night in 1962 in Hershey, Pa., when he scored 100 points against the New York Knicks. But Wilt liked to say that foul shooting wasn't what he was paid to do. It was as if the weakness were somehow calculated, a human foible affected to win the fans' favor. Yet if he were trying to endear himself to those predisposed to root against him, Wilt's good intentions often went for naught late in games, for to some observers he seemed to shrink from contact simply to preserve his record of having never once fouled out. Perhaps he needed the sorry foul shooting record to seem vulnerable, and the disqualification-free career to preserve his aura of invulnerability—so that in the

comforting interstices between those two poles he could be, however fleetingly, normal.

By the time he left Kansas, after two seasons, the college game had outlawed three things in part to curtail his effectiveness: taking off from the foul line and-dunking free throws, offensive goaltending, and the lobbing of inbounds passes from the baseline over the backboard to someone—guess who—who would summarily dunk them. While waiting out his eligibility for the NBA, Wilt toured with the Globetrotters. Then he embarked on the pro career that left the record books altered forever.

Over the course of the 1963–64 season coach Alex Hannum persuaded Chamberlain, then a San Francisco Warrior, that his fallaway shot was an unconscionable waste of his height (7' 1") and strength and that he should instead play, as Hannum put it, "like Bill Russell at one end of the court and like Wilt Chamberlain at the other." And Wilt did just that, scoring less and setting a record for assists by a center as the Warriors won the division. A year later, Wilt was sent to Philadelphia and the 76ers, where he soon found himself matched again with Hannum, and by 1967 a breathtakingly efficient Sixer team had won an NBA title. Chamberlain outscored Russell 29 to 4 in eliminating Boston, then led the Sixers to a six-game triumph over the very team that had traded him, the Warriors. He averaged 24 points, 24 rebounds and eight assists—as good an all-around season as any center has ever had. Finally, in 1972, playing for a Laker team that would go 69–13 and win 33 in a row and an easy NBA title, Wilt altered his role yet again, concentrating on defense and becoming in a strange way the team's Russell.

His stay in L.A. only reiterated how easily everything seemed to come to him. When he focused on passing, he set an assists record (1968). When he decided he wanted to shoot for percentage, he led the league (nine times). When he hunkered down and played defense, he made the All-Defensive team ('72 and '73). It seemed merely a matter of deciding what he wanted to do and doing it. Alas, he never resolved to master the game's gimme, the foul shot. It was a costly oversight: Seven times Russell's teams beat Chamberlain's in the playoffs, and on four of those occasions the series went seven games. In those four do-or-die affairs the combined Boston margin of victory was nine—and Wilt missed 24 free throws.

"Nobody roots for Goliath," Chamberlain had said, over and over, during the course of his career. Those four Games 7, it could be argued, constituted a nonrefundable deposit, Goliath's unsuccessful bid on a piece of the public's heart.

Bob Cousy

Even by the standards of the era in which he played, Bob Cousy was a little guy, 170 pounds and just a shade over 6' 1". But in its compensatory way nature had blessed him with long arms, large hands, powerful thighs and uncommon peripheral vision. Thus he could turn his size to his advantage, for it allowed him to see things from a perspective no one else had. No one before him had even conceived ways to exploit those alleys and openings, much less tried these daring new passes and dribbles, much less used them in games and to such good effect.

The son of Alsatian immigrants, Cousy spoke French until he was 10, only developing his distinctive New York accent after his family moved to Queens a year later. From his mother, a woman who kept canaries and parakeets, he took a lively spirit; from his father, a cab driver, he inherited a steady sense of control. He has always looked as if he belonged astride a bicycle, pedaling the Tour de France, and his high school coach must have thought that, too, for Cousy didn't make the team at Andrew Jackson High until the middle of his sophomore year. Young Bob had heard the coach was looking for a lefthander, and though righthanded, he had worked on both hands long enough to fool the coach into believing he was a southpaw. By his senior season he had become enough of a scorer to be named All-City.

Cousy was a playmaking substitute for Holy Cross during the Crusaders' 1946–47 NCAA championship season, and then a starting floor leader for three more seasons that were nearly as successful. With no big man, the Crusaders became adept at passing, cutting and running the give-and-go. Cousy was the ringleader. "They claim we sold basketball to New England," he has said, "but we may have also retarded it, by emphasizing the spectacular."

In the face of local pressure to draft Cousy in 1950 with a territorial choice, the Celtics' Red Auerbach, then coach and general manager, was unmoved. "Am I supposed to win," he asked, "or please the local yokels?" Instead he chose a big man, and Cousy wound up with the Chicago Stags. But the Stags collapsed before the season started, and Cousy was parceled out in a dispersal draft. The Celtics got "stuck" with the rookie. "Cousy," said Auerbach, ever stubborn, "will have to make the team."

At first Cousy's new teammates were every bit as bamboozled by the rookie's passes as were his opponents. But by midway through his second season Cousy had met the other Celtics halfway. He was named to the All-NBA team, the first of 10 straight times he would so qualify. In 1952–53, Cousy began a run of eight unbroken seasons leading the league in assists as Auerbach decided to showcase and exploit Cousy's skills in a fast-break system. Soon the Celtics' coach's comments about his young star took a different tone. "The only kick I have with Cousy," Auerbach said, "is that he makes practice sessions hard on a coach. All the other players just want to stand still and watch him." Wrote one sportswriter, "I saw him put salt and pepper on the ball, chew it up, and spit it into the basket."

As if to highlight the perfect balance he struck between winner and entertainer, Cousy left two games—one in the crucible of the playoffs, the other in the theme park of the All-Star Game—by which to appraise him. The playoff game, a victory in 1953 over Syracuse, took four overtimes; Cousy scored 50 points, including 17 of the Celtics' final 21. The All-Star Game came the next year, when he scored 10 of the East's 14 points in overtime. League pooh-bahs had to undo the MVP voting, which based on regulation play had already been won by Jim Pollard.

A decade later, in 1963, he was still dazzling crowds with behind-the-back passes, reverse dribbles and one maneuver all his own, a bit of legerdemain called the behind-the-back transfer that has no latter-day practitioner.

He had an uncanny ability to relax. Give him 10 minutes on a horizontal surface, and he could fall asleep. Yet when he applied himself, the game collectively shivered. Someone once ran into him on an off-day in a deserted high school gym, dashing from foul line to foul line. NBA defenders had learned to play him to pass when he reached the foul line, he explained, and he was working on his pull-up jump shot to better keep them off guard.

"If I were black, I'd be H. Rap Brown," said Cousy, who helped found the players' union in 1954 and has maintained his plainspoken reputation to this day. "No; I'd be dead."

In so many senses he was the game's first radical. Where George Mikan first drew the nation's attention to pro basketball, the Cooz riveted it. Yet Cousy was Everyman—someone who, when plying a city street, could get lost easily in a crowd. A reminder that you, too, could be a basketball star.

Julius Erving

Where baseball is chamber music and football big band, basketball is jazz, instinctual and improvisational. Julius Erving first came to light as a sort of cult musician, playing the out-of-the-way clubs of the old American Basketball Association. The ABA had no TV contract in those days, and so this extraordinary soloist began as a whisper, a rumor coursing its way through the hoops underground. Word had it that he had a style all his own. He had a handle, too. They called him the Doctor.

His contemporaries had flailed a bit at first, trying out as nicknames the Claw and Black Moses and Jewel. Yet when they finally settled on something—Julius had called a guy in the neighborhood the Professor, who had reciprocated with what Erving has been known as forevermore—it was perfect. Dignified, a practitioner, every bit a professional, Dr. J (ABA teammate Fatty Taylor added the initial) was as useful for the ideal he represented as for the player he was. "There have been some better people off the court," said Laker coach Pat Riley. "Like a few mothers and the pope. But there was only one Dr. J the player."

His beginnings hardly prefigured his ultimate hold on the game. Born to relatively comfortable surroundings in Roosevelt, N.Y., on Long Island, Erving snuck off to play college ball at the University of Massachusetts, in the out-of-the-way Yankee Conference. After two statistically impressive seasons there, both largely overlooked, he signed with the Virginia Squires for $500,000. While leaving the press conference announcing the agreement, the team's coach, Al Bianchi, turned to a companion and said, "My god, did you see those meat hooks!"

Physical features—not just the hands, but a long-stemmed build, and a magnificent thatch of Afro hair that ebbed and flowed with the prevailing fashion—helped set him apart. So did a knack for passing, shooting and even rebounding one-handed. But as much as anything, he came to symbolize the old-fashioned human virtues. By the end of his career, in a poll of sportswriters and sportscasters conducted to determine the nicest guy in sports, his name appeared on more ballots than anyone else's.

If Erving didn't actually force the merger of the two leagues, he was surely a spiritual transition figure. The unbridled inventiveness the Doctor represented bespoke the ABA, while the staid NBA happily welcomed the ambassadorial dignity of this Mr. Erving. By the time Magic and Larry and Michael made it into the NBA, the league that muddled through the '70s with money troubles had responded to the Doctor's care. It's curious how, amid all the questions about whether any arriviste ABA franchises were worthy of inclusion in the reconstituted, postmerger NBA, no one posed the most fundamental one: Did the NBA deserve the Doc?

Erving's ABA valedictory, the six-game series in 1976 in which his New York Nets beat the Denver Nuggets for the league's last championship, featured his 226 points, 85 rebounds and 13 blocks. Jordan would score more points in subsequent playoff series; but as spectacular as he can be, Jordan is a herky-jerky contortionist next to the Doctor. Seamless and organic, Erving's game found its inspiration in such forerunners as Elgin Baylor and Connie Hawkins. "He destroys the adage that I've always been taught—that one man can't do it alone," marveled Bobby Jones, the Denver defender assigned to him for that series.

With his move to the NBA, Erving "went public." He was no longer a cult act. Jones would eventually join him in Philadelphia, where together they anchored the frontcourt of Erving's sole NBA title team. Yet for the Doctor there would be two Philadelphia stories. One was written by the collection of misfits and free spirits that blew a two-game lead in the NBA Finals and lost to the Trail Blazers in 1977. From that Erving suffered. "Winning a championship," he said later, "is the only thing that will erase that first year, when we were the guys on the black horses, wearing black hats and bandannas."

Full erasure came six years later, with the Moses Malone–anchored crew that did eventually win it all, losing only one playoff game in three series. It was "We Owe You One," a misbegotten marketing slogan the Sixer management chose after the debacle of '77, finally getting paid up. The Sixers clinched their title in Game 4 against the Lakers in the most appropriate way possible, with Julius throwing in a dagger of an 18-footer late in the game. "I didn't find that shot," he said. "It found me."

One last time, just weeks before retiring in 1987, he reached back. Scoring 38 points in a home game against the Pacers, he seemed to telescope his career. The tomahawk dunks and converted alley-oops and spin moves conjured up the Doctor at his height. The finger rolls and feathery jumpers bespoke the Doc in descent. He came down gently and solidly. The essence of Julius Erving, the thing that placed his game in a different category from the commonplace juke artists and session jammers, always was his grace.

Magic Johnson

He had to win. If he didn't, the rest of his game might have seemed a thin act, cloying and beside the point. The smiles might have seemed insincere; the pumped fists might have looked like blind flailings; the French pastry might have tasted day-old. And then Earvin (Magic) Johnson wouldn't have been allowed to so conspicuously revel in making a blind half-court pass, or a double-pumped scoop layup in traffic, or a last-second bit of conjuring.

His nickname was part of that. He picked it up for his Promethean way with the pass, a skill he developed in the Boys Clubs and schoolyards around his home in Lansing, Mich., as a way of ingratiating himself to those who picked up teams. But his mother, a Seventh-Day Adventist, first heard the nickname and thought it blasphemous. "When you say Magic," Christine Johnson said, "people expect so much." His longtime coach with the Lakers, Pat Riley, added, "Magic is a stage name. It's unreal. That's what magic is—unreal. Nobody can be Magic for the rest of his life. When he was young, it was fun to be Magic, but what happens when he starts slipping? That's when the name can jump up and kick him in the butt."

He never did slip. In 1991 the AIDS virus abruptly yanked him down. He was the man who couldn't say no, who always wanted to oblige, whether the thrill-seeker was a paying customer in a mezzanine seat, or an admirer in a hotel lobby. The shock of his illness was all the more profound because Magic had prevailed so early, so often, as to seem invulnerable. He won a state championship at Lansing's Everett High in his senior year. Two years later, in his sophomore season at Michigan State, he won an NCAA title. A year after that he scored 42 points, grabbed 15 rebounds and added seven assists in the decisive game of the NBA Finals to lead the Lakers to a championship. He was an NBA rookie, and he had won three titles at three levels in four years. Magic he wanted? Magic it would be.

To look at Johnson then, and to look at him on the cusp of the '90s, is to see what seemed to be a charmed career. Yet his basketball life hadn't been entirely seamless even before he tested HIV-positive, even before his career sputtered to an end with the 1992 NBA All-Star Game (in which he won the game's MVP award) and the Barcelona Olympics and an abortive comeback attempt. He suffered and grew. At Michigan State, and in some of his early NBA playoff outings, there were late-game misadventures. He could front-run, sure, skeptics said, but let a game get tight, and Magic's smile would devolve into something pursed and grim, and his play would reflect his expression. A first-round miniseries loss to Houston in 1981 ended with Magic hoisting a point-blank airball in the closing seconds. Tragic Johnson, went the line.

Gradually, wary teammates and hardheaded scribes came around, unable to quarrel with his unsurpassed gifts. "He's the only player," said Julius Erving, "who can take only three shots and still dominate a game." Even Abdul-Jabbar, who was uncomfortable with Magic's exuberance early in his career, would come to acknowledge his debt to the younger man: "All he wants to do is get the ball to somebody else and let them score. If you're a big man, it's hard not to like somebody like that."

Soon people recognized what Johnson occasionally took pains to point out—that there are two of him. "It's like day and night," he said. "At home, away from the game, Earvin is much more laid back and quiet. Magic is just bubbly, energetic, an outgoing person."

The '80s were his decade. He had touched off the college game's prosperity in leading the Spartans to their 1979 title; then he had become the preeminent pro of his generation, winning nomination to the All-NBA first team nine straight times beginning in 1983, and adding three MVP awards at a time the competition—from Larry, Michael and Moses—was stiff. He put away for good carpings about his reliability with a game-winning hook shot in the lane that beat the Celtics in Game 4 of the 1987 Finals. It was perfect: He had developed the shot while goofing around, playing H-O-R-S-E with Abdul-Jabbar, pursuing what he believes to be the essence of the game—having fun.

At first the notion of someone 6' 9", with the skills of someone a half-foot smaller, not just leading the break, but orchestrating it, didn't seem altogether fair. Eventually Magic, who was once the avant-guard, became a prototype, such that the phrase "Magic Johnson–type"—it means someone with size and a handle—worked its way permanently into the game's lexicon. It was a combination so radical that a new statistic, the triple double, had to be invented to do justice to the breadth of his achievements.

"I don't jump very high, but I jump high enough," Magic had said. "I don't shoot very well, but I shoot well enough."

Enough, already. Enough to win.

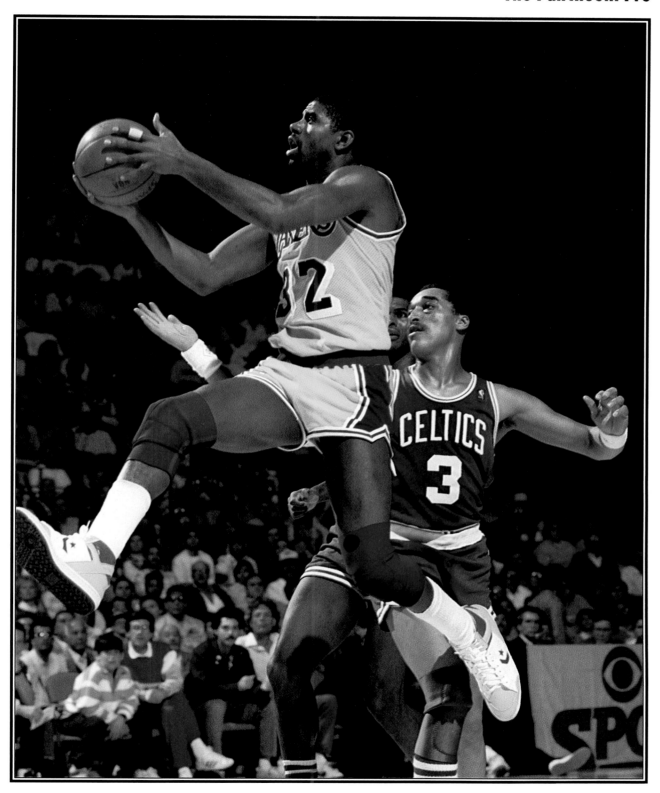

Michael Jordan

"You don't know what he's going to do," said Michael Cooper, the Lakers' stellar defender. "He goes right, left, over you, around and under you. He twists, he turns. And you know he's going to get that shot off. You just don't know when and how."

If there really is an inevitability to Michael Jordan—sooner or later, sometime, somehow, he's gonna get you—it escaped a number of people who pride themselves on detecting such things. Jordan wanted to go to UCLA, but the Bruins showed no interest in him when he came out of Laney High in Wilmington, N.C. And even after he had been the rare freshman starter at North Carolina, and thrown in the cold-blooded 16-footer in the final seconds that gave the Tar Heels the 1982 NCAA title over Georgetown, and led the U.S. Olympic team to the 1984 gold medal, and bagged college Player of the Year awards in his sophomore and junior seasons—even then, Jordan was only the third pick in the 1984 NBA draft.

Like so many Carolina stars before him, he blossomed as a scorer once he was given a chance to play unfettered against the man-to-mans mandated by the NBA. Yet he was so preternaturally competitive that he took as an insult scouting reports that, upon his arrival in the pros, had him pegged as a drive-all-the-time, only-goes-to-his-right, one-dimensional player.

Those reports quickly became so much rubbish. Jordan scored 37 points in his third pro game, 45 in his eighth and 25 or more in 10 of his first 15. In his second season, after missing all but 18 games with a broken foot, he dusted himself off for the Bulls' three-game first-round playoff series with Boston and averaged 43.7 points over that week, including a single-game playoff record of 63. The man his coach at the time, Doug Collins, called "easily the best practice player I've seen in my life" simply couldn't resist the game.

His scoring average of 37.1 for the 1986–87 season is a pro best for non-seven-footers and marked the first of seven straight seasons in which Jordan led the NBA in scoring. As a defender he had no peer in versatility, for he accumulated blocked shots and steals in comparably prodigious numbers. In 1988 he was named the NBA's Defensive Player of the Year, becoming the first scoring champion ever to do so.

"Night after night, year after year, he just carries this team," said the Bulls' John Paxson. "He never avoids it, never shirks it."

On his way to the top he had become the league's only one-man Fortune 500 conglomerate. His agent, David Falk, said, "If you were to create a media athlete and star for the '90s—spectacular talent, midsized, well-spoken, attractive, accessible, old-time values, wholesome, clean, natural, not too goody-two-shoes, with a little bit of deviltry in him—you'd invent Michael." Even after a tell-all book and several episodes with gamblers abruptly humanized Falk's client, Jordan still had a quiver of idiosyncracies, each capable of piercing the heart of the skeptical fan. An unprecedented "love of the game" clause in his contract allowed him to play ball anytime, anywhere, out of season, the opinion of Chicago management notwithstanding. He wore Carolina blue shorts under his NBA game uniform. When his utmost concentration was required he stuck out his tongue innocently, a tick he picked up from watching his father, James, concentrate on work in the backyard. He went back and got his degree at Chapel Hill—in geography, presumably so he could identify landmarks as he overflew them.

"What the fans on the road come to see," he noted early in his career, "is me get 50 and their team win." Yet through Jordan's first six pro seasons, the Bulls at best were playoff also-rans, nothing more. Eventually, when the clamor for him to lead his team to a title grew—when the public began to demand a ring as a condition for continuing to give him its unstinted admiration—Jordan didn't just deliver an NBA championship. He delivered three in a row.

As a college freshman, seeing the Tar Heel upperclassmen cry over their '82 NCAA title, Jordan had been mystified. "This was supposed to happen, right?" he would say in 1991. "You come to college and you win a championship. Now I've seen it from the opposite side. All the struggles, all the people saying, 'He's not going to win,' all those little doubts you have about yourself. And then, when you do it, it's just amazing."

Becoming an NBA champion was the final step in Jordan's ascent to his current position as the greatest in the game and, perhaps, in the history of his sport. His abilities were superhuman—we knew that. But now we knew that he shared an intangible quality with the game's most legendary performers: the ability to make his teammates better, individually and as a group.

His professional obligations fulfilled, there was nothing left for Jordan to do but to amuse himself up there, all alone on a plane of his own. As the Hawks' Dominique Wilkins said, "Can't nobody have done better."

130

George Mikan

George Mikan's uniform number, 99, like the man himself, seemed to push the limits of the game, as if basketball could barely accommodate the whole of him. He was 6' 10" and 245 pounds in an era when such dimensions were singular. Yet, as hard as it may be to believe, Mikan's size gave him no automatic license to dominate, for it came in a package that also included myopia, clumsiness and the sort of genial temperament that has never made for athletic greatness. He worked for his distinction as much as he was born to it. Mikan's legacy was pro basketball's first modern dynasty; the Minneapolis Lakers of the late '40s and early '50s were the game's Yankees, and Mikan its Ruth.

Raised on a farm in Will County, near Joliet, Ill., to parents of Balkan descent, George at first seemed unlikely to distinguish himself for much more than winning the county marbles championship, which he did at age 10. During an 18-month convalescence from a broken leg, he would grow more than six inches, but he would also be cut from his high school team in Joliet because "his feet didn't match."

When he enrolled at DePaul, the Chicago commuter school, in 1942, he did so with the intent of studying law. Only the stubborn naïveté of the Blue Demons' new coach, Ray Meyer, kept Mikan's career alive. Realizing that, as he would later put it, "a big man could score more points by accident than a little one could trying hard," Meyer put Mikan through a regimen of dance, jump rope and shadow boxing to improve his agility. He had him play catch alternately with a medicine ball and a tennis ball. And he drilled him in one-on-one against a 5' 5" teammate. "It was," said Meyer, "like watching a flower bloom." Ultimately Meyer added a peculiar exercise, known forever after as "the Mikan drill," that involved tossing up baby hooks from either side of the basket, with either hand, one after the other.

That's how Big George eventually dominated the game: as if he were still practicing his private little drill and defenses had been added to the mix merely to make the exercise a bit more challenging. Exploiting the six-foot-wide lanes of his era, Mikan set up in the low post, just a two-step post-and-wheel move away from an inevitable field goal. He was too efficient a foul shooter, and too stoic a character, for systematic hacking to pay off; it was a measure of Mikan's influence on the game that he forced defenses to double-team the post for the first time. By his final two seasons at DePaul, Mikan, now fully grown, easily led the nation in scoring, and in 1945 he averaged an astonishing 40 points over three games in leading the Blue Demons to the NIT title.

He signed a five-year, $62,000 deal with the Chicago Gears right out of college. But after one season the Gears' owner led a breakaway group that tried to form a new league with the Gears and Mikan as its cornerstone. Just weeks into its new season the Professional Basketball League of America folded, and in the ensuing dispersal draft, the NBL parceled Mikan out to Minneapolis.

Everyone had his own take on the man they called Scaffold. Bob Hope's was "a control tower that breathes." The Madison Square Garden marquee's was TONITE: GEO. MIKAN VS. KNICKS. "I used to like to pass him the ball, cut around him and then listen to the sound the guy guarding me made when he ran into George," says Swede Carlson, a former teammate of Mikan's. In 1951 the NBA paid Mikan the greatest homage, ordering the lane widened from six to 12 feet.

"George Mikan was the greatest competitor I've seen or been around in any sport," says Bud Grant, the normally taciturn former coach of the NFL's Minnesota Vikings, who was a Laker teammate. "I studied George back before I realized I'd someday make my living studying athletes, and he was amazing. He played hurt. He played when he'd had no sleep because of our travel schedule. And he always played at one speed—top." The Lakers' remarkable run of titles—one each in the NBL and BAA, and four of the NBA's first five—ended abruptly with Mikan's retirement.

He was only 29 when he left the game. That was too early for the competitor within himself, Mikan soon realized, because he launched an ill-advised comeback attempt after sitting out a year. But his influence was seminal. The Associated Press poll that in 1950 named Mikan the greatest basketball player of the first half of the century also picked Jack Dempsey, Jim Thorpe, Jesse Owens, Bill Tilden and Man o' War in their respective sports. When he quit after nine pro seasons, 166 stitches and at least 10 broken bones, there came this encomium, from New York Post columnist Milton Gross: "His presence made it possible for a game whose natural habitat was barrooms, barns and boxlike gyms to break out of its ghetto into the largest arenas in the land and take its place as a big-league professional sport."

Bob Pettit

"He's such a nice boy," said the mother of St. Louis Hawks owner Ben Kerner.

"He doesn't make a lot of noise," said Ed Macauley, another member of the Hawks' family.

"God bless Mommy," said little Susie Share, daughter of the Hawks' Chuck Share, before she went to sleep at night. "God bless Poppy. And God bless Bob Pettit."

Indeed, Bob Pettit was one of the game's greats in spite of a self-effacing manner rarely seen in superstars. His was a beneficent and dignified presence in pro basketball for the 11 seasons he played the game, from 1954 to '65. Yet he never placed lower than fifth in the league in scoring or rebounding in 10 of those seasons, and in eight of them he finished among the top four in the Most Valuable Player voting. Pettit was big, relentless and there—always there.

To be sure, he did elbow his way to a few firsts. He was first in the MVP balloting twice (in '56 and '59), first team All-NBA for each of his initial 10 seasons in the league and the first NBA player to score 20,000 points. And his Hawks in 1958 were the first team to interrupt the merciless reign of Bill Russell's Celtics. (That title, a blip on the Celtic green radar screen of the NBA's growth years, was truly Pettit's, for he scored 50 points in the decisive Game 6 of the championship series, including 19 of the Hawks' final 21.) But it was steady ubiquity that most characterized Pettit's career.

The sons of Louisiana county sheriffs—certainly a son of one named Robert E. Lee Pettit Sr.—don't normally escape the imperative of becoming football players. But after his first football scrimmage, when a ball carrier ran over his defensive position for a 65-yard touchdown, young Bob gave the game up. Having grown from 5' 9" to 6' 7" in just three years, he took his father's advice and devoted himself to playing at the hoop over the garage in the family's backyard. He would shoot, then do his homework, then take his reading lamp out into the dark and position it just so and shoot some more. After mastering the game's more solitary arts, Pettit threw himself into a church league. Emboldened by his success, Pettit, now a junior, tried out for and made the Baton Rouge High team from which he had been cut twice

before. In his senior season he led Baton Rouge to the state championship and was named to the All-State team as a center.

He spent his college years at hometown Louisiana State, and although he dominated his league for three seasons from the center position, it was Pettit's misfortune to come through the Southeastern Conference during the apogee of Kentucky and Adolph Rupp.

Pettit's future in the NBA was at forward, a position he would reinvent with his subtle skills. He wound up there partly because of his leanness and partly because the team that drafted him with a first-round selection in 1954, the Milwaukee Hawks, already had the 6' 11", 245-pound Share in the middle. A weight-training regimen, which ultimately added 30 pounds to his gawky frame, toughened Pettit sufficiently to enable him to win Rookie of the Year.

The rest of his career was played out in St. Louis, where the Hawks moved the next season. He followed his shots with a rare tenacity, making him the acknowledged best offensive rebounder in the league. Twice he played with casts protecting broken bones in his shooting hand. Knee, groin, back and stomach problems plagued but never sidelined him. A porkpie hat that rode squat atop his head and a favorite blue topcoat ("Big Blue" he called it, a nickname that friends began using for Pettit himself) helped make him less self-conscious about his height.

Pettit harbored an abiding belief that he was a role model. "You know," he told one St. Louis writer, "if Stan Musial had the measles, every kid who knows anything about baseball would want to have the measles."

It was with that in mind that he announced his retirement in 1965, at age 32, though he was still averaging 22 points a game and surely could have squeezed out a few more seasons. "My performance would be below my standards, and I don't think the fans would like to see this," he said. "I would never be content to play below my standards."

Kerner, the Hawks' owner, and Pettit had an extraordinary relationship. Kerner promised and regularly came through with bonus money. In return Pettit did everything from helping Kerner sell tickets in Milwaukee to setting new standards for the profession.

"There may have been greater players but none with greater desire or dedication," Kerner said, moments before breaking down in tears at the press conference announcing Pettit's retirement. "He is the pro's pro, the owner's dream."

Oscar Robertson

Oscar Robertson always seemed to have about him a sense of history. He was the great-grandson of a freed slave who, when he died in 1954 at age 116, was believed to have been the oldest living American. When Robertson's Crispus Attucks High School team in Indianapolis won the first of two state tournament titles, the Tigers became the first all-black school to do so. The basketball history the Big O made seems almost ordinary by comparison: 14 NCAA records set at the University of Cincinnati and a pro career in which he became, at 6' 5", the first great all-around player.

Born on a Tennessee farm, Robertson came north to Indianapolis with his family when he was three. At age eight he received his first basketball, a small one he washed with soap and water every night after playing on the earthen courts not far from the Robertson family's tarpaper shack. By age 11, one of the families for which his mother worked as a domestic had given young Oscar his first full-sized ball.

At Cincinnati, where he led the nation in scoring three years in a row, he came to be known as the Big O, partly because a work of James Thurber's, *The Wonderful 'O,'* was then enjoying wide popularity. His game was built on reflexes and quickness, attributes that were just beginning to emerge in a sport that had been marked hitherto by intricate group choreography. "If Oscar were a fighter," said his college coach, George Smith, "he could make a million." His only shortcoming seemed to be that, for all his efficiency and skill, or perhaps because of it, he played basketball with a certain joylessness. He once upbraided a university employee who, while promenading around the campus with him, took the leather ball that Robertson always seemed to carry and casually gave it a dribble on some outdoor concrete. "You'll ruin that ball," the Big O snapped. "You'll rub off the grain and throw it off balance."

In his first appearance in Madison Square Garden, as a Bearcat sophomore, he scored 56 points—a case, if ever there was one, of a performance matching the occasion. It prefigured what he would do as a pro, yet Jimmy Breslin, writing in the *New York Journal-American* in 1959, said with no little condescension: "He will make a fine professional back court man. But he will never be in a class with Elgin Baylor as a super star or what have you. And right here in New York Richie Guerin probably is a better back court man than Robertson will be as a professional."

It didn't take long for Breslin's foolishness to be exposed. When Robertson averaged 30.5 points a game as a rookie with the Cincinnati Royals in 1961, no one had ever scored so frequently from the backcourt. But the Big O did more than score; he also supplanted Cousy as the league's best playmaker and fought much taller men for rebounds night in and night out.

He had been diffident and wary in college, but his new wife, Yvonne, who took a job teaching first grade in Cincinnati, seemed to bring him out of his shell. Her first-graders delighted in calling her "Mrs. Oscar Robertson"; her husband soon became bold enough to lead the fledgling players' union. "My primary purpose," Yvonne Robertson's husband would say of his role as a Royal, "is to get the team moving, establish community out there and make some money."

Robertson would also say, "I didn't get a kick out of college basketball. It didn't excite me. But this game— the pro game—is plenty exciting." In 1961–62 he *averaged* a triple double: 31 points, 12 rebounds and 11 assists per game. He played in 12 All-Star Games and lost only one. But over and over again the Royals, like most of the rest of the league, proved to be mere foils for the Celtics. He was 31 in the summer of 1970 when Cincinnati traded him to Milwaukee. The Bucks' Jon McGlocklin, who was wearing Oscar's No. 14 at the time, offered to give it up. Oscar declined, choosing instead No. 1. "The only thing that matters in this game is being No. 1," he explained, "and we're aiming straight at it."

There had been no center to speak of in Cincinnati through all those 10 years; now, suddenly, he found himself with the prodigy from UCLA, Lew Alcindor. Injuries nagged at him over the length of that season. He was heavier. The points didn't come with quite the same ease. But he could still see the floor with clairvoyance, and in the Finals against the Bullets he controlled the backcourt colt, Earl Monroe. Oscar and Lew and a few spare parts proved to be enough. "Oscar respects people who can perform," said Alcindor. "Sometimes I think that's all Oscar respects."

With a ring at long last, the Big O earned a final measure of respect and yet another tie with history.

Bill Russell

If there had not been a Bill Russell, some coach would have tried to invent him for his instructive value. What a lesson: Here was a player who could dominate a game without scoring. By the time his 13-year career with the Boston Celtics ended, Russell had won 11 NBA titles, and no player had so come to symbolize the exaltation of the team over the individual. Say what you will about Red Auerbach, but the Celtics' longtime coach and major domo never coached a championship team without Russell on the roster. "Bill put a whole new sound in pro basketball," Auerbach said. "The sound of his footsteps."

Born in Louisiana, Russell and his family moved to Oakland when he was nine. He was a late bloomer at that city's McClymonds High School, and as a jayvee player he had been so unremarkable that he dressed only for every other game. Even as a senior, though he had grown to stand 6' 5", he was feckless on offense and really only distinguished himself as a defender and rebounder. His one scholarship offer came from the University of San Francisco, which under coach Phil Woolpert played a smart, controlled game. To this team, as it would to the Celtics several years hence, Russell's presence proved catalytic. Over his last two seasons at USF, the Dons won 55 games in a row and two NCAA titles.

In 1956, when Boston owner Walter Brown sent "Easy" Ed Macauley and the rights to Cliff Hagan to St. Louis for the Hawks' No. 1 draft choice, the Celtics had a reputation around the league for being a bunch of no-defense gunners stuck in a hockey-mad town. Boston had led the NBA in scoring over the five previous seasons but had won only one playoff series. In Russell, Auerbach believed, he had drafted an emphatic counterexample.

In his first meeting with Wilt Chamberlain, in Boston Garden in 1959, Russell grabbed 35 rebounds. By the early '60s, defense had become sanctified as the team's very soul. Russell himself most enjoyed the 1963–64 Celts, a good offensive team that was great defensively. They beat Wilt's San Francisco Warriors in five games for the title, a victory that would go down as yet another chapter in the Russell-Chamberlain rivalry. At 6' 9" and 220 pounds, Russell never could match Chamberlain's statistical accomplishments, but he has long been thought the greater of the two because of the Celtics' reign.

Russell was the first player to integrate what he called "the psych" into the game. He was briefly a high jumper at USF, a world-class one at that, and said, "There wasn't a guy I jumped against I couldn't beat if I had the chance to talk to him beforehand." Even his shot-blocking skills he used judiciously and with foresight. He would go up to an opponent and say, "Three tonight. Guess which three." Elvin Hayes called him the Ghost, because, Hayes explained, "you wouldn't see him anywhere, and he'd come out of nowhere to block your shot." He once told Bill Bridges to bring salt and pepper to a game, for he was going to make him eat basketballs. "Sure Red Auerbach makes mistakes, the entire Boston team makes mistakes," said Cincinnati Royals general manager Pepper Wilson. "But they can get away with it because they have the world's largest eraser in Bill Russell."

Russell blocked shots hitherto thought impossible to block: Bob Pettit's twisting jumpers, Neil Johnston's hooks, even Chamberlain's fallaways. Basketball, he had decided, was a game of habits, and as a defender his goal was to induce an offensive player, of his own volition, to deviate from those habits. "If he is thinking instead of doing," Russell said, "he is yours."

As a personality Russell was iconoclastic and prickly. He came at the world differently: lefthanded, black, with a beard. His brow seemed to come prefurrowed, as if he worried unduly about things. For a long time he had to vomit before he could play—to Celtic teammates, it became a reassuring sound—and take sleeping pills before he could sleep. He concerned himself, too, with the world roiling around him, and thus it was wholly appropriate that, in the watershed year of 1968, Russell not only anchored the middle of the Boston lineup, but—as the first black coach of a major league team in the modern era—led the Celtics to a championship.

"I'm moody and demanding, and in some ways inconsiderate," he once said. Yet for an angry young man he had a disarmingly light touch, and a laugh that the *Saturday Evening Post* once said sounded in pitch and tone like "thunder . . . played on an English horn instead of a kettle drum."

Russell recognized sooner than most great players when the fire within him had begun to flicker. Late in his career he noted, "Now I just throw up for the playoffs." He bowed out soon thereafter.

How, someone asked the retired Russell, might he have done against Kareem Abdul-Jabbar?

"Young man," he replied, "you have the question backward."

Jerry West

By all accounts, including his own, Jerry West's 14 seasons as an NBA player were gloriously happy ones, notwithstanding the nerves that addled him before and after games, and the disappointment with which most of those seasons ended. West couldn't have envisioned a more wondrous way to spend one's young adulthood than to travel the land with a brotherhood of ballplayers, always wearing the colors of the Los Angeles Lakers, and play the game he had learned in its humblest form.

"I think I became a basketball player because it is a game a boy can play by himself," he writes at the beginning of his autobiography. Indeed, on winter nights he would shoot baskets on the dirt court outside the family home in Chelyan, W. Va., until his fingers cracked and bled. (Contrary to legend, his father was not a miner, but an electrician, and a reasonably prosperous one at that; and the West home wasn't in Cabin Creek, although their mail went there.) On March 24, East Bank Consolidated High School still sometimes changes its name to West Bank Consolidated to commemorate the day in 1956 that West led the school to the state title. West Virginia coach Fred Schaus courted him literally on the porch swing out front of the Wests' home, so charming Cecile West that she decreed her son would go to Morgantown.

The Mountaineers lost the 1959 NCAA championship game to the California team of Pete Newell, the coach who had to talk West out of quitting the 1960 Olympic team after one bad practice. For someone who would be known as Mr. Clutch, West seemed only moderately confident early in his career; he was actually surprised at being drafted in the first round. "I didn't think I was good enough to play in the NBA," he has said.

Oh, how wrong he was. He had form so classic that the NBA's logo for the past quarter century has been a silhouette of West dribbling straight at you with his opposite hand. Yet he always seemed to be on the emotional edge, as if in imminent peril of being exposed. He became nauseous before games, and his face broke out in freshets of sweat; after games he would often lay awake until 3 or 4 a.m., trying to come down from the ompetitive high if he had won or trying to sort out the night's glitches if he had lost. He got off his jump shot in

a trice, as if a forbidding hand was forever poised to come sweeping out of nowhere and swat it away if he didn't.

He was notoriously superstitious, driving the same, idiosyncratic route to the Forum via a maze of side streets for every home game. His perfectionism was such that he once stormed off the course during a celebrity golf tournament, enraged at his poor performance. His fussy standards were his only weakness, according to Schaus, who took the job as the Lakers' coach only after being assured that the team would draft West.

Like Oscar Robertson, with whom he was compulsively compared throughout his career, West won only one championship—late in his career and only after being joined by a dominant center, this one named Chamberlain. There is no challenging his mantle as Mr. Clutch, of course; but it is worth noting that, if he had scored 10 more points in five particular games, West would have won four more NBA championships and an NCAA title. (At least one of those near misses surely shouldn't be counted against him: West's 60-foot heave in Game 3 of the 1970 NBA Finals merely forced an overtime with the Knicks, rather than beating them, because the three-point shot was then only an ABA curiosity. In what has been called the most egregious anticlimax of all time, New York came back to win that game and, eventually, the series.)

West may never have been better than during the Lakers' 1969 loss to the Celtics in the Finals, where his play was so remarkable that he was named MVP of the series. And to this day there may be no individual opponent the Bostonians of that dynastic era respect more than Zeke from Cabin Creek. At his own expense, Bill Russell flew to L.A. in 1971 to address the Forum crowd on Jerry West Night. "The greatest honor a man can have is the respect and friendship of his peers," Russell told West in front of the gathered crowd. "You have that more than any man I know. If I could have one wish granted, it would be that you would always be happy."

It was a pulled muscle in that roiling middle of his being, his stomach, that led West to retire in 1974. Russell's wish for him seemed elusive over the next decade as West struggled with real life after basketball fantasy. But in 1982 he became general manager of the only professional team with which he has ever been associated, and soon became pro basketball's preeminent executive, guiding the Lakers to seven appearances in the NBA Finals, three of which ended in championships. Still obsessive-compulsive, still atop the game, Mr. Clutch now had a clutch of rings for one hand and was working on a few more for the other.

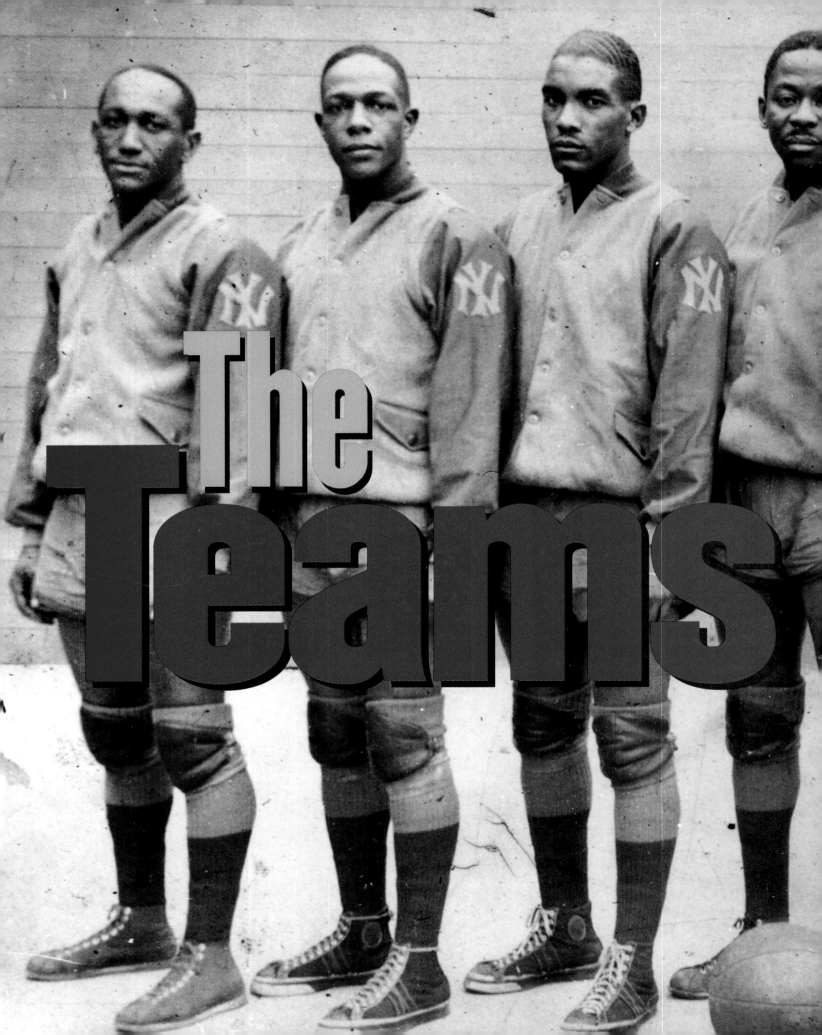

The Teams

Some more celebrated than others, these are the college and pro teams that made basketball history

The St. John's Wonder Five

Sixty years after they made their mark, no single name stands out from among the five members of the St. John's team that lost only eight games between 1927 and '31. This is testament both to how well they blended into a unit—and also to how unchronicled college basketball was as it moved from the '20s into the '30s.

Several large and unlikely coincidences created the team that would become known as the Wonder Five.

Each of the starters—Mac Kinsbrunner, Matty Begovich, Allie Schuckman, Max Posnak and Rip Gerson—showed up in Queens as freshmen in the fall of 1927. James (Buck) Freeman, who had just taken over as the St. John's coach, devised a system for testing each of the many candidates who came out for the team. He picked the five best all-around athletes; they turned out to be splendidly suited for basketball.

Kinsbrunner was the showman of the Five, a 5' 8"

Four of the Wonder Five were present for this team photo of the 1929-30 squad (front row, left to right: Begovich, Schuckman, Kinsbrunner, Posnak and reserve James Collins).

ball handler who in one game against Clair Bee's Rider College dribbled out most of the final 11 minutes. Schuckman, also 5'8" and a deft dribbler, was a sure and quick shot, too. Posnak, 6', was the team's best passer, and the 6'5" Begovich was peerless at center; he perfected the useful art of directing the ball to a teammate off the tap at a time when a center jump followed every basket. Gerson, 5'11", was the flintiest defender, always matched up against the opponent's leading scorer.

Gerson best personified the team's essence, for St. John's devoted most of each practice to defense, particularly a scientific switching scheme not unlike that of the professional Celtics. Even as Rhode Island was shattering the point-a-minute barrier by averaging 40 points per game for the 1930–31 season, the Johnnies held fast. In four seasons only one team broke 40 against them in a game, and that was the semipro Crescent Athletic Club, which did it while the Wondrous Ones were still freshmen.

Freeman was a persnickety man who sweated such details as how the team's oranges were sliced. He had a penchant for borrowing from other coaches, then adapting and refining those precepts into his own coherent philosophy. He believed that if his five players ate, studied and socialized together, they would develop a chemistry that might help them perform better on the floor. He believed, too, in scouting and set up a network of informants who helped him vet future opponents. And he believed in ball control, well before Henry Iba came along and turned the precepts of deliberate basketball into a religion. Much of the difficulty St. John's opponents had in scoring resulted from Freeman's credo: "Keep the ball away from them; the longer the better."

By the time the Wonder Five had entered their junior year, a New York newspaperman, as slack-jawed as the rest of the city, had given them their nickname. St. John's lost only once during that 1929–30 season, to Providence 31–21. Stung, Freeman told his team, "Let's not lose any more." They didn't—not that year, or for 13 games of the next season either, to give them 27 consecutive wins. After NYU knocked them off midway through their senior season, the Redmen won their last eight games to finish up the season at 21–1. Overall they went 86–8, with six of the losses coming when the team was still a collection of underclassmen. Only the far more celebrated dynasties at Kentucky and UCLA would string together so impressive a record over four years.

After graduation the Wonder Five decided to stick together, barnstorming as a unit for a couple of years before joining the American Basketball League, where they competed for five seasons as the Brooklyn (later New York) Jewels. They had switched boroughs, but their appeal was still the same. Sometimes the Jewels would play on an 80-foot-long stage at the Paramount Theatre in downtown Brooklyn, functioning as a sort of live trailer to the first-run feature film to come later that evening, and attendance would triple over a normal movie night.

But their professional career was a trifling epilogue to what they had accomplished as college kids. By lording over basketball in the Northeast for four seasons, the Wonder Five set the stage for the college game's growth through the '30s, when a sportswriter-turned-promoter named Ned Irish would start up his doubleheaders at Madison Square Garden, and the National Invitation Tournament and NCAA tournament would be established to determine who was the best college team in the land.

There had been lively arguments on that topic before the Wonder Five came along, and there would be similar debates after they moved on to the pros. But for those first couple of years of the Depression, when Freeman's boys were at their height, there were no arguments at all.

The Kentucky Wildcats

John Crigler of the Fiddlin' Five drove past Elgin Baylor in the 1958 NCAA title game; Rupp (opposite), though slightly mellower in his later years, remained a curmudgeon.

The fortunes of Adolph Rupp's Kentucky teams of the '40s and '50s seemed to describe the undulations of the bluegrass country they called home: They came to grace, then fell from it, then earned back a measure of grace once more. Throughout, they were loved unconditionally by a state where capacity crowds flock to open practices and where there's still a hoop outside the governor's mansion.

In the down-home argot of the people who worshipped them, the championship Wildcats came with nicknames, in two editions. The first and most talented agglomeration was the Fabulous Five, winners of NCAA titles in 1948 and, with adjustments in personnel, in '49 and '51, though by then the bloodlines to the original group had thinned out. The second, the Fiddlin' Five, won another crown in 1958, despite an intervening scandal that forced the shutdown of the program for an entire season. All four teams were forged in the crucible of Rupp's practices, humorless and largely silent affairs marked by two predominant sounds—the squeak of sneakers and the sharp voice of the cantankerous coach. Each workout would begin the same way, with the team running through their 10 basic sets, and a player permitting the ball to touch the floor at his peril. "If they want to talk," Rupp liked to say, "we've got a student union for visiting purposes."

The beginnings of the Fabulous Five can be traced to 1946, when Kentucky beat Rhode Island for the NIT title behind a tiny blur of a guard named Ralph Beard. But it wasn't until the fall of 1947 that the parade of talent started coming through Lexington's Memorial Coliseum. It began with 6' 7" Alex Groza, a prodigious scorer and rebounder who had spent time in the service. Two more World War II vets, 6' guard Kenny Rollins and 6' 2" forward Cliff Barker, also won starting spots. And the ebullient Wallace (Wah Wah) Jones, an All-Southeastern Conference pass receiver, rounded out the lineup. With Beard only 19 years old, and Barker already 26, it was a mix curious enough to challenge even as experienced an alchemist as Rupp. A typical Kentucky basket would begin with Groza ripping a rebound off the glass and finding Jones upcourt. Jones would in turn hit Rollins just past midcourt. By now Beard, the quickest Wildcat of all, might be angling in for a

layup; Rollins was sure to find him. "Cruel and cold-blooded," Rupp would call the team that gave him his first NCAA title by beating Baylor in the finals that spring.

Dale Barnstable stepped in for Rollins the next fall, and in 1949 the Cats won again, beating Bob Kurland and Oklahoma A&M 46–36. Henry Iba's teams normally made it their business to frustrate opposing offenses, but this time the Aggies were the ones being held to two baskets in the second half. In 1951 Rupp made his recombinant formula work yet again. Cliff Hagan and Frank Ramsey had arrived from the in-state towns of Owensboro and Madisonville, respectively, and 7' Bill Spivey led the Wildcats to a 68–58 victory over Kansas State, scoring 22 points and grabbing 21 rebounds to assure title No. 3 for the Baron.

Soon enough, however, the accomplishments of the Fabulous Five and even Rupp himself would be besmirched by college basketball's unraveling scandals. In 1952, Beard, Groza and Barnstable admitted taking money from gamblers who wanted them to control the point spread in several games, including the Wildcats' inexplicable loss to Loyola of Chicago in the 1949 NIT. The NCAA forced Kentucky to call off its 1952–53 season, and the Cats passed up the 1954 tournament when three of their senior stars were declared ineligible for postseason play. Rupp was defiant. He wouldn't leave the game, he vowed, "until the man who said Kentucky can't play in the NCAA hands me the national championship trophy."

Rupp's revenge would come four years later, when his Fiddlin' Five—Vernon Hatton, John Crigler, John Cox, Ed Beck and Adrian Smith—came together. Even Rupp didn't expect the "barnyard fiddlers" to prosper as they did in the face of a "Carnegie Hall schedule." They lacked size and speed, and lost six games, more than any champion to that time. But the NCAA had booked the regionals and the Finals into Lexington and Louisville, respectively, and several upsets helped open up the draw. Kentucky's balance undid Seattle and Elgin Baylor in the finals, and the man who said Kentucky couldn't play in the NCAA did indeed hand the Baron another championship trophy.

The **USF** Dons

Defensive specialist Russell showed his offensive touch on this move to the basket against UCLA in the 1956 NCAA tourney; a celebration was in order (opposite) after the Dons' first title in '55.

148

The Dons of the University of San Francisco gave no indication in the fall of 1954 that theirs would turn out to be perhaps the greatest college team of all time. In four previous seasons, under the guidance of a former high school coach named Phil Woolpert, the teams representing this humble Jesuit school had gone a nondescript 44–48. This edition of the Dons had a young center named Bill Russell, a spindly-legged kid who had shown some promise during the 1953–54 season, and a combative guard named K.C. Jones, who had been impressive before coming down with appendicitis. But no other major college had offered either a scholarship, and no one thought to include USF in its preseason Top 10.

Besides, this was a team with no gym in which to practice. The players gathered hastily around one o'clock each afternoon at St. Ignatius High School, where Woolpert had coached a few seasons before; some couldn't get out of classes until two, and all had to vacate the gym by three so the schoolboys could take the floor.

Woolpert, a gaunt and nervous man, refused to see this as a handicap. As a result of the arrangement, he said, "the boys are always eager for more work." Three games into the season the Dons learned a lesson so well that they wouldn't lose again for two years. They lost to UCLA 47–40, as Bruins center Willie Naulls outplayed Russell.

Russell wept in the locker room afterward. "It's my fault," he said.

"It's not your fault," Woolpert told him. "It's everybody's fault."

A week later USF beat UCLA in the rematch. By January the Dons had cracked the Top 10; by February they had slipped past Kentucky into the No. 1 spot. In the starting lineup two 6' 3" senior forwards, Jerry Mullen and Stan Buchanan, joined 5' 10" defensive specialist Hal Perry, a junior walk-on and the only Don who didn't come from the Bay Area. (At a time when *Brown* v. *Board of Education* was still causing a stir, half the roster was black, and Woolpert occasionally played an unheard of five blacks at a time.)

The most outstanding defender, of course, was Jones. Indeed, before the NCAA title game against LaSalle,

Woolpert decided to assign the 6' 1" Jones to guard Tom Gola, the 6' 7" Explorers star and college player of the year. Jones limited Gola to 16 points, while Russell, free to roam the middle, blocked 11 shots.

The following season was one long victory tour. The 1955–56 Dons weren't merely the first team to go undefeated since the NCAA was formed; they won by an average of 20 points, held opponents to fewer than 53 a game and suffered one of their closest calls, a 33–24 victory, when a desperate California team decided to hold the ball. The season's only suspense centered around whether the Dons could negotiate the tournament without Jones, who had to sit out the NCAAs because of an eligibility ruling related to the partial season he played at the time of his appendectomy. Here USF flaunted its depth: Gene Brown, a 6' 3" reserve with a fine touch, scored consistently in double figures throughout the tournament. Despite falling behind 15–4 at the outset of the title game against Iowa, the Dons won once again 83–71.

The USF streak would run for 60 games over exactly two years, from Dec. 17, 1954, until the same date in 1956. The first 55 victories came while Russell patrolled the middle. Even Woolpert couldn't deny the impact of what his players had learned during those stolen moments in the St. Ignatius High gym. "This team is the finest I've ever seen," he said. "I can say that in all honesty now. It has done everything asked of it."

Two profound basketball influences had now sprung up by the Bay: the Luisetti one-hander and, 20 years later, the Russell swat. Woolpert had fought Russell—fought his pride and stubbornness, often kicking him out of practice, once even threatening him with suspension if he didn't perform better in class. Yet Russell shook off his doubts and insecurities and fulfilled his promise, going on to become perhaps the most dominant player in history. Woolpert, by contrast, became a prisoner of the promises that success always seem to make. Burned out, he left San Francisco in 1959 and coached briefly in the American Basketball League, before moving to a little town on Washington's Olympic peninsula. There he took a job driving a school bus.

The **UCLA** Bruins

In the 1968 NCAA semifinals, Alcindor led the Bruins to a 101–69 rout of Houston and Elvin Hayes (44) to avenge UCLA's only loss that season; Wooden (opposite) savored the '75 title—his last—the most.

Study old film of UCLA's NCAA championships and the same thing strikes you over and over again. There is joy when the final seconds tick down and another title is assured, but there is no delirium. This is not because the Bruins have become jaded from winning, from accumulating the titles that would eventually total 10 over 12 seasons and seven in a row. Rather, they are acting out one of the many precepts coach John Wooden drummed into them—that for every peak there is a valley. Keep your cool at the peaks, and the valleys will be more tolerable.

Between 1964 and '75, with only two exceptions, UCLA lived in the game's mountain aeries. From the first NCAA title, won by an undersized outfit that astonished college basketball by going 30–0, until the last championship, the one Wooden savored the most because no one expected it, the Bruins scaled those summits with simplicity. Hold the ball in triple-threat position. Know your range and launch your shots from within it. Don't pass to the man, pass to the spot on the body. When a shot goes up, don't merely "block out," but charge the ball.

It has been said that, to succeed, a team must have piano movers in addition to piano players. The system that Wooden devised worked so well that even the names of the piano movers appeared on the nightclub marquee in Westwood. No other college program has made such celebrities out of players who were largely practitioners of a single skill. Keith Erickson, the bounding athlete, played goalie at the back of the 2-2-1 zone press. Lynn Shackelford was the master of a very specific kind of shot, the corner jumper. Swen Nater spent four years as the best practice center in history and went on to a prosperous pro career. Greg Lee, if he did nothing else, lofted lob passes to Bill Walton.

There were stars, too, players like Walt Hazzard, Lew Alcindor, Sidney Wicks and Walton, with megawatt talents; and there were slightly lesser lights like Gail Goodrich, Lucius Allen, Keith Wilkes and Curtis Rowe. But every Bruin, no matter how gifted or contrary, accepted without question the same building blocks in Wooden's Pyramid of Success.

To win championships more or less annually, from the presidency of Lyndon Johnson through that of Gerald Ford, a coach must adapt. Wooden did. He won with little guys, the blue-collar workers in the "Glue Factory," the 2-2-1 press that marked the 1964 and '65 teams. He won with the 7' 2" Alcindor in the middle—which any coach could have done, of course, albeit not necessarily for three consecutive years, from 1967 through '69. He won with points coming from the forwards, Wicks and Rowe, in 1970 and '71. By the time Walton and Richard Washington came through Pauley Pavilion, leading the Bruins to NCAA crowns in 1972, '73 and '75, college basketball had become so inured to UCLA's success that it begged for an explanation when the guys from Westwood didn't win. (In 1966 illness and injury sidelined most of the key starters at one point or another; in 1974 Wooden recognized at midyear an absence of hunger and told the press so.) "Just another UCLA bullfight," said Pan American coach Abe Lemons after watching Walton's 21-for-22 shooting performance humble Memphis State in the '73 final. "In the end the matador sticks it in you and the donkeys come on and drag you out."

In many ways Wooden was a paragon of orthodoxy. "What we do is simple," he once said. "We get in condition, learn fundamentals and play together."

Yet he believed in the educational value of making mistakes; one of the Bruins' most emphatic victories, their 101–69 rout of Houston in the 1968 semifinals, came after an early-season loss to the Cougars. Wooden learned, installing a diamond-and-one defense that utterly frustrated the Cougars' Elvin Hayes in the rematch.

So then: 1964, 30–0 with no player over 6' 5"; '65, the first team to win back-to-back NCAA titles without a dominant big man; '67, 30–0 again, with four sophomores and two juniors; '68, the first team to win back-to-back titles twice; '69, the first team to win three straight; '70, the first team to win four straight; '71, the first team to win five straight; '72, the first team to win six straight; '73, the first team to win seven straight; and '75, the first team to win 10 of 12.

UCLA achieved first after first—so many firsts that, surely, the Bruins will be the last such team.

The **Buffalo** Germans

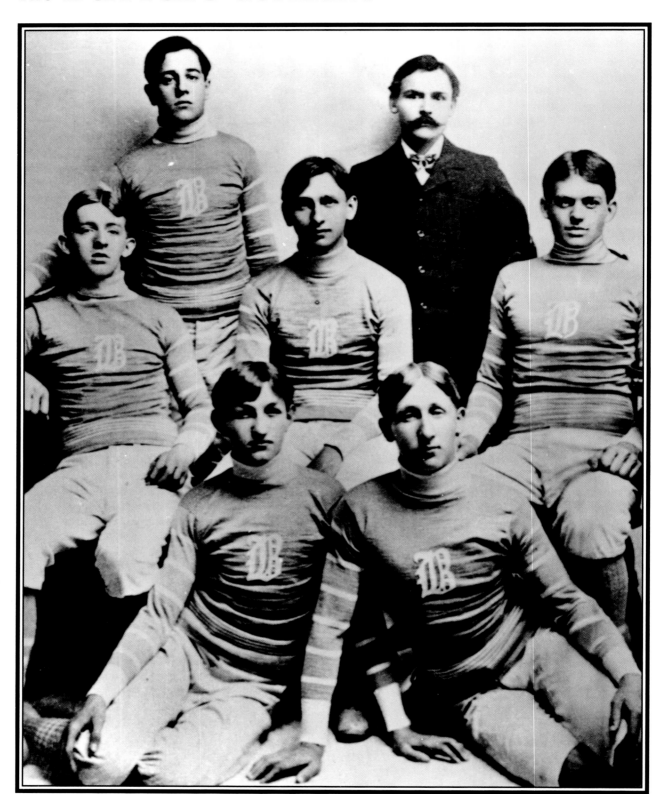

The 1902 Buffalo Germans (back row, left to right: John Maier, Burkhardt; middle: Henry Faust, Heerdt, Eddie Miller; front: George Redlein, William Rohde).

They weren't much older than the game itself, the 14-year-olds who mustered in 1895 at the YMCA on Genesee Street on Buffalo's East Side. The names bespoke the German neighborhood from which they had been culled: Reimann, Heerdt, Rohde, Faust, Haas. Fred Burkhardt, the "Y" physical director and coach of these boys who would become known as the Buffalo Germans, had learned the game from Naismith himself.

In 1901, barely in their 20's, the Germans set a new and enduring standard for the rout, beating Hobart College 134–0. That same year they coasted to the championship of the national AAU tournament, which by coincidence was held in their hometown at the Pan-American Exposition. In the final, three key players, confused about the correct starting time, were late, leaving three other Germans to take on St. Joseph's of Paterson, N.J., three-on-five. Seven minutes in, with Buffalo somehow holding the score to 1–1 despite its disadvantage, the Germans' Eddie Miller pedaled madly up to the grass court on his bicycle. He stripped off his warmup and dashed into the game. Two minutes later captain Al Heerdt arrived and played out the rest of the half in street clothes. With a quorum at last, the Germans shut out St. Joe's the rest of the way and won 10–1.

Thus began the legend of basketball's first great team. Three years later it was enhanced at the Olympic Games in St. Louis, where the Germans won the competition in basketball, then a demonstration sport, and accepted their anointment as the finest team in the world. Certainly the city of Buffalo considered them such: Upon their return from the 1904 Games, the victors were paraded through downtown in a horse-drawn carriage.

By 1905 the Germans had turned professional. Despite many invitations, they declined to join any particular league, choosing to barnstorm instead. Their record—over 29 seasons, nine of them as amateurs, the Germans would go 792–86—was all the more remarkable because of the frequency with which they hit the road. They might play in a drafty armory with a high ceiling one night and a cramped Masonic temple the next. Basketball in this era was loosely organized, with officials likely to grant the home team the benefits of the doubt as to rule interpretations or close calls. In addition, the Germans traveled with only six players; over one stretch, when injuries hit, they lost seven straight games.

Yet these grand Teutons also won prolifically, thanks to a combination of moxie, epoxy and conditioning. (Physically imposing they weren't; they had been together for a dozen years before suiting up their first

player over six feet: Harry Miller, the 6'3" kid brother of charter member Ed.) Over three seasons, beginning in 1908, they won 111 straight games, by an average score of 54–18. Their competition, drawn from the mosaic of incipiently industrialized America, might have been a college team, a YMCA team or a pickup brigade of townies. The Germans would typically play a three-game series, sometimes making as much as $500 per "stand." Once, they beat Jim Thorpe's Carlisle Indians as part of a doubleheader—and then won the other game in the twin bill against another team. Not until 1911 did Buffalo finally lose, in Mohawk, N.Y., to a team representing a National Guard unit based in Herkimer.

The Germans finally succumbed to the more organized game, joining the American Basketball League upon its founding in 1925. They entered a second-generation complement of players who fell well short of the standards set by pioneers like Heerdt and Miller, both of whom played until 1915. Buffalo finished near the bottom of the standings and withdrew before the 1926–27 season. Finally, in 1929, the team disbanded. Incredibly, they had lost just six times at home over 30 years before the ABL misadventure. And those six losses had come by a total of 13 points.

Historians suspect that the Germans weren't as invincible as their record and reputation make it seem. They didn't tour particularly far afield, owing to Buffalo's location away from the population centers of the East and Midwest and to the players' need to stay close to home for their day jobs. Furthermore, during their record winning streak, they didn't play a single team from the three top professional leagues of the era. But on longevity and cohesiveness alone, the Germans merit their place as one of only four teams enshrined in the Hall of Fame. To demonstrate that a team develops a sort of ineffable magic when it comes together at age 14 and stays together for decades, the original Germans gathered in 1931 for a reunion game. On that day, some 36 years after its inception, that team of 51-year-olds beat a much younger Tonawanda side by a point.

In 1944, the story goes, Nat Holman brought his CCNY team to Buffalo to play Canisius College. The City kids won, and Holman invited Heerdt into his locker room afterward. "I want you to meet the greatest basketball player of all time," he told his players. "Al Heerdt of the Buffalo Germans."

Heerdt corrected him. "No," he said. "Not Al Heerdt, the greatest basketball player. Al Heerdt of the Buffalo Germans, the greatest basketball team."

153

The Original Celtics

What a heady feeling it must have been to be an Original Celtic during the '20s—to ply the rails and highways of America with no coach to speak of, responsible only to your teammates, getting paid handsomely to come up with new, crowd-pleasing ways to interpret this immature game. Five out of every six times they took the floor the Original Celtics came away victorious, though rarely by scoring much, for they so loved to pass that they seemed to shoot only reluctantly. With their innovation and guile, they stand to basketball as the old Baltimore Orioles of

Hughie Jennings and John McGraw—who popularized the hit-and-run and the drag bunt—do to baseball.

The game's historians credit the Celtics with inventing or popularizing the give-and-go and post play on offense and the rudiments of the zone defense. Their young center, 6' 5" Joe Lapchick, became so adept at winning the tap that the Celtics ran set plays off the center jump. There was an élan to this team, too. Nat Holman, a master passer and feinter who could dribble out the clock with ease, is believed to be the first player

to practice histrionics in order to draw a foul. George (Horse) Haggerty, 6' 4" and 225 pounds, was the game's first "enforcer," a man as willing to use body language on an official as on an opponent. For strategic guidance, the Celtics looked to rugged Johnny Beckman, their coach on the floor, whose intuitive feel for the game was legendary. Beat the Celtics twice in a row, and they would literally give you the shirts off their backs—which weren't exactly coveted, inasmuch as the distinctive Shamrock jerseys would go unwashed for days because of the team's full schedule.

Original Celtics is a misnomer, for the team was in fact derivative, beginning in 1914 as the New York Celtics, drawn from a 12-square-block area on Manhattan's West Side. The club was dissolved with the outbreak of World War I, only to reorganize, at the urging of a promoter named Jim Furey, after the Armistice. The New York Celtics' founder refused to give Furey permission to use the team's full name, so Original they became.

Part hustler, part visionary, Furey secured for his team the 71st Street Armory as a home court and, for the 1921–22 season, signed his players to the first exclusive contracts in the game's history. Heretofore professionals had little allegiance to any particular team, getting paid by the game and moving like mercenaries to wherever an owner's word seemed reliable. By guaranteeing substantial money over a full season, Furey gave his players an incentive to stay. The longer they stayed, the more they jelled. As they jelled, their reputation spread.

And as the Celtics' reputation spread, more and more people flocked to watch the pinball passes and labyrinthine screens that were leaving crowds amazed. Furey's salaries of up to $10,000 a season were a sound investment.

One night in Chattanooga in 1926 they happened upon the pivot play. A big lug on the home team had set up on defense at the top of the foul lane. This inconvenienced the Celtics, whose intricate patterns often traversed the middle. Dutch Dehnert decided to take up a position with his back to the basket, right in front of this "standing guard," and urged his teammates to feed him the ball. When they did, Dehnert sent it back to them instantaneously. The fans screamed their approval. Soon Dehnert took a pass from the right, another Celtic bolted for the basket from the left, and Dehnert found him for a layup. Frustrated, the Chattanoogan tried to "front" Dehnert—at which point Dutch wheeled past him for an easy layup. The pivot play was both functional and riveting to watch. Before long the posters were bidding people to SEE THE ORIGINAL PIVOT PLAY STARRING THE ONE AND ONLY 'DUTCH' DEHNERT!

The Celtics had played briefly in two professional leagues during the early 1920s, but so dominated them that, from '23 through '26, they chose to schedule their more than 100 games a season on a free-lance basis. When the American Basketball League formed in 1925, the Celtics declined to join, preferring instead to cut their own separate deals for exhibitions, which they would typically win with ease, even against the occasional ABL club. The league resented this and the following season barred its members from playing against Furey's team. The Celts had no choice but to join up. They won the ABL title easily in '27 and '28. But with large numbers of fans turning out only to see one team, the cry went up to "break up the Celtics." This the league did, dispersing them among four teams for the 1928–29 season.

After the breakup Holman and Haggerty met each other in an ABL game that might serve as the Celtics' epitaph. With six seconds to play, Holman's team trailed Haggerty's by a point, as Horse held the ball. "Hey, Horse!" Holman yelled to his former teammate. Haggerty instinctively threw Holman a lead pass, and the original Original Celtic dashed to the far basket for the winning points.

Haggerty lost the game that night, but in his error he affirmed something more profound.

The **Harlem Rens**

As black as basketball is today, the sport produced only two Negro teams of national renown through its first half century. One, the Harlem Globetrotters, owned and managed by a white entrepreneur, eventually dissolved into a minstrel show that has since clouded its legacy. The Renaissance Big Five, on the other hand, black-owned and very serious, is enshrined as a unit in the Hall of Fame.

The Rens were named for Harlem's Renaissance Casino, whose second-story ballroom served as their home court. But the Rens rarely played there, becoming barnstormers out of necessity, for no existing pro league would accept a black team into its ranks. Yet the road proved to be hostile too. Fans spat on them, and hotels and restaurants routinely turned them away, forcing them to log many additional miles in search of lodging. They existed this way for more than a quarter century, from the flush beginnings of the Roaring '20s to the advent of the cold war, winning several mythical world championships—and one real one—over that span. By the time they disbanded in 1949, the Rens had gone 2,588–529. In one remarkable 86-day stretch during the 1932–33 season they won 88 straight games.

To make ends meet, the Rens had to play every day and sometimes twice on Saturdays and Sundays. Thus they rarely substituted during a game, preferring to play an iron five and give the other two players the day off. They would set up a base in, say, Chicago, where they could be assured a friendly hotelier, and make day trips into the small towns of the heartland, where some folks were as curious about what black people looked like as they were about the fast, clean game that these men played. Sometimes white coaches from nearby schools would sit in the stands, diagramming the Rens' plays. The team bus turned into a hostelry when the team couldn't find lodging, and a commissary—cold cuts and bread were passed around, and sandwiches improvised—if a restaurant turned them away.

On pro basketball's time line, the Rens pick up roughly where the Buffalo Germans leave off. Bob Douglas, a West Indian émigré who had discovered the game as a teenager in Harlem, founded the team in 1922. It first came to prominence four years later by splitting a six-game series with the Original Celtics. By 1932 the Rens were exclusively a touring team, and between '32 and '36, with the same seven-man nucleus, they won 473 games and lost only 49. Some of those losses were surely attributable to bigoted officiating.

Their hallmarks weren't unlike those of their white counterparts across town, Holman's Celtics: intricate

teamwork, simple passes, defense, speed. Their captain, 5' 7" Clarence (Fat) Jenkins, was a blur of a playmaker, and Bill Yancey, his running mate, played suffocating defense. (Over the summer, they played outfield and shortstop, respectively, in the Negro Leagues.) James (Pappy) Ricks, the team's designated shooter, was so accurate that he would launch into shotmaking exhibitions in the midst of games, occasionally congratulating himself on his exceptional marksmanship by shaking his own hands above his head.

Up front the Rens were huge for their era. Charles (Tarzan) Cooper, 6' 4", was "the best center I ever saw," according to Joe Lapchick of the Celtics. And with the addition in 1932 of 6' 5" Wee Willie Smith, a Clevelander who was unique on the team in that he didn't come from Philadelphia or New York, the Rens became nigh unbeatable.

Eventually the Rens' reputation grew such that every black youngster in the land wanted to play for the team, and Douglas received referrals from a network that expanded with every new city the team visited. Two more stars had joined the Rens by 1939, when they went 112–7 and won their world title, at an 11-team tournament in Chicago. One of the newcomers, Johnny (Boy Wonder) Isaacs, took over at the point from Jenkins, who was now the coach, while William (Pop) Gates played Ricks's shooting role. The tournament, held in Chicago Stadium in front of overflow crowds, was the Rens' one chance to test themselves against the very best white teams. They met the test splendidly.

Because of the economic conditions of the era in which they played, and a well-founded suspicion with which they

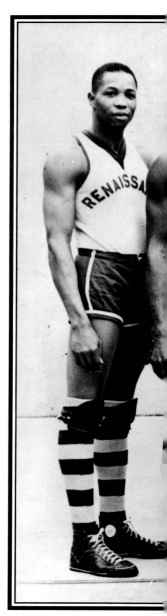

Wee Willie Smith (far left), Charles (Tarzan) Cooper (second from left) and Clarence (Fat) Jenkins (second from right) were the bulwark of the Rens teams in the mid-'30s.

regarded the world, the Rens may have had no more important member than Eric Illidge, Douglas's feisty aide-de-camp. Part traveling secretary, part bursar, part chief scout, he packed a pistol and became expert at counting heads; the gun was to make sure no one shortchanged the visitors, who were usually paid a percentage of the gate. The Rens never took the floor until Illidge had been handed their rightful share.

On those rare occasions when the team played at home, they received nothing but approbation. Their season opener was always at a packed Renaissance Casino ballroom. Jimmie Lunceford's orchestra might be in the bandstand at courtside. Well-to-do Harlemites, regally turned out in tuxedos and evening gowns, paid a pricey $2 a head to gain admission and danced long after the game had ended. For one night a year, in contrast to their hand-to-mouth, often demeaning existence on the road, the Renaissance Big Five foreshadowed the stylish and proud African-American spectacle that professional basketball would become.

The Minneapolis Lakers

On this night in 1949, Mikan and his teammates had two causes for jubilation: Mikan's 48-point performance and the team's 101–74 rout of the Knicks.

158

During the heyday of the Minneapolis Lakers, professional basketball grew in sudden and profound ways. The molded ball replaced the old sewn-and-laced one. The foul lane was widened to its current dimensions. The National Basketball League and Basketball Association of America passed from the scene, and the ambivalence of the opposing crowd toward the gifted big man—shall we root against George Mikan or simply behold his grace?—began to take root. This all happened in the span of seven seasons, from 1947 through '54, during which the Lakers won the last World Tournament in Chicago (1948), an NBL title (1948), the final BAA championship before that league's integration into the NBA (1949) and four of the first five NBA crowns (1950, '52, '53 and '54). Modern pro basketball was being buffeted about chaotically through this period, with leagues forming and reforming like DNA molecules and the Lakers themselves jumping from league to league. But Minneapolis's sustained excellence made them the single constant of the era, a product the game's elders could sell to a skeptical public.

The Lakers featured prototypes of two species that would one day distinguish the NBA: a forerunner of Calvin Murphy and Spud Webb in the diminutive Slater Martin; and the first dominant big man, a forebear of Wilt Chamberlain and Kareem Abdul-Jabbar, in Mikan. Martin, 5' 10", came from Texas, where he had learned an aggressive game that would one night hold Rochester's Bob Davies without a point. Mikan was a foot taller than Martin; he had made his mark as a collegian at DePaul and now sat atop pro basketball's salary structure with a five-figure deal.

But Minneapolis also had Jim Pollard, a 6' 4" jump shooter who had starred at Stanford and with the Lakers' original incarnation, the Detroit Gems. In 1949 the team added 6' 7" Vern Mikkelsen, an erstwhile center whom coach John Kundla converted into an agile and skilled forward. The resulting frontcourt was formidable: If the Lakers' first option, a pass dumped in to Mikan, failed to result in a score, Pollard and Mikkelsen frequently salvaged matters with an offensive rebound. Minneapolis Auditorium featured a court that was smaller than most, and the robust Laker front line—Mikan weighed 245 pounds and Mikkelsen 230—was perfect for such close quarters.

Minneapolis during the postwar era was a friendly, heretofore minor league town, and its citizens embraced their first big league franchise all the more warmly after the Lakers began lording imperiously over the sport. Only two members of the Lakers' 1953 championship team, Mikkelsen and Myer (Whitey) Skoog, were native Minnesotans, but everyone on the team stayed in town during the off-season, as local businesses conducted a civic-spirited bidding war to offer them jobs in the community. (One Laker, an intense and quiet reserve named Bud Grant, would go on to become head coach of a future Twin Cities big league enterprise, the NFL's Minnesota Vikings.)

Maurice Podoloff, the 5' 3" hockey arena operator who cobbled together the NBA out of the NBL and BAA, knew well the importance of bringing Minneapolis into his new league for the 1949–50 season. At home Minneapolis routinely drew crowds of 4,000 to 5,000, more than any other NBA franchise except Syracuse. But Podoloff knew that Mikan would pack arenas on the road, too. Mikan was clean-cut, a law student during the off-season, the epitome of the professional, who in years to come would enhance the NBA's image while point-shaving scandals were sullying the reputation of the college game.

The beginning of the end of the Minneapolis dynasty may be traceable to Nov. 22, 1950, when the Fort Wayne Pistons froze the ball and ended the Lakers' 29-game home winning streak with a 19–18 victory. That game led to the enactment three seasons later of the 24-second rule. Curiously enough, the shot clock, although designed to avert fiascoes like the Fort Wayne freeze, actually would have frustrated Mikan and Minneapolis. The Lakers were a notorious ball-control outfit, renowned for working as much time off the clock as necessary to make sure their big man had set up near the basket. ("Waiting for Mikan," the joke around the league went, as in *Waiting for Godot*.) Mikan quit before he had to play under the new rule, after the Lakers won their final title with a seventh-game defeat of Syracuse in 1954. He was 29, tired of the professional grind and ready to launch his law career.

Minneapolis finished second in its conference for three straight seasons after Mikan's retirement, and the interest of Twin Citians began to waver. Then, in 1958, the Lakers finished in last place, and the fans who had never known professional hoops without success turned indifferent. In 1959 owner Bob Short briefly jump started the fortunes of the franchise by signing a rookie named Elgin Baylor. But a year later Short moved the team to Los Angeles.

It would take the Los Angeles Lakers, as great as they were, a dozen years to win their first NBA championship. It took the Minneapolis Lakers only five years to win four.

159

The Auerbach Celtics

Havlicek drove to the hoop against Chamberlain in the 1968 eastern division finals, a series that ended as most of them did in those days: with Russ and Red (opposite, seven years earlier) celebrating a win.

They were really Bill Russell's Celtics, because Red Auerbach—coach, general manager, president, guiding spirit and medicine man—never won a title until the Bearded One arrived in Boston. But then who brought Russell to Boston? Auerbach did. And in their clannishness and competitiveness, their savvy and intuition, the Celtics who won 11 NBA titles between 1957 and '69, including eight in a row, perfectly reflected the man in charge. He was a man who "dresses British and thinks Yiddish," in the words of one of his players, K.C. Jones. Whose habit of lighting a cigar to signal the salting away of a victory was, according to another Celtic, Bob Cousy, "the single most arrogant act in sports." Who brushed off a request from a network producer for a postgame interview after one of those titles by saying, "Where were you guys in February?"

Suspicious, surpassingly loyal, skeptical—Auerbach was all of these. He enforced the ethic of "team first" so fastidiously that, when Bill Sharman once ate a pregame candy bar without sharing it, Auerbach gave him a good reaming out. "Show me a good loser," he liked to say, quoting Rockne, "and I'll show you a loser." On the few occasions he lost, Auerbach proved himself to be no hypocrite. He was a stinking lousy loser. But he coached so many players to so much success that a rookie in Boston today

doesn't have much choice in uniform numbers: 1, 2, 6, 10, 14, 15, 16, 17, 18 (twice), 19, 21, 22, 23, 24, 25—all have been retired.

A good part of Auerbach's genius was his contrarianism. He won with guards who couldn't shoot (Don Chaney, K.C. Jones), forwards who couldn't move (Bailey Howell, Don Nelson) and starters who, rather than starting, finished (Frank Ramsey, John Havlicek). When he realized the abundance of Cousy's gifts, he adapted Boston's theretofore lumbering style to accommodate the little guard he had once disparaged. Then in 1956, recognizing how perfectly a shot-blocking, rebounding center would dovetail with that fast break, he traded for the draft rights to Russell. Just months later Auerbach would get his first license to do what he would be accused of enjoying all too much—rubbing others' noses in his triumphs. Led by Cousy and Sharman and rookies Russell

and Tom Heinsohn, the Celtics won the first of their titles, in a seven-game championship series, over Hagan, Macauley and the Hawks.

The Celtics enjoyed extraordinary stability during their run, despite consignment to second-class status in Boston Garden, the musty building that they have come to personify. (Their landlord, the hockey Bruins, had dibs on the city's sporting heart during the wintertime.) The cast didn't change much over the Celtic era, save for the late-season acquisitions, picked up for a song, that always seemed to push the team into playoff shape. (After getting Howell for Mel Counts in 1966, the Celts didn't make another body-for-body trade during their reign.) Boston had seven set plays, no more, and everyone in the league knew exactly what they looked like. Indeed, they knew them by number. Still, no one could find a way to stop them.

Even as ownership changed—seven different men took their turns looking over Auerbach's shoulder and through his cigar smoke between 1963 and '69—two constants prevailed: Red and Russell. The first articulated the standards, the second exemplified them. Those black shoes? The Celts wore them not for distinction or even the psych factor, but because white shoes got dirty faster, had to be replaced sooner, and therefore didn't make sense. "The Guys," Russell called the team of which he was the selfless soul.

In *The Centaur,* which he wrote at the very time the Celtics enjoyed their hegemony over the league, John Updike describes how a good basketball team should look: "Every shoelace, every hair, every grimace of concentration, seems unnaturally sharp, like the details of stuffed animals in a large lit case. Indeed, there is a psychological pane of glass between the basketball floor and the ramp of seats." Perhaps Updike, the Harvard man, took his inspiration from the hometown team. For his description perfectly fits these Celtics—the epitome of the basketball *team;* but a group, too, whose devotion to itself outstripped that of the puck-crazy Boston public to it. The Celtics of this most turbulent era in American life played for themselves and each other, with breathtaking consistency.

The 1969–70 New York Knicks

Frazier displayed his effortless style against Bob Weiss of the Bulls; Holtzman (opposite) blended his players into a unit whose whole was greater than the sum of its parts.

"See the ball," their coach, Red Holzman, would bark out as his New York Knickerbockers played defense. *"See the ball!"*

Holzman favored two other imperatives: "Move without the ball" and "Hit the open man." Add to them the fevered urgings of the sellout crowds that filled Madison Square Garden—19,500 hardbitten New Yorkers would chant *"Dee-fense! Dee-fense!"* through thick cigar smoke—and the Knicks' success seemed reducible to sloganeering.

In fact, the legend of the 1969–70 Knicks—augmented by the mythmaking powers of the New York media—rested on four very simple precepts: on offense, passing and movement; on defense, effort and awareness. After 11 previous appearances in the NBA playoffs without a championship, the Knickerbockers finally came together with the 1968 trade that brought them the workhorse forward, Dave DeBusschere. As the '60s drew to a close, New York's advertising and journalistic communities, warmed to the selfless and multiracial result, holding it up as an example of what professional basketball could be. Synergy, they called the team's accomplishments—the whole is equal to more than the sum of its parts.

The Knicks were Team Everyman, ordinary people who nonetheless played extraordinary basketball. DeBusschere poured each of his six feet, six inches into every game. The captain, Willis Reed, was a combination of strength and finesse, a good offensive center but not so dominant a force that he had to be the single focus. Walt Frazier, the stylish guard, directed the offense with sangfroid and ran amok through opposing offenses. Dick Barnett, the sinistral shooter with the sloe eyes, had a cocky signature line, "Fall back, baby!" he would utter as he squeezed off his soft jumper. And Bill Bradley, after an interlude as a Rhodes scholar at Oxford, found a system in which his intuition and perpetual motion were welcome.

The reserves, the Minutemen, included Cazzie Russell, the energetic streak shooter; Dave Stallworth, the bounding frontcourtman who had suffered a heart attack but found more inside a damaged ticker than most others could summon from unscarred ones; Nate Bowman and Phil Jackson, the ungainly backup centers; and Mike Riordan, the irrepressible guard with an outer-borough attitude.

Two events bracket that season like bookends, suggesting that the Knicks' run was preordained, payback perhaps for 23 years of futility. One portent came early, in Cincinnati, as New York won its 18th straight game, an NBA record at the time. Trailing by five points with 16 seconds to play, the Knicks conjured up a series of baskets to pull within a point. Then Frazier tossed in two free throws as two seconds remained to put the game away.

The other magical moment came after a 60–22 regular season, in Game 7 of the NBA Finals. Reed had strained his thigh in Game 5, which New York had nevertheless come back to win; in Los Angeles for Game 6, the Lakers had run wild as Reed watched. Back in New York, with the help of cortisone, the captain limped on to the floor just before tip-off. The crowd studied each of his warmup shots, cheering wildly as they swished through.

When Reed hauled himself down the floor on New York's first possession, Frazier found him at the top of the key. The Knicks' center zinged in an outside shot. A minute later, after hauling down a defensive rebound, he ran downcourt, took a return pass, stopped, popped and drained another 20-footer. Reed didn't score again, but the Knicks rode the prevailing emotional frenzy like a wave. Frazier took over, scoring 36 points and passing off for 19 assists, and the Lakers were brought to heel.

The Knicks would win another title after a two-year interregnum, beating Los Angeles even more emphatically in 1973. Earl Monroe, thought to be an incorrigible solo performer, blended in alongside Reed, Frazier, DeBusschere and Bradley, as did another newcomer, Jerry Lucas. Looking back at those two titles, Bradley wrote these words in *Sports Illustrated*: "The sudden rush of awareness that a group has become a meshed team provides each member with a remarkable sense of power. Each game is eagerly anticipated. Road games suddenly become like a paid vacation. You begin to see in your teammates good qualities that before went unnoticed.... Other groups that are further back along the road toward unity look foolish against the confident effort of a well-blended team."

The **1971-72** Los Angeles Lakers

Chamberlain skied high for a rebound against Kareem Abdul-Jabbar in the western conference finals; West (opposite) had his usual picture-perfect shooting form in '72, but he also led the league in assists.

164

It began 10 games into the season, on Nov. 5, 1971, the very day Elgin Baylor announced his retirement and young Jim McMillian stepped into the starting lineup. The Los Angeles Lakers, a curious mixture of new blood and old fogeys, of McMillian and Gail Goodrich on the one hand and Jerry West and Wilt Chamberlain on the other, ripped off 33 consecutive victories. They went more than two months without losing. They won one game in which Chamberlain scored all of three points. When they won their 21st straight, breaking the Milwaukee Bucks' previous mark, they refused to drink the champagne awaiting them in the locker room; No. 33, a 44-point defeat of Atlanta, was close to a perfect game. "The most amazing thing about the streak has been our consistency," said the Lakers' coach, Bill Sharman, at the time. "Only five or six have been close, and real luck only figured in one of them." The Bucks finally ended the run, on Jan. 9 in Milwaukee, but by then the Lakers hadn't merely set an NBA record that will probably never be broken but also established the standard for every other major league sport as well.

The team coalesced at a time when pro basketball was at its most chaotic, with players jumping leagues and franchises switching cities willy-nilly. Los Angeles was a fairly discombobulated club in its own right: The Lakers had reached the Finals in seven of the previous 10 seasons with nothing to show for it, as their heavy-handed owner, Jack Kent Cooke, kept trying out coaches in the hope of finding one who could get along with Chamberlain.

Sharman was the latest to audition, arriving in L.A. in the summer of 1971 from the ABA, where his precise and hyperorganized style had led the Utah Stars to a title. His predecessor, Joe Mullaney, had left substantial turbulence in his wake, actually calling West, 33, and Chamberlain, 35, "over the hill." Yet Sharman remained unperturbed, coaching much as he played, with the attitude of a self-made man. First, he stripped the game down, installing late-morning shootarounds on the days of games and a fast-breaking system. Then he met individually with his two superstars, selling them on his ideas, and prevailing on them to bring their gripes to him, not the press.

Sharman asked West to focus on defense and playmaking, and the great jump shooter led the league in assists. He appointed Chamberlain captain, and asked the Dipper to block shots and rebound; the most prolific scorer in league history went on to clear more boards than anyone in the NBA that season, averaging 18.6 per game. Often Wilt would touch the ball only once on a Laker possession—on the defensive glass—before hurling it downcourt where Goodrich, whom Sharman encouraged to release to the far end, scored often enough to lead the team in that category.

The team's two other starting pieces fit perfectly. McMillian was a catalyst, a 6' 5" defender and spot-up shooter playing in an era when small forwards of that size could prosper. Power forward Happy Hairston played rugged defense and, working alongside Chamberlain, pulled down 1,000 boards of his own.

The '72 Lakers had a long bench, too. Virtually all the substitutes—among them Flynn Robinson, Leroy Ellis, Keith Erickson and a Laker lifer named Pat Riley—were ex-NBA starters picked off the waiver wire or acquired for cash or low draft choices.

It was as if that old Celtic, Sharman, had turned Wilt into Russell, and the rest of the team fell into line, turning themselves into knockoffs of Auerbach's finest and most selfless players. In going 69–13 (81–16 counting playoff games) the Lakers outscored their opponents by an average of more than 12 points a game, which is still a record. All that remained was for the Lakers to win a title, for without one the streak would have been no more than a tantalizing footnote in a history of L.A. futility. Chamberlain sprained his wrist after the Lakers had taken a 3–1 lead over New York in the Finals. But after soaking it the night before in a whirlpool, Wilt picked off 29 rebounds and the MVP award as the Lakers finished the job in Game 5.

Finally at the summit after one of the game's marathon climbs, the Lakers still reflected the even temper of their coach, a man whose most violent act all season was, in West's words, "throwing down a pile of towels." They allowed themselves some champagne—but they drank it out of glasses.

The Bird Celtics

Johnson (3), Bird and Parish gave Boston a powerful presence on the parquet; Bird (opposite) celebrated his first Celtics title in 1981.

It would take a dozen years for Red Auerbach to rebuild another truly great team after the end of the Russell era. But when he finally did, he did it suddenly, on the ruins of the 1978–79 season in which the Celtics went a franchise-worst 29–53 and moved their chief chronicler, Bob Ryan of *The Boston Globe,* to write, "For 20 years the Celtics stood for something. The only thing they stand for now is the anthem."

The nucleus of Larry Bird, Robert Parish and Kevin McHale stood tall as Boston won NBA titles in 1981, '84 and '86. As great as Bird was, he was also virtually 6' 10". When he lined up alongside McHale, also 6' 10", and the 7' Parish, every team had to guard him with a small forward, most of whom Bird mercilessly took to school. He, Parish and McHale all had better-than-average footspeed, but the monument to the Celtics of the '80s should be a vertical one.

Bird was the proton of that nucleus, the prodigy Auerbach had picked a year early, when he was still a junior at Indiana State but nonetheless eligible for the draft. As the Celtics muddled through the 1978–79 season, selling out Boston Garden only once, Bird enjoyed a sceptered senior year, leading the Sycamores into the NCAA finals. "People made such a big deal of us using a first-round draft choice on Bird and having to wait a year before we got anything to show for it," Auerbach would say. "But I've found time goes by quickly."

Auerbach's aura had been dimmed by his lackluster recent drafts, and by his having to fire one of his own, former Celtics forward Tom Heinsohn, as coach in 1978. Acquiring Bird seemed to imbue Red once again with the managerial magic. He looked outside the Celtics family for his new coach, and settled on Bill Fitch, a martinet known for his touch with young teams.

Fitch got through to the 1979–80 Celtics. Bird meshed with veterans like Cedric Maxwell, Dave Cowens and Tiny Archibald, and Boston inverted its won-lost record from the previous season, going a league-best 61–21 before being eliminated in the conference finals. Then Auerbach pulled another heist. In a single transaction, one that a poll of general managers would pick as the most lopsided deal in NBA history, he picked up both Parish

and the draft rights to McHale from Golden State for two lesser picks in the first round that year. Parish took over for Cowens in the middle and flourished; McHale soon proved to be one of the league's ablest sixth men, an efficient scorer and shot blocker. That spring the Celtics beat Houston in six games for the title.

Boston stumbled in the playoffs in the next two seasons, as Fitch's severe manner began to alienate the Bird-Parish-McHale triumverate. In 1983, after losing four straight playoff games to Milwaukee, Auerbach sent a washed-up Rick Robey to Phoenix for the defensive-minded Dennis Johnson and replaced Fitch with the easygoing K.C. Jones, who in turn ceded much of the leadership to Bird. "It's embarrassing," McHale would say, "not to play the way Larry wants you to play." The rest of the Celtics fell into line, and they beat the Lakers in a seven-game series.

Whether the 1986 NBA champions were the best Celtics team ever can be debated. They probably were the most talented one; they won 67 regular-season games and another 15 in the playoffs, had a bench that seemed to go on forever and shot more than 50% as a group. Veterans like Johnson, Danny Ainge, Scott Wedman, Jerry Sichting and Bill Walton produced seasons few thought they had in them. As a group, these Celtics had Auerbach's fingerprints all over them. They played much better than they looked, which was pasty and arthritic; and there was the usual complement of reconditioned veterans, led by Walton, who had phoned Auerbach as a free agent over the summer and begged for a spot on the team.

But the nucleus, the three players who had turned Boston's fortunes around, was still intact. The supreme proton turned in perhaps his finest season, springing for two triple doubles during the Finals, which ended with another six-game dispatching of the Rockets.

If this was going to be the last Boston title for a while, it wasn't a bad one by which to be remembered. "They are the epitome of the way it's supposed to be," said Norm Sonju, G.M. of the Dallas Mavericks, a team that was still hunting for a championship. "I will never, ever be satisfied until we get to be that kind of team."

The Showtime Lakers

Abdul-Jabbar unleashed this majestic sky-hook against the Sixers in the 1982 NBA Finals; in '80, MVP Magic (opposite), just a 20-year-old rookie, posed with the first of his five championship trophies.

The nightclub on Wilshire Boulevard was called the Horn, and Jerry Buss loved to go there to unwind during the early 1960s, after he had begun building the real estate empire that one day enabled him to buy the Los Angeles Lakers. Before the opening act the lights would dim, an emcee would take the stage, and the entertainment would begin to the strains of a song called *It's Showtime*.

In 1979, Buss did buy the Lakers, and in assembling the team that went on to win five titles through the 1980s—and the first back-to-back championships since the Celtics' run more than two decades earlier—he never forgot the Horn. He created a team that matched its milieu perfectly. L.A.'s fast break could have been choreographed by Cecil B. deMille. A cadre of cheerleaders in spandex worked the sidelines. Dancing Barry cut up the aisles. Sundry celebrities filled the courtside seats, happy to be idolizers rather than idols for once.

Two Lakers entranced Jack Nicholson, Dyan Cannon, Tom Selleck and the rest of the Forum regulars: Earvin (Magic) Johnson, the 6' 9", state-of-the-art point guard with the batteries-not-included smile who had joined the team the same year Buss bought it; and 7' 2" Kareem Abdul-Jabbar, whom a 12-year-old Johnson had scored an autograph from eight years earlier in the tunnel at Detroit's Cobo Arena after a Bucks-Pistons game. The two instinctively knew that they needed to share the spotlight, that each was essential to the team's reaching championship form—and that this town would judge them both by how many NBA titles they won and how stylishly they did it.

The Lakers' reign began with a pratfall—coach Jack McKinney's bicycle accident in November 1979—that allowed assistant Paul Westhead to take over and coach the team to the title the following spring. Magic, just a rookie, clinched the 1980 championship while filling in at center, scoring 42 points in Philadelphia as Kareem nursed a bad ankle back in L.A. "The team was just maturing then, winning on talent," Pat Riley, then an assistant, would say. "They hadn't really become a team yet."

The Lakers betrayed their immaturity a year later in losing a first-round miniseries to Houston. The following November, Westhead was fired, essentially at the insistence of Magic, who felt that Westhead wasn't allowing the Lakers free rein to run. (How ironic that charge would seem today in light of Westhead's eventual reputation as the guru of the running offense.) But under Riley's guidance that season, the Lakers began to develop into a multifaceted and even-tempered team. They beat the 76ers in the 1982 Finals, jump starting their break with a thorny half-court trap. Then in 1985, after coming to terms with losses to Philadelphia and Boston in two intervening trips to the Finals, they integrated Byron Scott into their lineup to replace the traded Norm Nixon and won a decisive championship series game in Boston Garden, interring for good the jinx of eight previous playoff failures against the Celtics.

That 1985 team may have been the most dazzling of them all. Abdul-Jabbar, despite playing his 16th season, dominated the Finals such that he won the MVP award, and Magic's touch was evident in two NBA records set by those Lakers: best field goal percentage, team, season (.545), and most assists, team, season (2,575). But in some quarters L.A.'s next two—the back-to-back 1987 and '88 championships—are more impressive, because they came after Riley decided to wean the team off Abdul-Jabbar, then 40, as the primary half-court option. Certainly the last two titles clinched the reputation of Riley as a master at persuading great players to subjugate their egos.

Again and again, Riley found a cause for his players to rally around. In '82 it was the challenge of proving that they were men now, who had learned from their failures as boys. In '85 it was to bury the canard that the Lakers were all glitz and glamour, while their Eastern Conference foes carried the lunch buckets. In '88 it was the proposition that they were mentally tough enough to defend a championship, where the last 17 teams to try had failed. Indeed, in the locker room after the 1987 title, still wet from champagne after beating the Celtics, Riley guaranteed a repeat. And when the Lakers did indeed win in '88, beating Detroit despite the pressure of that prophecy, they assured that they would be remembered as much for their substance as for their style.

The Jordan **Bulls**

Jordan (opposite and shooting at right against Dennis Rodman and the Pistons in 1991) came to appreciate the value of his supporting cast, including Paxson (5), Pippen (under basket) and Cartwright (behind Jordan).

By the dawn of the '90s, Michael Jordan seemed to have everything: fame, wealth, respect and skills so incandescent that few doubted he had become the game's preeminent player. But there remained one thing he lacked and hungered for. He had been a professional for five seasons, but the Chicago Bulls, the troupe with which he toured, had yet to win an NBA championship.

At the beginning of the 1989–90 season the Bulls hired Phil Jackson as their coach. Quirky, taciturn and a dabbler in counterculture, Jackson had been a reserve forward on two New York Knicks teams that won NBA titles with unselfish ball movement. During his first year in charge the Bulls won 55 games, yet for the second straight season they met their appointed demise against Detroit in the Eastern Conference finals. Soon Jackson came to a realization. For four years Jordan had won the NBA scoring crown, in the process accounting for almost a third of the Bulls' points. Yet only once since the introduction of the 24-second clock in 1954, had a league scoring champion led his team to a title. (In 1971, Kareem Abdul-Jabbar did so with the Milwaukee Bucks.) Something had to be done.

Jackson knew the other Bulls chafed under the team's heretofore Michael-centric style. "The Jordanaires," wags called the rest of the team, as if they were some kiddie chorus on a Saturday-morning TV show. So Jackson decided to install a halfcourt offense, the sideline triangle, which Bulls assistant Tex Winter had developed at Kansas State before Jordan was born. Bulls who had hitherto stood around slackjawed during Jordan's nightly levitations would now have specific roles to play. "No, Michael doesn't need the triangle," Jackson said. "The offense limits him, no doubt about it. But we've let Michael clear out and try to win it by himself. And we've come up short."

Jordan resisted the triangle at first. But Jackson, the son of a Pentecostal minister, never stopped preaching the gospel of team play. And so Jordan and Jackson coexisted in delicate balance—the coach with his higher truth of championship basketball, which Jordan so desperately sought; the superstar with his worldly gift, the ability to manufacture baskets when Jackson's offense broke down.

Even as Jackson invested new confidence in them, and they responded, those Bulls whom Jordan called "my supporting cast" still seemed slight somehow. Their center, Bill Cartwright, was known chiefly for a fadeaway jumper. Power forward Horace Grant rebounded and defended with a small forward's frame. When he was a rookie, B.J. Armstrong, who by the team's third championship season had become the starting point guard, was barred admittance from the Bulls' practice facility by a well-meaning secretary who believed him to be underage. Even Scottie Pippen, the wondrous wingman who blossomed into a Dream Teamer in Jordan's shadow, could be rendered useless from time to time by migraine headaches. But with each successive title Jordan came to appreciate more and more the value of each of these parts, all of whom general manager Jerry Krause had brought to Chicago without the benefit of a lottery pick. After the Bulls won their first crown, the Walt Disney Company asked Jordan to film a postgame commercial. He insisted that the other four starters be included.

It's remarkable how the defining moments of Chicago's titles involved actors other than the marquee lead. In 1991, John Paxson knocked down five clutch jumpers in Game 5 to eliminate Los Angeles. In '92, a S.W.A.T. team including Scott Williams, Bobby Hansen, and Stacey King touched off a Game 6 fourth-quarter rally that finished off Portland. In '93 it was Paxson again, bottoming out a three-pointer in Game 6 with seconds to play, and then Grant, blocking a shot moments later, who beat Phoenix.

Were those Bulls a great team, or just a good team with a surpassingly great player? Their accomplishments should render the question moot. Consider that only the Minneapolis Lakers of the early '50s, and the Boston Celtics of the early '60s, had won three rings in a row. Not since the start of the 1990–91 season, when their title run began, did this Chicago team lose so many as three straight games. Never before had so dominant an NBA champion been built around a player in the backcourt.

With his third title only seconds old, that player didn't glory in it. He dashed instead into the crowd, after the game ball. Jordan did indeed now have everything, everything except a token of it all. And of course he wound up getting that, too.

The Highlights

These are the milestones—a chronology of the sport from the peach basket era to the days of dunk, with a few scenic stops in between

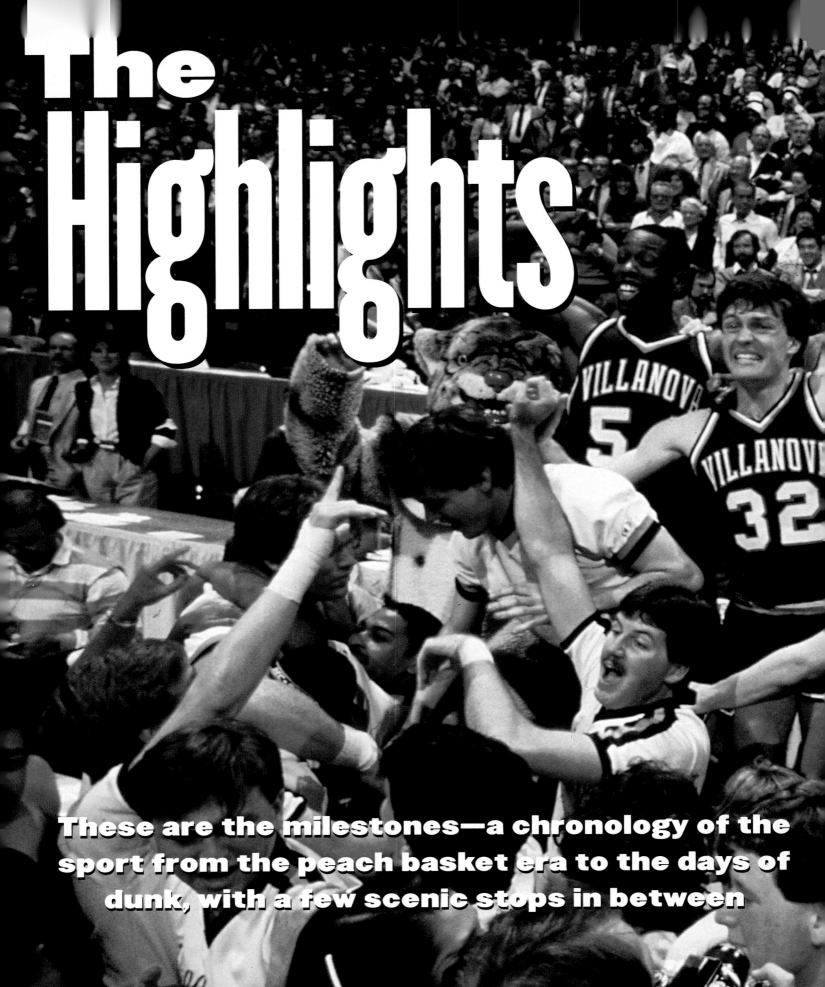

1891

Dr. James Naismith directs a custodian to tack two baskets to the balcony of the gymnasium at the YMCA Training School in Springfield, Mass., and the game of basketball is born. Naismith had asked for two boxes, but only peach baskets could be found. The balcony just happens to be 10 feet off the ground.

1894

A wheel manufacturer in Chicopee Falls, Mass., produces the first basketball, fashioned from four odd-sized panels of tanned cowhide and stuffed with a rubber bladder. The game has heretofore been played with the much smaller soccer ball.

1895

Hamline College of St. Paul, Minn., wins the first college game, defeating the Minnesota State School of Agriculture 9–3. There are nine players on each side. A year later, in the first five-to-a-side college game, the University of Chicago will beat Iowa 15–12.

1896

Teams from Trenton, N.J., and Brooklyn play the first pro game, in Trenton. After being driven from its home court by a YMCA ruling aimed at curbing rowdyism and "un-Christian-like" behavior at basketball games, the Trenton side is forced to rent the local Masonic Temple. The team takes out newspaper ads to promote the game, and attracts enough paying spectators to turn a profit. The Trentonians win 16–1, and

This outdoor game took place in Springfield in 1892, when hoops was truly *basket* ball.

when the gate receipts are split, each player receives $15.

1897

Basketball teams are required to field five players to a side. The original game had engaged nine on each team, and one exhibition, played at Cornell soon after basketball's invention, had 100 players on the floor at the same time.

1898

Six teams from the Delaware River Valley, including the pioneering Trentonians, form the first professional circuit: the National Basketball League. Players earn $2.50 for games at home and $1.25 for games on the road.

1904

The Buffalo Germans win the first national tournament, an exhibition at the Olympics in St. Louis. Culled nine years earlier from an ethnic neighborhood on Buffalo's east side, the Germans will become the game's first dynasty, playing together until 1929 and winning 90.2% of their games.

1917

The Converse Rubber Co. introduces its All-Star basketball shoe. Several years later a former pro named Chuck Taylor will begin driving around the country giving clinics and selling "Connies" out of the trunk of his Cadillac. In 1936 Converse will honor the game's No. 1 proselytizer by adding his name to the shoe.

1925

Passaic (N.J.) High's 159-game winning streak, which spanned more than five

The early basketball was a marvel to behold—it even included laces for easy gripping.

years, ends in a loss to Hackensack (N.J.). Passaic's coach, Ernest Blood, and star, John Roosma, who will go on to star at Army, are both eventually inducted into the Hall of Fame.

1927

The Harlem Globetrotters' long history begins when five black players and Abe Saperstein, a 5' 3" immigrant Jew, climb into a Model T Ford and drive the 50 miles from Chicago to Hinckley, Ill., for a game. Two years later the Trotters, whose uniforms Saperstein has fashioned in his father's tailor shop, introduce their

fancy passing and ball handling routines. The legerdemain is designed to entertain and not alienate the local communities from which their opposition is taken, and thus assure a return engagement.

1928

Carr Creek, a high school in the Appalachians with an enrollment of eight male students, captures the country's imagination by nearly winning the Kentucky state championship. The Creekers, who lose in the tournament final to Ashland in four overtimes, have no gym. They perfect their running, pressing style on an outdoor court carved out of a mountainside by mule-drawn shovels.

1931

At the urging of New York City mayor Jimmy Walker, who wants to raise money for relief efforts during the Depression, sportswriter Ned Irish promotes the first tripleheader in Madison Square Garden. The arena will soon become a mecca for college basketball. Two years later a Garden septupleheader—seven games, lasting all day—will attract 20,000 fans.

1934

An article appears in *Scholastic Coach* magazine entitled "Basketball: The Athletic Fad This Year."

1936

In the first Olympic basketball tournament, in Berlin, the United States wins the gold medal by defeating Canada 19–8. The final is played in a quagmire, on an outdoor court in the rain. James Naismith is on hand to watch the action.

1936

Hank Luisetti, bringing his revolutionary running one-hander to the East for the first time, helps Stanford end Long Island University's 43-game winning streak with a 45–31 victory in Madison Square Garden. "That's not basketball," huffs CCNY coach Nat Holman. "If my boys ever shot one-handed, I'd quit coaching." But Luisetti scores 15 points and dominates the game, and the Garden crowd gives him a standing ovation as he leaves the floor.

1937

The jump ball after every basket is eliminated.

1937-38

The National Association for Intercollegiate Athletics (NAIA) tournament and National Invitation Tournament (NIT) are established. Warrensburg College, now Central Missouri State University, defeats Morningside College 35–24 for the first NAIA title in 1937, and Temple beats Colorado 60–36 in Madison Square Garden for the championship of the inaugural NIT in '38. Both the NAIA tournament and the NIT will retain their relationships with the cities in which they are born, Kansas City and New York, respectively.

1939

In the first National Collegiate Athletic Association (NCAA) tournament, Oregon defeats Ohio State 46–33 in Evanston, Ill. Not until the '50s will the NCAAs surpass Madison Square Garden's NIT as the most prestigious major-college postseason tournament.

1939

In late November, just as the basketball season begins, James Naismith dies, in Lawrence, Kans. He is 78.

1940

The first live telecast of a basketball game—a matchup between Fordham and Pittsburgh, from Madison Square Garden—is broadcast to several hundred TV sets in New York City by play-by-play man Allen William Walz. There is a 20-minute blackout due to technical

Stanford's Luisetti won a host of converts when he brought the one-hander to the East.

problems during the broadcast, which ends with the Rams winning 57–37.

1945

Clarence (Big House) Gaines is hired, at age 22, to coach at Winston-Salem State College in North Carolina. At his first coaching clinic, someone asks him if he is the janitor; 45 seasons later, Gaines will win his 800th game and join Kentucky's Adolph Rupp as the only coaches at four-year colleges to break that barrier.

1946

Maurice Podoloff, a 5' 2" Russian immigrant, lawyer, hockey executive and operator of the New Haven (Conn.) Arena, leads a consortium of fellow arena managers in founding the Basketball Association of America. Three years later the BAA's 11 teams will absorb six surviving National Basketball League franchises, and the result will be called the National Basketball Association. Podoloff will become the new organization's first president. "I never cared for basketball," he will say. "I was hired to do a job."

1946

Holcombe Rucker, a 19-year-old future Harlem schoolteacher, founds his amateur basketball league in New York City. Two of his associates, Bob McCullough and Fred Crawford, will continue the mission of the league—to promote athletics and education by adding the trappings of order to raw, inner-city pickup games—after Rucker's death of cancer in 1965. A generation of playground legends, including such cult figures as Herman (Helicopter) Knowings, Joe (the Destroyer) Hammond, "Sidecar" Jackie Jackson and

Earl (Goat) Manigault, will make their mark in "the Rucker."

1948

College coaches are first permitted to speak to players during timeouts, notwithstanding the instincts of the game's inventor. "Basketball is not a game that can be coached," Naismith had once said. "It can only be played."

1949

The Minneapolis Lakers defeat the Harlem Globetrotters in Minneapolis 68–53 to end the Trotters' streak of 146 straight victories that season. Three years later Seattle University will beat the Globetrotters in a charity game, and the line of demarcation between entertainment and serious basketball will be forever drawn.

1950

Duquesne's Chuck Cooper becomes the first black man drafted by the pros when he is chosen by Boston with its second-round pick. But because of the vagaries of the schedule, Earl Lloyd of West Virginia State, whom Washington has drafted in the eighth round, is the first black man to play in the NBA that season. Nat (Sweetwater) Clifton, a former Globetrotter signed by New York, also begins his career during the 1950–51 season.

1951

Seventy-five thousand spectators—the largest basketball crowd to date—pack the Olympic Stadium in Berlin, the same structure in which Adolf Hitler refused to shake the hand of gold medalist Jesse Owens in 1936, to watch the Globetrotters. At halftime a helicopter alights on the infield and Owens himself emerges. "Fifteen years ago on this field Hitler refused to offer you his hand," says West Berlin mayor Ludwig Shreiber in greeting Owens. "Now I give you both of mine."

1951

College basketball's most wrenching point-shaving scandal comes to light when Manhattan College's Junius Kellogg reports a bribe offered to him by gamblers. Investigators will uncover fixing that affected nearly 100 games over four seasons and touched Bradley, Toledo, CCNY, NYU, Manhattan, LIU and Kentucky.

1954

Clarence (Bevo) Francis of Rio Grande College in Ohio scores 113 points in a game against Hillsdale. "The Hillsdale players beat him to death," a sportswriter who watched the game would say. "But there was nothing they could do about the jump shot. They'd keep fouling him and he'd keep making them." Francis will be expelled from school later in the season for skipping classes.

1954

Chicago's DuSable High becomes the first black-coached all-black team to reach the finals of the Illinois state tournament. The Panthers lose in the final 76–70 to a downstate school, Mount Vernon High. "For years Illinois had been playing a sleepy-time-gal kind of game," DuSable coach Jim Brown will say. "We came in and woke it up."

1954

Tiny Milan High, with an enrollment of just 73 boys, wins the Indiana state title

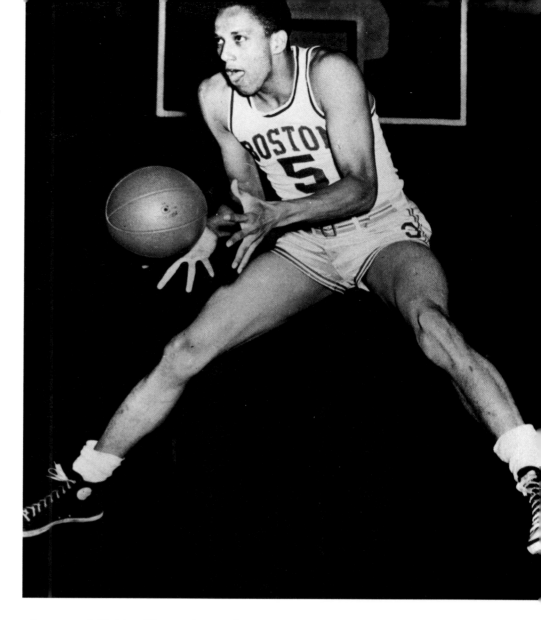

when guard Bobby Plump throws in a shot at the buzzer. The 1986 film *Hoosiers* will be based on "the Miracle of Milan."

1954

With stalling tactics threatening to spoil the appeal of the pro game, Danny Biasone, a bowling alley proprietor who owns the Syracuse Nationals, invents the 24-second clock. "Teams were taking about 60 shots in a game if nobody screwed around," Biasone will say. "I figured if the teams combined for 120 shots and the game was 48 minutes

Cooper's second-round selection by the Celtics made him the first black player drafted in the NBA.

long, I should divide 120 into 2,880 seconds. The answer was 24."

1956

San Francisco wins its 55th straight game and second straight NCAA title, defeating Iowa for the championship 83–71. Before the 1954–55 season no one had picked the Dons in a top 10 poll, and neither of the team's two stars, local products Bill Russell and K.C. Jones, had received scholarship offers from any other school.

1960

Danny Heater of Burnsville (W.Va.) High scores a national high school record 135 points in a 173–43 victory over Widen High. Heater achieves the mark in a 30' by 50' gym, and with the help of teammates who are hoping he can catch the eye of the college scouts. Heater receives one offer—from Richmond—but will wind up dropping out of school to support his family after their home is destroyed by a fire.

Anatomy of Wilt's wondrous night: 36 for 63 from the field and a surprising 28 of 32 free throws.

1962

The Libyan national team dresses the tallest player ever, eight-foot Suleiman Ali Nashnush.

1962

Philadelphia's Wilt Chamberlain scores 100 points in an NBA game when, with 46 seconds to play, he takes a pass from teammate Joe Ruklick and tosses in a short jump shot. Television isn't on hand to record Chamberlain's achievement, and no film footage of it exists today. Curiously, Knick center Darrall Imhoff, upon being called for fouling Chamberlain in the first quarter, says to one of the referees, "Why don't you just give him 100 points and we'll go home!"

1962

Tommy Boyer of Arkansas, although blind in his right eye, wins the NCAA free throw shooting title. Boyer's single-season percentage of .933 is the best in NCAA competition up to that time.

1962

For the second year in a row Cincinnati wins the NCAA title with a victory over Ohio State. After being frustrated in the national semifinals in 1959 and '60, and despite the loss of Oscar Robertson, the Bearcats use defense and patience to turn back the Buckeyes of Jerry Lucas and John Havlicek in the '61 and '62 finals.

1963

Walter Garrett of West End High in Birmingham, Ala., scores all of his team's points in a 97–54 defeat of Glenn Vocational. Garrett's teammates refuse to shoot, and by the end of the game all five Glenn defenders devote themselves to keeping Garrett from scoring 100.

1964

Coach John Wooden and the UCLA Bruins, a team with no player taller than 6' 5", complete an undefeated 30–0 season and begin their run of 10 NCAA titles in 12 years.

1966

Texas Western, with an all-black starting five, defeats all-white Kentucky 72–65 in the NCAA title game. The Miners, whose school will eventually change its name to Texas–El Paso, defeat the game's most notorious white supremacist, Adolph Rupp, in what will

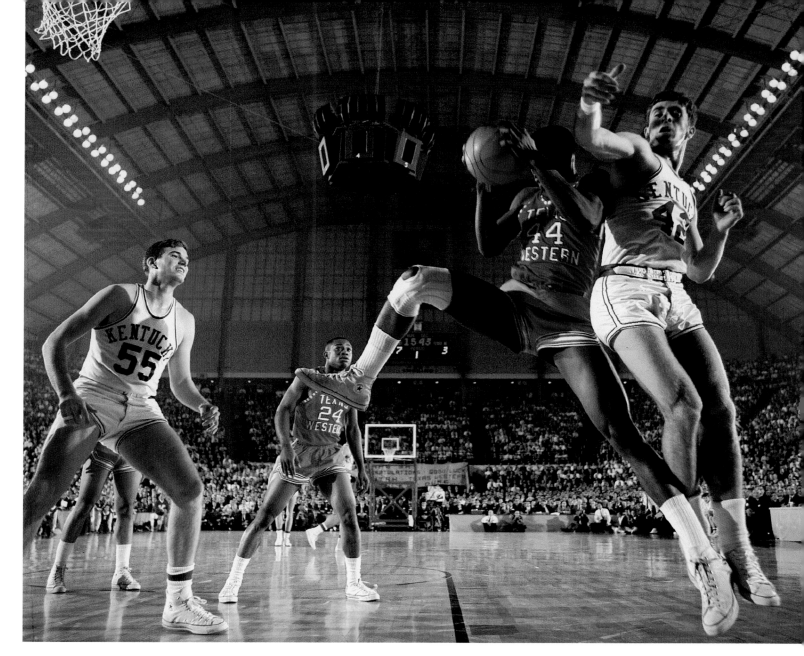

be called the *Brown v. Board of Education* of college basketball.

1967

Billing itself as "The Lively League," the American Basketball Association is founded by a group of businessmen, mostly from California. At the inaugural press conference, commissioner George Mikan says the ABA will not raid its more established counterpart for players, but, "if they are free, we want to talk to them." One league coach will describe the ABA's red, white and blue ball as looking as if it "belongs on the nose of a seal."

1968

Houston ends UCLA's 47-game winning streak with a 71–69 victory in the Astrodome before 52,693 fans, the largest college basketball crowd to that time. Scoring 39 points, the Cougars' Elvin Hayes outplays UCLA star Lew Alcindor. In the national semifinals later that season, Alcindor will hold

The Miners' Harry Flournoy beat future Laker coach Pat Riley (42) to the ball in the historic '66 showdown.

Russell (bottom) and John Havlicek had the Lakers boxed out during the '69 NBA Finals.

Hayes to 10 points in the Bruins' 101–69 victory.

1969

Spencer Haywood, the Mississippi-born son of a mother who works as a domestic and a father who is deceased, forswears his junior season in college and signs with the ABA's Denver Rockets. Haywood's move shocks the NBA, but paves the way for a policy that ultimately permits "hardship" cases. Haywood and the Seattle SuperSonics will file suit against the NBA for not letting him play until his college class had graduated.

1969

Two Tennessee high schools, Chattanooga East Ridge and Voltewah, play through 16 overtimes, a record at any level of competition. East Ridge wins 38–37.

1969

The Boston Celtics, led by player-coach Bill Russell, win their 11th NBA title in 13 years with a 108–106 victory in Game 7 in Los Angeles. Lakers owner Jack Kent Cooke's balloons, inflated and stowed in the rafters of the Forum in anticipation of a victory celebration, are left there to shrivel.

1971

The Harlem Globetrotters, after a 100–99 loss to the New Jersey Reds on Jan. 5, begin a winning streak that will cover more than 7,000 games and still be intact as basketball turns 100.

1972

The Lakers, despite the advancing age of their nucleus of West and Chamberlain, both of whom are in their mid-30's, win 33 consecutive games, an NBA record. The Lakers' mark, which shatters the previous record of 20, may never be equaled in any pro team sport.

1974

UCLA's NCAA-record 88-game winning streak ends in South Bend, Ind., when Notre Dame's Dwight Clay throws in a corner jump shot in the final seconds for a 71–70 win.

1974

North Carolina State, led by College Player of the Year David Thompson, beats Maryland 103–100 in overtime in the finals of the ACC tournament. Because only the conference champion can go to the NCAAs, the Terrapins, including such stars as Tom McMillen, Len Elmore and John Lucas, must stay home. Even after N.C. State defeats UCLA in the national semifinals of the same season in double overtime, and then beats Marquette in the NCAA title game, Wolfpack guard Monte Towe will say, "Nothing can compare to beating Maryland in the ACC finals."

1974

The Original, Takin' It to the Streets, All-World Gus Macker Three-on-Three Tournament is founded in the driveway of the McNeal family in Lowell, Mich. As much a festival of puckish humor as it is a serious competition, the Macker eventually takes to the road, spawning a nationwide vogue in half-court three-on-three tournaments.

The Lakers' Jim McMillian went to the hoop against Seattle during L.A.'s 33-game winning streak.

One of the UCLA surprises in '75 was Dave Meyers, who made this block in the NCAA final.

Benson grabbed this ferocious rebound against UCLA early in Indiana's undefeated season.

1975

John Wooden wins his 10th and last NCAA cahampionship two days after announcing he will step down as UCLA's coach. Wooden will call this Bruin team one of his favorites because the title, clinched with a 92–85 defeat of Kentucky in the final game, was so "unexpected."

1976

Indiana, led by Quinn Buckner, Kent Benson and Scott May, caps an undefeated season with an 86–68 defeat of Michigan in the NCAA title game. The championship is Hoosier coach Bob Knight's first of three.

1976

A class-action suit, brought against NBA owners in 1970 by Players Association president Oscar Robertson, is settled out of court and achieves for all veteran players the right to genuine free agency. The landmark agreement, known as the Robertson Settlement, ushers in an era of labor peace in the NBA unprecedented in professional sports.

1976

Boston and Phoenix play the longest game in NBA Finals history, a three-overtime, four hour and 20 second affair in Boston Garden. The Celtics prevail 128–126 after midnight, then go on to defeat the Suns in Phoenix in Game 6 to clinch their 13th title.

1976

The NBA and ABA agree to merge, with the NBA absorbing four of the upstart league's franchises—the Denver Nuggets, Indiana Pacers, New York Nets and San Antonio Spurs. In its nine years, four months and 15 days of existence, the ABA lost an estimated $40 million. But through its legacy of innovative rules, marketing and entertainment sense, and belief in putting the players first, the ABA will help catapult its older counterpart to new and unforeseen successes.

1979

ESPN, the 24-hour all-sports cable television network, is founded. College basketball will become the staple of its wintertime programming and launch the broadcast career of adenoidal analyst Dick Vitale.

1979

Former Providence College basketball coach Dave Gavitt, hoping to capitalize on the strong college basketball tradition and lucrative metropolitan media markets along the East Coast, founds the Big East Conference. By the end of its first decade, six of the league's first nine members will have reached the NCAA Final Four, and a 10th school, Miami, will be added to the conference to annex yet another large eastern market.

1979

Larry Bird's Indiana State Sycamores and Magic Johnson's Michigan State Spartans hook up in the NCAA title game in front of the largest TV audience for basketball, then or since. The Spartans' 75–64 victory—and the subsequent arrival in, and tonic effect on, the NBA of Bird

The scoreboard told the tale as the Celts and Suns began the third OT in their playoff marathon.

in, and tonic effect on, the NBA of Bird and Magic—is a watershed in the growth of the game at both the collegiate and professional levels.

1979

The NBA, taking a lesson from the defunct ABA, adopts the three-point shot, at the distance of 23' 9". The rule will open up pro offenses, produce a raft of exciting finishes and foster the emergence of the indispensible three-point shooter, a category that will enable several otherwise marginal players to survive.

The '79 NCAA matchup between Johnson and Bird (33) was a watershed in the game's growth.

1980

The NCAA tournament committee decides to "balance" the regional brackets, sending teams around the country for first-round games based primarily on strength and not geography. The result is a string of unprecedentedly exciting tournaments through the '80s that turn the three weeks in March into a hot television property.

1982

Virginia's Ralph Sampson and Georgetown's Patrick Ewing meet in a made-for-TV game on Ted Turner's SuperStation WTBS. In this clash of seven-footers, Sampson outscores, outrebounds and outblocks the younger Ewing as the Cavaliers win 68–63.

1982

Tiny Chaminade University, an NAIA school in Honolulu with an enrollment of 900 students, upsets No. 1–ranked Virginia and Sampson 77–72. Six foot eight inch Tony Randolph, an old high school nemesis of the Cavs' center, scores 19 points for the Silverswords.

1982

Centralia (Ill.) High becomes the first high school to win 1,500 games. The Orphans, so nicknamed because the school's longtime coach was a fan of the Lillian Gish film *Orphans of the Storm*, have won three state titles and produced such players as former Southern Illinois star and NBA player Dick Garrett and former Bradley star and Harlem Globetrotter Bobby Joe Mason.

1983

North Carolina State defeats heavily favored Houston and the Cougars'

imposing 7' center, Akeem Olajuwon, 54–52 for the NCAA title. The Wolfpack wins on a dunk at the buzzer of a teammate's airball by forward Lorenzo Charles and by employing coach Jim Valvano's strategy of intentionally fouling Houston's inept free throw shooters over the game's final minutes.

1983

NBA owners elect David Stern, the league's executive vice-president and former general counsel, to replace Lawrence O'Brien as commissioner. Stern will preside over unprecedented growth, prosperity and internationalization of the league, and in 1990 will sign a $27.5-million deal to stay on until at least 1995.

1984

The NBA and its players, acting after several years of behind-the-scenes discussions between Stern and Players Association executive director Larry Fleisher, reach a settlement that guarantees the players at least 53% of the league's gross revenues in exchange for a cap on player salaries. In *The New York Times,* respected labor writer A.H. Raskin calls the arrangement "one of the most innovative in any area of labor-management relations."

1985

Villanova shoots a torrid 79% to stun favored Georgetown 66–64 and win the NCAA championship in the final collegiate appearance of the Hoyas' Patrick Ewing.

**Charles' dunk capped the
Wolfpack's improbable win over
Houston for the NCAA title.**

1985

Spurred by the sluggish final of the 1982 ACC tournament, in which North Carolina beat Virginia 47–45 after stalling for most of the second half, and emboldened further by successful experimentation in several conferences over the previous few seasons, the NCAA rules committee adopts the 45-second clock.

1986

The NCAA rules committee approves the three-point shot, at the relatively short distance of 19'9". The committee's chairman, Dr. Edward Steitz, is reviled in the press as "the Three's Stooge," and the shot is called "the Doctor's J." But the three-pointer, if not its distance, soon gains wide acceptance for the excitement it brings. Before his death in 1990, Steitz could say, justifiably, "The dunk is no longer basketball's home run. The three-point shot is."

1986

Nancy Lieberman plays three scoreless minutes for the Springfield Fame of the United States Basketball League in a game against Staten Island, becoming the first woman to play in a men's professional game.

1989

At a special session in Munich, the membership of FIBA, basketball's international governing body, adopts a rule that will permit NBA players to compete in heretofore "amateur" competitions, including the Olympic Games. "We see this as our triumphant entry into the 21st century," says Boris Stankovic, FIBA's executive secretary. "The borders in basketball have fallen." In accordance with this development,

FIBA, while retaining its acronym, changes its name from Federation Internationale de Basketball Amateur to Federation Internationale de Basketball.

1990

Lisa Leslie, a 6'5" senior at L.A.'s Morningside High, scores 101 points in the first half of a game against South Torrance. Plagued by fouls and injuries, the South Torrance players elect to quit at halftime, thus preventing Leslie from breaking Cheryl Miller's single-game high-school record of 105 points.

1990

CBS agrees to pay $1 billion to broadcast the NCAA tournament over the next seven years.

1991

Michael Jordan leads Chicago to its first NBA championship. It is a definitive answer to those critics who recognized Jordan's skills but doubted his ability to win. Jordan averages 31.2 points per game against the Lakers in the Finals and is named the series' MVP.

1993

With their victory over the Phoenix Suns in the NBA Finals, the Chicago Bulls join the Bostons Celtics and the Minneapolis Lakers as the only teams in NBA history to win three consecutive titles. Michael Jordan scores 41.0 points per game—an alltime Finals high—and is named the series' MVP, also for the third straight year. Scottie Pippen contributes to the cause with 21.1 points per game.

Jordan levitated for two against Sam Perkins and the Lakers in the 1991 NBA Finals.

Lieberman's 1986 appearance was the first for a woman in a men's professional contest.

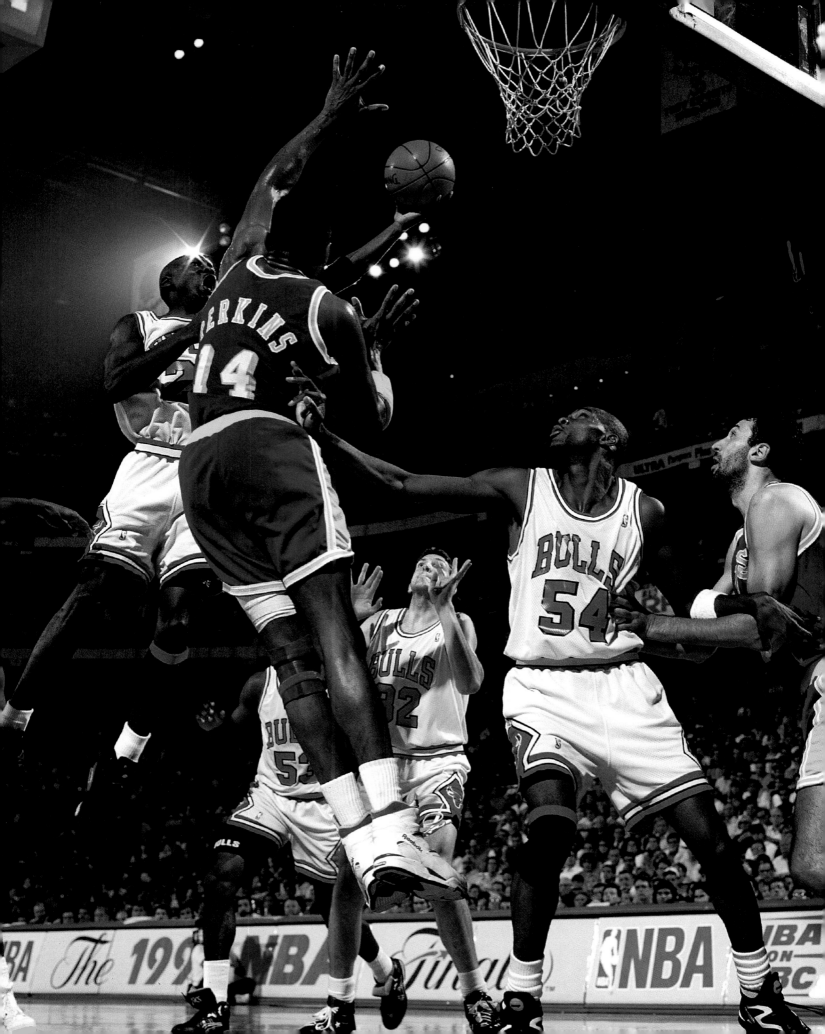

The Ecumenical Game

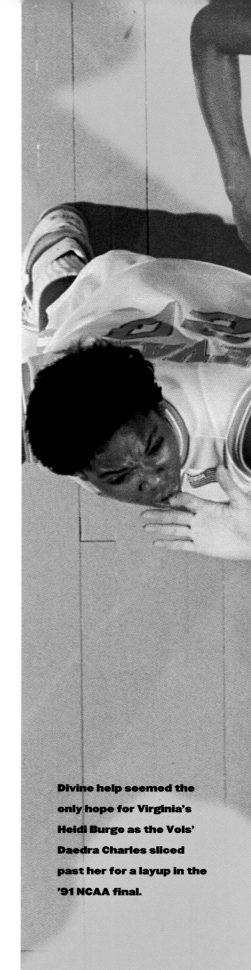

Baseball still doesn't have a worldwide reach. Women have too much sense to play football. Soccer hasn't yet penetrated the United States as a spectator sport. And—outside certain precincts in Canada, anyway—most fans think hockey keeps score with the 10-point must system. That leaves basketball as the team sport to bind the world.

From the beginning hoops didn't merely tolerate diversity. Within weeks of its invention the sport had gone forth and introduced itself to people quite different from the male North Americans (and one Japanese) who played in the original game. Women tipped off the first game in Springfield, Mass., in March 1892. (Two years later James Naismith would marry Maude Sherman, one of the players in that game.) Soon thereafter basketball made its way south across the border to Mexico, and by 1893 it had spread to Europe, with Asia (1894), South America (1896), Australia (1900) and Africa (1920) soon to follow.

Now this game, invented by a Canadian, is played by 250 million people worldwide and followed passionately by some 300 million more. In China it is the national sport; in Bhutan, the king has a private coach. Women have likewise claimed the game as their own. They have done this not merely stateside, in places like Des Moines, where 15,000 fans flock to Super Saturday of the Iowa Girls State High School Tournament every year, but in places like France and Brazil, too, where showwomen like Jackie Chazalon and Hortência have galvanized the attention of sports fans of both sexes.

Divine help seemed the only hope for Virginia's Heidi Burge as the Vols' Daedra Charles sliced past her for a layup in the '91 NCAA final.

The Ecumenical Game

That basketball today is claimed by people of every gender and nationality can be traced to two instances of sheer serendipity. One occurred in 1895, when a woman named Clara Baer, who was a physical education instructor at Newcomb College in New Orleans, wrote Naismith to request a copy of the rules for his new game. With his reply, Naismith included a diagram sketching out the ideal positions of the players. Baer misunderstood, thinking the indications meant that players were confined to certain stations. And so Baer, a keen proselytizer for the game among physical educators of women, began the development of the six-to-a-side, three-on-offense, three-on-defense women's rules that would prevail during the first 75 years of the game's life. Even after the misunderstanding was pointed out to her, Baer stuck to the modified rules for "basquette," the Frenchified name she used. She considered the all-court game played by the men to be too strenuous for women and continued to promote the circumscribed version so, as she put it, "a delicate girl, unaccustomed to exercise, and for the most part averse to it, would become interested in spite of herself." Given the patronizing attitudes toward women that prevailed in American society around the turn of the century, it's likely basketball would have remained a largely male pastime if Baer hadn't adopted her gentler version of the game.

Basketball's rapid spread overseas owes much to the vagaries of chance as well. For another new sport was also played at the Training School in Springfield, a game played with a ball and a net called volleyball, invented by William G. Morgan, a colleague of Naismith's, in 1895. This game also could have been spread overseas with missionary zeal. But because Naismith's game had been created four years earlier, it became the diversion of choice for the school's evangelical efforts. Had the timing been different, there might be volleyball nets, instead of basketball hoops, in schoolyards the world over.

1893

At a YMCA gym on the rue de Trevise in Paris, two teams play the first European game. The referee wears, literally, a black hat, which he doffs after each basket in a sort of salute. The players refer to the sport as "the game from Texas."

1893

Two intramural teams at Smith College in Northampton, Mass., just north of Springfield, play the first women's collegiate game. No men are allowed to watch, because the participants are wearing bloomers.

1899

The first women's rules, influenced by Clara Baer and Naismith himself, who concurred with Baer's beliefs, divide the court into three sections, forbid players to steal the ball from one another and provide for the assessment of a personal foul on any player leaving the section to which she is confined. According to the introduction to the rules, "a number of girls who play without division lines have developed hypertrophy of the heart."

1915

The Edmonton Commercial Grads are founded in Alberta, Canada, by John Percy Page. Until 1940 the Grads, a women's team whose members all graduated from the same high school, will go 522–20 while barnstorming through North America and Europe, defeating men's teams seven of the nine times they meet. Page summarily drops from the team anyone who marries, yet only 38 different women play for the Grads over those 25 years.

1924

Marie Boyd of Lonaconing Central High in Maryland scores 156 points in a 163–3 victory. Her total, a single-game high school record, is partly the result of Baer's rules, under which only three players may shoot.

1931

Babe Didrikson, the Olympic track star, leads the Dallas Golden Cyclones to the 1931 AAU women's tournament title by scoring 106 points over five games, including the decisive basket with 20 seconds to play.

1936

Basketball is an official part of the Olympic program for the first time, at the Games in Berlin. The United States wins the gold medal by defeating Canada 19–8 outdoors during a rainstorm, as James Naismith looks on. "The tournament proved two things," reports *The New York Times*. "First, it is now clear that basketball no longer is merely an American game, but a genuine world game. The tournament proved, in the second place, however, that North America

Bloomers kept the men away from the first women's college game in 1893; Didrikson (below) was a hoops ace for Dallas.

still is unthreatened in its basketball supremacy."

1937

The six-to-a-side rules are adopted for women. The following season the court will be redistricted into two sections, rather than the three that have prevailed officially since 1899.

1946

The Toronto Huskies of the Basketball Association of America become the first professional team to

The Soviets were a happy bunch after their upset of the U.S. in the 1972 Olympics.

have its headquarters outside the United States.

1955

Nera White, playing for Nashville Business College, is named an AAU All-America, the first of 15 consecutive times she will be so honored. White, who plays the rover position in six-to-a-side competition, will win 10 AAU tournament MVP awards and lead NBC to as many national titles. When the Hall of Fame finally inducts its first female player, it will very likely be she.

1971

The rules are amended to reduce the number of players on a women's team from six to five. Several states, most notably Iowa, retain the old rules.

1972

In the first championship of the Association for Intercollegiate Athletics for Women (AIAW), Immaculata College defeats West Chester State 52–48 to claim the first women's national collegiate title. Immaculata, a school outside Philadelphia with an enrollment of 800, will win the first three AIAW crowns and produce such future women's coaches as Teresa Shank Grentz, Marianne Crawford Stanley and Rene Muth Portland. The AIAW will exist until the early 1980s, when the NCAA takes over women's athletics and forces the fledgling organization out of business.

1972

The Soviet Union beats the United States 51–50 in Munich for the gold medal, the first time the Americans have ever been beaten in Olympic play. The Soviets win on a disputed layup at the buzzer, after the U.S., which had trailed by 10 points late in the game, rallies to take a one-point lead with three seconds remaining.

1976

By virtue of a perfect 5–0 record in Olympic play, the Soviets are awarded the first Olympic gold medal in women's basketball.

1984

The women's game officially adopts a basketball 29 inches in circumference, about an inch smaller than the regulation men's ball.

1985

University of Miami head coach Bill Foster, a white Southern Baptist, fills out his coaching staff with four Americans—a black, a Hispanic, a Jew and an Asian.

1985

Lynette Woodard, an All-America at the University of Kansas, becomes the first woman to play for the Harlem Globetrotters.

1987

Cheryl Myers of Lakeland (Ind.) Christian Academy throws in a 77-foot shot during a victory over Elkhart Baptist. The basket is the longest by a woman at any level.

1987

Brazil, behind the shooting of flamboyant forward Oscar Schmidt, defeats the U.S. for the gold medal at the Pan American Games in Indianapolis.

1992

With an average margin of victory of almost 44 points a game, the American "Dream Team" of one collegian and 11 NBA multimillionaires—Michael Jordan, Magic Johnson, Larry Bird and Charles Barkley among them—sails through the eight-game Olympic tournament in Barcelona to the gold medal.

Among the dreamiest of the 1992 Olympic Dream Teamers: (from top) Bird, Jordan, Scottie Pippen and Johnson.

The Future

It will be remembered that the manly art of stalling, the slow break and the sleepy, center-feed style of play which came into general use during the last few years so slowed up the game that last season the customers stayed away very briskly. There is no percentage in paying a dollar to sleep on a hard board seat behind a stanchion when you can sleep free on a soft bed at home. If you have a home these days.

—Red Smith, December 1932

Basketball is for the birds—the gooney birds. The game lost this particular patron years back when it went vertical and put the accent on carnival freaks who achieved upper space by growing into it. They don't shoot baskets anymore, they stuff them, like taxidermists.

—Shirley Povich, December 1958

So take *that*, hoops. Smith of *The New York Herald Tribune* and Povich of *The Washington Post*, perhaps the two greatest sportswriters of your era, trashing you at two intervals of your development. We don't know quite how to break this to you—and, yes, we agree that *Red and Shirley* sounds

The Future

like a sitcom—but . . . well, who's to say they weren't correct? Who's to say that, at 40, you weren't boring, and that, a quarter century later, you weren't still rigged in favor of the pituitary cases?

In your defense, all we can do is summon Dave Kindred, who's widely considered to be the heir to Smith and Povich as today's preeminent sports voice in American newspapers. "No other game has changed so much so quickly," Kindred wrote as basketball turned 100. "And for the better. Always a nice little game, basketball now is the best game."

Kindred went on: "Red Smith . . . described himself as a man who 'would rather drink a Bronx cocktail than speak well of basketball.' Red wrote that valentine in the late '40s, which explains everything, of course. Michael Jordan's parents hadn't even met."

As Dolores and James Jordan enter their fourth decade of matrimony, basketball has outstripped its critics utterly. The customers show up very briskly. The

professional season still lasts too long, and the colleges still unjustly exploit and indenture young players, and a basketball game will sometimes backslide into unseemly bogarting. But basketball surely is not categorically boring. Nor can one say that the big fella has it made—not when speed and spring will more consistently win out than height; and not when the Detroit Pistons won back-to-back NBA titles in 1989 and '90 with a center who shot outside jumpers, and with playoff MVPs (Joe Dumars and Isiah Thomas) who stood 6' 3" and 6' 1", respectively.

Where, then, does "the best game" go from here?

To a concave backboard, some say, off which rebounds will carom at unpredictable angles. To recessed foul lanes, say others, so the closer you get to the basket, the higher the rim will be.

More likely, the three-point shot will be standardized at 20' 6" for the high schools and colleges, to match the international distance. A widened lane and lengthened court will further reward speed and quickness over power and bulk.

Coaches and general managers everywhere will look for versatility. The first 7' point guard will suit up, and, somewhere, a coach will play five seven-footers at the same time. There will always be those who, like the Portland Trail Blazers in 1984, draft a Sam Bowie before a Jordan, but they will be left at the station. Height won't mean nearly as much as what you can *do* with your height, whatever it may be. Consider 5'7" Spud Webb on the subject of elbows: "You just keep throwing them. And by the third quarter their shins are so sore that you can run right by them."

Not that the players won't get bigger. (Or stronger. Or faster. Or better.) The height of the average NBA player, 6'3" in 1948, is now more than 6'7", and certain to increase beyond that. Similarly, the league-wide field goal percentage, .284 in 1948, has now hit .474. But when you consider that players at the very highest level of the game are still missing more shots than they make, you have to figure that there's plenty of room for improvement there, too.

As the NBA expands from its current total of 27 franchises, cries will go up that quality is being diluted. Yet at the height of the NBA-ABA war, in 1972, there was enough talent to stock two major leagues. And foreign-born NBA players, unthinkable a decade ago but now so commonplace that no one gives them a second thought, will further expand the pool of eligible players.

Some of those non-Americans may well be playing for hometown teams in the NBA as the internationalization of the game continues apace. It's not hard to imagine a game in Red Square between the Soviet national team and an NBA squad. An annual, eight-team tournament that would crown a world professional champion. Perhaps even a world superleague.

Among things that probably won't happen: raising the rim beyond its familiar 10 feet. The case for the 12-foot basket has been made intermittently throughout the century, first when Bob Kurland began dominating the college game during the '40s, and more recently when Lew Alcindor matriculated at UCLA. But that clamor has quieted for now. With his Slam-Dunk title, Spud established that little guys don't need to be patronized. And even those who agree with the intent of so radical a change—to cut the little guy a break—now concede two things: that the three-point shot has gone a long way toward doing that already, and that a raised basket will only be a tougher target for the small outside shooter to reach. "Let's say shooting percentage goes down 20% with a higher basket," says Red Auerbach, who has never been accused of seeking charity for the underdog. "That's 20% more rebounds in a game, and most of them will belong to the big man. It is simply ridiculous to think that a higher basket would make the big man less important."

Besides, who would want fewer dunks?

Basketball goes forth into its second century with one great advantage: It was invented. On Dec. 20, 1891, it didn't exist; on Dec. 21, it did. Thus it hasn't been handed down through generations like a precious heirloom, with some mystical pedigree so intimidating that no one dared mess with the game's warp or woof. And Naismith, who remained a member of the rules committee well after that group's formation in 1898, encouraged the tinkering process that strengthened the game through the first few decades of its life. Luther Gulick, Naismith's old boss at Springfield and the head of the original rules committee, wrote in the introduction to the first rules guide, published in 1898:

"Each game has its own evolution, that is somewhat independent of the rules, for we always find, even in the most strictly enforced athletic games, that the actual playing rules do not and cannot conform exactly to the printed rules. . . . This represents the evolution of the game itself, and it is the business of the rules committee to understand and formulate this unconscious development of the game, as well as to endeavor to meet the evils that this evolution will inevitably bring to the front."

When those evils cropped up, the keepers of the game rose to meet them. After travesties like the Fort Wayne freeze in 1950 and the North Carolina–Virginia ACC tournament final in '82, the game's legislators introduced shot clocks. When Kurland started playing goalie in front of the basket, they enacted the goaltending rule. As congestion began to develop around the basket, the NBA widened its lane—from six feet to 12 feet in 1952, and to the current 16 feet in '64—and the colleges adopted the three-point shot. Upon beholding the joyless character of the game without the dunk, the legislators recognized their original mistake in banning it and brought it back.

Soccer languishes because its elders would sooner put up with World Cup matches decided on penalty kicks than alter substantially the laws of the game. Basketball, by contrast, has always understood that rules aren't chiseled into some Rosetta stone. They are, rather, a kind of contract between the players and the spectators. And, at some point, all contracts come up for renewal.

It's not particularly important whether hindsight proves every rule change to be wise, though most certainly have been. What's most important is that basketball remain malleable, always evolving, and in the process continue to exalt the superb players whose skills force the rule makers' hand.

Happy 100th, hoops. May you have a hundred happy hundreds more.

Appendix:
The Champions

Season	Champion	Series win-loss	Eastern Div./Conf. champ. & win-loss record		Western Div./Conf. champ. & win-loss record		NBA Finals MVP
1946-47	Philadelphia	4-1	Philadelphia	35-25	Chicago	39-22	no award given
1947-48	Baltimore	4-2	Philadelphia	27-21	Baltimore	28-20	no award given
1948-49	Minneapolis	4-2	Washington	38-22	Minneapolis	44-16	no award given
1949-50	Minneapolis	4-2	Syracuse	51-13	Minneapolis	51-17	no award given
1950-51	Rochester	4-3	New York	36-30	Rochester	41-27	no award given
1951-52	Minneapolis	4-3	New York	37-29	Minneapolis	40-26	no award given
1952-53	Minneapolis	4-1	New York	47-23	Minneapolis	48-22	no award given
1953-54	Minneapolis	4-3	Syracuse	42-30	Minneapolis	46-26	no award given
1954-55	Syracuse	4-3	Syracuse	43-29	Fort Wayne	43-29	no award given
1955-56	Philadelphia	4-1	Philadelphia	45-27	Fort Wayne	37-35	no award given
1956-57	Boston	4-3	Boston	44-28	St. Louis	34-38	no award given
1957-58	St. Louis	4-2	Boston	49-23	St. Louis	41-31	no award given
1958-59	Boston	4-0	Boston	52-20	Minneapolis	33-39	no award given
1959-60	Boston	4-3	Boston	59-16	St. Louis	46-29	no award given
1960-61	Boston	4-1	Boston	57-22	St. Louis	51-28	no award given
1961-62	Boston	4-3	Boston	60-20	Los Angeles	54-26	no award given
1962-63	Boston	4-2	Boston	58-22	Los Angeles	53-27	no award given
1963-64	Boston	4-1	Boston	59-21	San Francisco	48-32	no award given
1964-65	Boston	4-1	Boston	62-18	Los Angeles	49-31	no award given
1965-66	Boston	4-3	Boston	54-26	Los Angeles	45-35	no award given
1966-67	Philadelphia	4-2	Philadelphia	68-13	San Francisco	44-37	no award given
1967-68	Boston	4-2	Boston	54-28	Los Angeles	52-30	no award given
1968-69	Boston	4-3	Boston	48-34	Los Angeles	55-27	Jerry West, L.A.
1969-70	New York	4-3	New York	60-22	Los Angeles	46-36	Willis Reed, N.Y.
1970-71	Milwaukee	4-0	Baltimore	42-40	Milwaukee	66-16	Kareem Abdul-Jabbar, Mil.
1971-72	Los Angeles	4-1	New York	48-34	Los Angeles	69-13	Wilt Chamberlain, L.A.
1972-73	New York	4-1	New York	57-25	Los Angeles	60-22	Willis Reed, N.Y.
1973-74	Boston	4-3	Boston	56-26	Milwaukee	59-23	John Havlicek, Boston
1974-75	Golden State	4-0	Washington	60-22	Golden State	48-34	Rick Barry, G.S.
1975-76	Boston	4-2	Boston	54-28	Phoenix	42-40	JoJo White, Boston
1976-77	Portland	4-2	Philadelphia	50-32	Portland	49-33	Bill Walton, Portland
1977-78	Washington	4-3	Washington	44-38	Seattle	47-35	Wes Unseld, Wash.
1978-79	Seattle	4-1	Washington	54-28	Seattle	52-30	Dennis Johnson, Seattle
1979-80	Los Angeles	4-2	Philadelphia	59-23	Los Angeles	60-22	Magic Johnson, L.A.
1980-81	Boston	4-2	Boston	62-20	Houston	40-42	Cedric Maxwell, Boston
1981-82	Los Angeles	4-2	Philadelphia	58-24	Los Angeles	57-25	Magic Johnson, L.A.
1982-83	Philadelphia	4-0	Philadelphia	65-17	Los Angeles	58-24	Moses Malone, Phil.
1983-84	Boston	4-3	Boston	62-20	Los Angeles	54-28	Larry Bird, Boston
1984-85	Los Angeles	4-2	Boston	63-19	Los Angeles	62-20	Kareem Abdul-Jabbar, L.A.
1985-86	Boston	4-2	Boston	67-15	Houston	51-31	Larry Bird, Boston
1986-87	Los Angeles	4-2	Boston	59-23	L.A. Lakers	65-17	Magic Johnson, L.A.
1987-88	Los Angeles	4-3	Detroit	54-28	L.A. Lakers	62-20	James Worthy, L.A.
1988-89	Detroit	4-0	Detroit	63-19	Los Angeles	57-25	Joe Dumars, Detroit
1989-90	Detroit	4-1	Detroit	59-23	Portland	59-23	Isiah Thomas, Detroit
1990-91	Chicago	4-1	Chicago	61-21	L.A. Lakers	58-24	Michael Jordan, Chicago
1991-92	Chicago	4-2	Chicago	67-15	Portland	57-25	Michael Jordan, Chicago
1992-93	Chicago	4-2	Chicago	57-25	Phoenix	62-20	Michael Jordan, Chicago

Year	Champion	Score	Runner-Up	Thitd Place	Fourth Place	Site	Outstanding Player Award
1939	Oregon	46–33	Ohio State	*Oklahoma	*Villanova	Evanston, Ill.	no award given
1940	Indiana	60–42	Kansas	*Duquesne	*Southern Cal.	Kansas City, Mo.	Marvin Huffman, Ind.
1941	Wisconsin	39–34	Wash. State	*Pittsurgh	*Arkansas	Kansas City, Mo.	John Kotz, Wisc.
1942	Stanford	53–38	Dartmouth	*Colorado	*Kentucky	Kansas City, Mo.	Howard Dallmar, Stanford
1943	Wyoming	46–34	Georgetown	*Texas	*DePaul	New York City	Ken Sailors, Wyoming
1944	Utah	42–40	Dartmouth	*Iowa State	*Ohio State	New York City	Arnold Ferrin, Utah
1945	Oklahoma St.	49–45	NYU	*Arkansas	*Ohio State	New York City	Bob Kurland, Oklahoma St.
1946	Oklahoma St.	43–40	North Carolina	Ohio State	California	New York City	Bob Kurland, Oklahoma St.
1947	Holy Cross	58–47	Oklahoma	Texas	CCNY	New York City	George Kaftan, Holy Cross
1948	Kentucky	58–42	Baylor	Holy Cross	Kansas State	New York City	Alex Groza, Kentucky
1949	Kentucky	46–36	Oklahoma St.	Illinois	Oregon State	Seattle	Alex Groza, Kentucky
1950	CCNY	71–68	Bradley	N. Carol. St.	Baylor	New York City	Irwin Dambrot, CCNY
1951	Kentucky	68–58	Seattle	Temple	Kansas State	Minnepolis, Minn.	no award given
1952	Kansas	80–63	St. John's (NY)	Illinois	Santa Clara	Seattle, Wash.	Clyde Lovellette, Kansas
1953	Indiana	69–68	Kansas	Washington	Louisiana St.	Kansas City, Mo.	B.H. Horn, Kansas
1954	La Salle	92–76	Bradley	Penn. State	Southern Cal.	Kansas City, Mo.	Tom Gola, La Salle
1955	San Francisco	77–63	La Salle	Colordao	Iowa	Kansas City, Mo.	Bill Russell, San Francisco
1956	San Francisco	83–71	Iowa	Temple	SMU	Evanston, Ill.	Hal Lear, Temple
1957	North Carolina	54–53	Kansas	San Francisco	Michigan State	Kansas City, Mo.	Wilt Chamberlain, Kansas
1958	Kentucky	84–72	Seattle	Temple	Kansas State	Louisville, Ky.	Elgin Baylor, Seattle
1959	California	71–70	West Virginia	Cincinnati	Louisville	Louisville, Ky.	Jerry West, West Virginia
1960	Ohio State	75–55	California	Cincinnati	NYU	San Francisco	Jerry Lucas, Ohio State
1961	Cincinnati	70–65	Ohio State	**Vacated	Utah	Kansas City, Mo.	Jerry Lucas, Ohio State
1962	Cincinnati	71–59	Ohio State	Wake Forest	UCLA	Louisville, Ky.	Paul Hogue, Cincinnati
1963	Loyola (Ill.)	60–58	Cincinnati	Duke	Oregon State	Louisville, Ky.	Art Heyman, Duke
1964	UCLA	98–83	Duke	Michigan	Kansas State	Kansas City, Mo.	Walt Hazzard, UCLA
1965	UCLA	91–80	Michigan	Princeton	Wichita State	Portland, Ore.	Bill Bradley, Princeton
1966	UTEP	72–65	Kentucky	Duke	Utah	College Park, Md.	Jerry Chambers, Utah
1967	UCLA	79–64	Dayton	Houston	North Carolina	Louisville, Ky.	Lew Alcindor, UCLA
1968	UCLA	78–55	North Carolina	Ohio State	Houston	Los Angeles	Lew Alcindor, UCLA
1969	UCLA	92–72	Purdue	Drake	North Carolina	Louisville, Ky.	Lew Alcindor, UCLA
1970	UCLA	80–69	Jacksonville	N. Mexico St.	St. Bonaventure	College PArk, Md.	Sidney Wicks, UCLA
1971	UCLA	68–62	**Vacated	**Vacated	Kansas	Houston	**Vacated
1972	UCLA	81–76	Florida State	North Carolina	Louisville	Los Angeles	Bill Walton, UCLA
1973	UCLA	87–66	Memphis State	Indiana	Providence	St. Louis	Bill Walton, UCLA
1974	N.C. State	76–64	Marquette	UCLA	Kansas	Greensboro, N.C.	David Thompson, N.C. State
1975	UCLA	92–85	Kentucky	Louisville	Syracuse	San Diego	Richard Washington, UCLA
1976	Indiana	86–68	Michigan	UCLA	Rutgers	Philadelphia	Kent Benson, Indiana
1977	Marquette	67–59	North Carolina	UNLV	N.C.-Charlotte	Atlanta	Butch Lee, Marquette
1978	Kentucky	94–88	Duke	Arkansas	Notre Dame	St. Louis	Jack Givens, Kentucky
1979	Michigan State	75–64	Indiana State	DePaul	Penn	Salt Lake City	Earvin Johnson, Michigan St.
1980	Louisville	59–54	**Vacated	Purdue	Iowa	Indianapolis	Darrell Griffith, Louisville
1981	Indiana	63–50	North Carolina	Virginia	Louisiana State	Philadelphia	Isiah Thomas, Indiana
1982	North Carolina	63–62	Georgetown	*Houston	*Louisville	New Orleans	James Worthy, North Carolina
1983	N.C. State	54–52	Houston	*Georgia	*Louisville	Albuquerque, N.M.	Akeem Olajuwon, Houston
1984	Georgetown	84–75	Houston	*Kentucky	*Virginia	Seattle	Patrick Ewing, Georgetown
1985	Villanova	66–64	Georgetown	*St. John's (NY)	**Vacated	Lexington, Ky.	Ed Pinckney, Villanova
1986	Louisville	72–69	Duke	*Kansas	*Louisiana State	Dallas	Pervis Ellison, Louisville
1987	Indiana	74–73	Syracuse	*UNLV	*Providence	New Orleans	Keith Smart, Indiana
1988	Kansas	83–79	Oklahoma	*Arizona	*Duke	Kansas City, Mo.	Danny Manning, Kansas
1989	Michigan	80–79	Seton Hall	*Duke	*Illinois	Seattle	Glen Rice, Michigan
1990	UNLV	103–73	Duke	*Arkansas	*Georgia Tech.	Denver	Anderson Hunt, UNLV
1991	Duke	72–65	Kansas	*North Carolina	*UNLV	Indianapolis	Christian Laettner, Duke
1992	Duke	71–51	Michigan	*Cincinnati	*Indiana	Minneapolis	Bobby Hurley, Duke
1993	North Carolina	77–71	Michigan	*Kentucky	*Kansas	New Orleans	Donald Williams, North Carolina

* *Tied for third place*
** *Athletes representing St. Joseph's (Pa.) in 1961, Villanova (runner-up) in '71, Western Kentucky (third place) in '71, UCLA in '80 and Memphis State in '85 were declared ineligible after the tournament. Under NCAA rules, the ineligible athletes' records were deleted and the teams places in the standings were vacated.*

ABA Champions

Season	Champion	Series win–loss	Eastern Div. champ. & win-loss record		Western Div. champ. & win-loss record		Regular season MVP
1967-68	Pittsburgh	4–3	Pittsburgh	55–24	New Orleans	48–30	Connie Hawkins, Pittsburgh
1968-69	Oakland	4–1	Indiana	44–34	Oakland	60–18	Mel Daniels, Indiana
1969-70	Indiana	4–2	Indiana	59–25	Los Angeles	43–41	Spencer Haywood, Denver
1970-71	Utah	4–3	Kentucky	44–40	Utah	57–27	Mel Daniels, Indiana
1971-72	Indiana	4–2	New York	44–40	Indiana	47–37	Artis Gilmore, Kentucky
1972-73	Indiana	4–3	Kentucky	56–28	Indiana	51–33	Billy Cunningham, Carolina
1973-74	New York	4–1	New York	55–29	Utah	51–33	Julius Erving, New York
1974-75	Kentucky	4–1	Kentucky	58–26	Indiana	45–39	Julius Erving, New York & George McGinnis, Indiana
1975-76	New York	4–2	One Division; NY (55–29) beat Denver (60–24) in finals				Julius Erving, New York

NBA Regular Season MVP

1955-56	Bob Pettit, St. Louis
1956-57	Bob Cousy, Boston
1957-58	Bill Russell, Boston
1958-59	Bob Pettit, St. Louis
1959-60	Wilt Chamberlain, Philadelphia
1960-61	Bill Russell, Boston
1961-62	Bill Russell, Boston
1962-63	Bill Russell, Boston
1963-64	Oscar Robertson, Cincinnati
1964-65	Bill Russell, Boston
1965-66	Wilt Chamberlain, Philadelphia
1966-67	Wilt Chamberlain, Philadelphia
1967-68	Wilt Chamberlain, Philadelphia
1968-69	Wes Unseld, Baltimore
1969-70	Willis Reed, New York
1970-71	Kareem Abdul-Jabbar, Milwaukee
1971-72	Kareem Abdul-Jabbar, Milwaukee
1972-73	Dave Cowens, Boston
1973-74	Kareem Abdul-Jabbar, Milwaukee
1974-75	Bob McAdoo, Buffalo
1975-76	Kareem Abdul-Jabbar, Los Angeles
1976-77	Kareem Abdul-Jabbar, Los Angeles
1977-78	Bill Walton, Portland
1978-79	Moses Malone, Houston
1979-80	Kareem Abdul-Jabbar, Los Angeles
1980-81	Julius Erving, Philadelphia
1981-82	Moses Malone, Houston
1982-83	Moses Malone, Philadelphia
1983-84	Larry Bird, Boston
1984-85	Larry Bird, Boston
1985-86	Larry Bird, Boston
1986-87	Magic Johnson, L.A. Lakers
1987-88	Michael Jordan, Chicago
1988-89	Magic Johnson, L.A. Lakers
1989-90	Magic Johnson, L.A. Lakers
1990-91	Michael Jordan, Chicago
1991-92	Michael Jordan, Chicago
1992-93	Charles Barkley, Phoenix

NBA Regular Season Scoring Champions

Year	Champion	Pts.	Year	Champion	Pts.
1946-47	Joe Fulks, Phil.	1389	**1970-71**	K. Abdul-Jabbar, Mil.	*31.7
1947-48	Max Zaslofsky, Chi.	1007	**1971-72**	K. Abdul-Jabbar, Mil.	*34.8
1948-49	George Mikan, Minn.	1698	**1972-73**	Nate Archibald, K.C.-O.	*34.0
1949-50	George Mikan, Minn.	1865	**1973-74**	Bob McAdoo, Buffalo	*30.6
1950-51	George Mikan, Minn.	1932	**1974-75**	Bob McAdoo, Buffalo	*34.5
1951-52	Paul Arizin, Phil.	1674	**1975-76**	Bob McAdoo, Buffalo	*31.1
1952-53	Neil Johnston, Phil.	1564	**1976-77**	Pate Maravich, New O.	*31.1
1953-54	Neil Johnston, Phil.	1759	**1977-78**	George Gervin, S.A.	*27.2
1954-55	Neil Johnston, Phil.	1631	**1978-79**	George Gervin, S.A.	*29.6
1955-56	Bob Pettit, St. Louis	1849	**1979-80**	George Gervin, S.A.	*33.1
1956-57	Paul Arizin, Phil.	1817	**1980-81**	Adrian Dantley, Utah	*30.7
1957-58	George Yardley, Det.	2001	**1981-82**	George Gervin, S.A.	*32.3
1958-59	Bob Pettit, St. Louis	2105	**1982-83**	Alex English, Denver	*28.4
1959-60	Wilt Chamberlain, Phil.	2707	**1983-84**	Adrian Dantley, Utah	*30.6
1960-61	W. Chamberlain, Phil.	3033	**1984-85**	Bernard King, N.Y.	*32.9
1961-62	W. Chamberlain, Phil.	4029	**1985-86**	Dominique Wilkins, Atl.	*30.3
1962-63	W. Chamberlain, S.F.	3586	**1986-87**	Michael Jordan, Chicago	*37.1
1963-64	W. Chamberlain, S.F.	2948	**1987-88**	Michael Jordan, Chicago	*35.0
1964-65	W. Chamberlain, S.F.-Phil.	2534	**1988-89**	Michael Jordan, Chicago	*32.5
1965-66	W. Chamberlain, Phil.	2649	**1989-90**	Michael Jordan, Chicago	*33.6
1966-67	Rick Barry, S.F.	2775	**1990-91**	Michael Jordan, Chicago	*31.5
1967-68	Dave Bing, Detroit	2142	**1991-92**	Michael Jordan, Chicago	*30.1
1968-69	Elvin Hayes, S.D.	2327	**1992-93**	Michael Jordan, Chicago	*32.6
1969-70	Jerry West, L.A.	*31.2		*scoring champion based on average	

NIT Champions

(All games played at Madison Square Garden)

Year	Champion	Runner-Up	Score
1938	Temple	Colorado	60–36
1939	Long Island Univ.	Loyola (Ill.)	44–32
1940	Colorado	Duquesne	51–40
1941	Long Island Univ.	Ohio Univ.	56–42
1942	West Virginia	W. Kentucky	47–45
1943	St. John's (NY)	Toledo	48–27
1944	St. John's (NY)	DePaul	47–39
1945	DePaul	Bowling Green	71–54
1946	Kentucky	Rhode Island	46–45
1947	Utah	Kentucky	49–45
1948	St. Louis	NYU	65–52
1949	San Francisco	Loyola (Ill.)	48–47
1950	CCNY	Bradley	69–61
1951	BYU	Dayton	62–43
1952	La Salle	Dayton	75–64
1953	Seton Hall	St. John's (NY)	58–46
1954	Holy Cross	Duquesne	71–62
1955	Duquesne	Dayton	70–58
1956	Louisville	Dayton	93–80
1957	Bradley	Memphis State	84–83
1958	Xavier, Ohio	Dayton	78–74
1959	St. John's (NY)	Bradley	76–71
1960	Bradley	Providence	88–72
1961	Providence	St. Louis	62–59
1962	Dayton	St. John's (NY)	73–67
1963	Providence	Canisius	81–66
1964	Bradley	New Mexico	86–54
1965	St. John's (NY)	Villanova	55–51
1966	BYU	NYU	97–84
1967	S. Illinois	Marquette	71–56
1968	Dayton	Kansas	61–48
1969	Temple	Boston College	89–76
1970	Marquette	St. John's (NY)	65–53
1971	North Carolina	Georgia Tech.	84–66
1972	Maryland	Niagara	100–69
1973	Virginia Tech	Notre Dame	92–91
1974	Purdue	Utah	97–81
1975	Princeton	Providence	80–69
1976	Kentucky	N.C.-Charlotte	71–67
1977	St. Bonaventure	Houston	94–91
1978	Texas	N.C. State	101–93
1979	Indiana	Purdue	53–52
1980	Virginia	Minnesota	58–55
1981	Tulsa	Syracuse	86–84
1982	Bradley	Purdue	67–58
1983	Fresno State	DePaul	69–60
1984	Michigan	Notre Dame	83–63
1985	UCLA	Indiana	65–62
1986	Ohio State	Wyoming	73–63
1987	Southern Miss.	La Salle	84–80
1988	Connecticut	Ohio State	72–67
1989	St. John's (NY)	St. Louis	73–65
1990	Vanderbilt	St. Louis	74–72
1991	Stanford	Oklahoma	78–72
1992	Virginia	Notre Dame	81–76
1993	Minnesota	Georgetown	62–61

NCAA Women's Champions

Year	Champion	Runner-Up	Score	Outstanding Player
1982	La. Tech	Cheyney St.	79–62	Janice Lawrence, La. Tech.
1983	Southern Cal.	La. Tech.	69–67	Cheryl Miller, Southern Cal.
1984	Southern Cal.	Tennessee	72–61	Cheryl Miller, Southern Cal.
1985	Old Dominion	Georgia	70–65	Tracy Claxton, Old Dominion
1986	Texas	Southern Cal.	97–81	Clarissa Davis, Texas
1987	Tennessee	La. Tech.	67–44	Tonya Edwards, Tennessee
1988	La. Tech	Auburn	56–54	Erica Westbrooks, La. Tech.
1989	Tennessee	Auburn	76–60	Bridgette Gordon, Tennessee
1990	Stanford	Auburn	88–81	Jennifer Azzi, Stanford
1991	Tennessee	Virginia	70–67	Dawn Staley, Virginia
1992	Stanford	W Kentucky	78–62	Molly Goodenbour, Stanford
1993	Texas Tech	Ohio State	84–82	Sheryl Swoopes, Texas Tech

Olympic Medalists

Men:

Year	Site	Gold	Silver	Bronze
1936	Berlin	U.S.	Canada	Mexico
1948	London	U.S.	France	Brazil
1952	Helsinki	U.S.	U.S.S.R.	Uruguay
1956	Melbourne	U.S.	U.S.S.R.	Uruguay
1960	Rome	U.S.	U.S.S.R.	Brazil
1964	Tokyo	U.S.	U.S.S.R.	Brazil
1968	Mexico City	U.S.	Yugoslavia	U.S.S.R.
1972	Munich	U.S.S.R.	U.S.	Cuba
1976	Montreal	U.S.	Yugoslavia	U.S.S.R.
1980	Moscow	Yugoslavia	Italy	U.S.S.R.
1984	Los Angeles	U.S.	Spain	Yugoslavia
1988	Seoul	U.S.S.R.	Yugoslavia	U.S.
1992	Barcelona	U.S.	Croatia	Lithuania

Women:

Year	Site	Gold	Silver	Bronze
1976	Montreal	U.S.S.R.	U.S.	Bulgaria
1980	Moscow	U.S.S.R.	Bulgaria	Yugoslavia
1984	Los Angeles	U.S.	Korea	China
1988	Seoul	U.S.	Yugoslavia	U.S.S.R.
1992	Barcelona	Unified Team	China	U.S.

Photography credits

Front Cover
John W. McDonough

Back Cover
Heinz Kluetmeier

Front Matter
1, Walter Iooss Jr.; 2-3, Damian Strohmeyer

The Roots of the Game
7, World Wide Photos; 8, Bruce Roberts; 9, Rich Clarkson; 10, Manny Millan; 11, John Iacono; 12, Charlie Samuels; 13, Brad Trent

The Elements
14-15, Hy Peskin; 16-17, Manny Millan; 19, Leviton-Atlanta; 20, Jerry Wachter; 21, Manny Millan; 22-23, Walter Iooss Jr.; 25, Naismith Memorial Basketball Hall of Fame; 26, Walter Iooss Jr.; 27, Manny Millan; 28-29, Sheedy & Long; 31, Walter Iooss Jr.; 32, Peter Read Miller; 33, Manny Millan; 34-35, Hy Peskin; 37, Ron Koch/NBA Photos; 38, Walter Iooss Jr.; 39, John W. McDonough; 40-41, Manny Millan; 43, Peter Read Miller; 44, Manny Millan; 45, Andrew D. Bernstein/NBA Photos; 46-47 John W. McDonough; 49, Rich Clarkson; 50-51 Walter Iooss Jr.; 52-53, Richard Mackson; 55, Richard Mackson; 56, David E. Klutho; 57, Heinz Kluetmeier; 58-59, John W. McDonough; 61, Tony Triolo; 62, John W. McDonough; 63, John W. McDonough; 64-65, Walter Iooss Jr.; 67, Andy Hayt; 68, John W. McDonough; 69, John W. McDonough; 70-71, Walter Iooss Jr.; 73, UPI/BETTMAN NEWSPHOTOS; 74, Richard Mackson; 75, John Biever; 76-77, Louis Psihoyos; 78, no credit; 79, Craig Molenhouse; 80, Brian Lanker; 81, J.R. Eyerman/LIFE;

The Pantheon
82-83, Sheedy & Long; 85, George Silk/LIFE; 87, Walter Iooss Jr.; 91, Manny Millan; 93, Naismith Memorial Basketball Hall of Fame; 95, Manny Millan; 97, Myron Davis/LIFE, inset, Associated Press; 99, Associated Press; 101, Rich Clarkson; 103, UPI/BETTMAN NEWSPHOTOS; 105, Leviton-Atlanta;

107, John Biever; 109, James Drake; 111, Sheedy & Long; 113, Rich Clarkson; 115, Brian Lanker; 117, Neil Leifer; 119, Sheedy & Long; 121, Manny Millan; 123, Walter Iooss Jr.; 125, John G. Zimmerman; 127, John D. Hanlon; 129, Manny Millan; 131, Andrew D. Bernstein/NBA Photos; 133, Associated Press; 135, Associated Press; 137, James Drake; 139, James Drake; 141, Marvin E. Newman

The Teams
142-143, Naismith Memorial Basketball Hall of Fame; 144, St. John's University; 146, Courier Journal and Louisville Times; 147, John D. Hanlon; 148, Associated Press; 149, Associated Press; 150, Rich Clarkson; 151, Rich Clarkson; 152, Naismith Memorial Basketball Hall of Fame; 154, Naismith Memorial Basketball Hall of Fame; 157, Naismith Memorial Basketball Hall of Fame; 158, UPI/BETTMAN NEWSPHOTOS; 160, Walter Iooss Jr.; 162, Walter Iooss Jr.; 163, Walter Iooss Jr.; 164, Sheedy & Long; 165, Walter Iooss Jr.; 166, Carl Skalak; 167, Peter Read Miller; 168, Richard Mackson; 169, Manny Millan; 170, Manny Millan; 171, John W. McDonough

The Highlights
172-173, Richard Mackson; 174, Naismith Memorial Basketball Hall of Fame; 175, Naismith Memorial Basketball Hall of Fame; 176, Naismith Memorial Basketball Hall of Fame; 177, Naismith Memorial Basketball Hall of Fame; 179, Naismith Memorial Basketball Hall of Fame; 180, Associated Press; 181, James Drake; 182, Sheedy & Long; 183, Sheedy & Long; 184, top Rich Clarkson, bottom James Drake; 185, Manny Millan; 186, Rich Clarkson; 187, Rich Clarkson; 188, John D. Hanlon; 189, Manny Millan;

The Ecumenical Game
190-191, Damian Strohmeyer; 193, top Naismith Memorial Basketball Hall of Fame, bottom UPI/BETTMAN NEWSPHOTOS; 194, Neil Leifer; 195, John W. McDonough

The Future
196-197, Joe McNally; 198, Joe McNally

204

Index